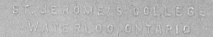

# A KOREAN VILLAGE

## Between Farm and Sea

Vincent S. R. Brandt

Harvard University Press
Cambridge, Massachusetts
1971

© Copyright 1971 by the President and Fellows of Harvard College

All rights reserved

Preparation of this volume has been aided by a grant from the
Ford Foundation

Library of Congress Catalog Card Number 73–162857

SBN 674–50565–4

Printed in the United States of America

21605

# ACKNOWLEDGMENTS

The research that forms the basis of this study was partially financed by a National Defense Foreign Language fellowship. Subsequently the National Institutes of Health provided a fellowship to cover the period during which I wrote up the results of my field investigation as a Ph.D. thesis. I am most appreciative of the assistance provided in both instances.

The form and theoretical viewpoint of the original thesis were discussed with a number of persons at Harvard University. In particular, Professors John Pelzel, Douglas Oliver, David Maybury-Lewis, and Ezra Vogel made valuable comments and suggestions. Professors Pelzel, Oliver, and Edward Wagner read the draft, and I am extremely grateful for their critical insight. Professor Wagner saved me from many errors of orthography and of fact. Also, he and Professor Vogel made valuable suggestions for improving the style and tightening the organization of the argument. The manuscript benefited greatly later on from the detailed comments of Professors Lee Man Gap, Hahm Pyong Choon, Felix Moos, James Palais, and Steven Piker.

My greatest debt, of course, is to the many Koreans both in Seoul and in the countryside who offered me hospitality and friendship as well as a means of learning about their country.

V. S. R. B.

Putney, Vermont

# CONTENTS

**1** Introduction   1

The Village of Sŏkp'o   1
Rural Korea: Homogeneity and Contrast   7
Villagers and the Nation   11
Change   15

**2** Problem and Theory   19

Establishing the Problem   20
The Concept of Structure   23
The Model   25
Some Theoretical Comparisons in
  Social Anthropology   29

**3** Environment and Economy   37

Residence Patterns   39
Resources   41
Neighborhoods   45
Agriculture   49
Fishing   60
Other Economic Factors   66

**4** Class, Status, and Mobility   88

Fifty Years Ago   88
The Contemporary Scene   91
Mobility   99
Hierarchy, Leadership, and Status   102
Discussion   106

**5** Lineage and Household   108

Structure of the System   108
Kinship Ideology and Ritual   115
Marriage Rules and Affinal Relations   121
Wives and the Status of Women   124
Behavior among Kin   136
Summary   142

6  Beyond Kinship: The Anatomy of Solidarity   144

  Interpersonal Relations   146
  Values and Sanctions   171
  Topography and Interaction   181
  Summary   182

7  Conflict and Malintegration   184

  Sources of Conflict   187
  Malintegration   189
  Social Control   197
  Examples of Disputes and Their Settlement   201
  Discussion   211

8  The Individual and the Community   214

  Small Lineages   214
  Migrants to Sŏkp'o   217
  Large Lineages   220

9  Ideology and Solidarity: A Structural Interpretation   230

  Lineage Orientation — The Ideal   230
  The Other Ideology   231
  Effects of the Environment   233
  Ideology, Behavior, and Solidarity in Sŏkp'o   234
  Inadequacies of the Model   235
  Village Organization, Cooperation, and Conflict   237

  Bibliography   241
  Glossary   245
  Index   247

# TABLES

1. Population and number of households in Sŏkp'o in four different years.  44
2. Age and sex distribution of Sŏkp'o population, 1966.  44
3. Size of Sŏkp'o households by neighborhood, 1966.  45
4. Number of Sŏkp'o households in each lineage by neighborhoods and sections, 1966.  45
5. Amount of arable land per household in Sŏkp'o, the county, the province, and the nation, 1966.  54
6. Economic classification of Sŏkp'o households (including factors in addition to land).  56
7. Analysis of indebtedness of certain villagers in Sŏkp'o by neighborhood, with reasons given for going into debt.  74
8. Number of acres of land owned in Sŏkp'o by lineage of household.  143

# MAPS

1. South Korea  3
2. Sŏsan County  4
3. Sŏkp'o  40

# ILLUSTRATIONS

Panorama of the village, taken from the path to the bus
  line   Frontispiece
Roof-tree ceremony   21
Carrying water   47
Hauling nets   62
Dividing the catch   64
Roof building   70
Annual *sije* ceremony   118
Informal drinking and singing party   146
Cooking noodles at the wedding   151
Grain harvest   155
Mending nets on the beach   160
Thrashing barley   226
Preparing a roof covering   227

# A KOREAN VILLAGE
## Between Farm and Sea

# 1

## INTRODUCTION

Just south of the thirty-seventh parallel in Korea a long, jagged peninsula extends westward far out towards China into the Yellow Sea. At its extreme northwestern tip lies Sŏkp'o, a fishing and farming village of slightly more than a hundred households.* This book is an attempt to describe the way of life of the residents of that village in terms of their membership in groups and the way they get along (or fail to get along) with one another as individuals.

### THE VILLAGE OF SŎKP'O

The T'aean peninsula as a whole is mountainous with hilly extensions reaching everywhere to the water. The pattern is reproduced at Sŏkp'o and its adjoining coast on a somewhat reduced scale. The village lies between steep 400- and 500-foot hills that in many places plunge sharply to the beach or cliffs. Because of this rugged topography footpaths must climb and descend precipitously, the connecting passes between valleys being only slightly below the highest hilltops.

Tidal range is great in this part of the world, averaging about 26 feet. On the shallow, heavily indented, eastern side

*The name "Sŏkp'o" is fictitious.

1

of the village, low water exposes miles of mudflats which the incoming tide transforms into an extensive bay with fiord-like fingers that reach deep into the mountains. On the ocean side to the west, coves headed by sandy beaches alternate with rocky promontories. Here the difference between high and low tide, while still dramatic by American standards, is less readily apparent. Numerous offshore islands complete a landscape of spectacular beauty.

Although only about 60 sea miles from the port of Inchŏn, which provides a gateway to the nearby metropolitan and industrial heart of the country around Seoul, Sŏkp'o is remote and seldom visited by outsiders (see Map 1). Land transportation in this part of South Ch'ungch'ŏng Province is difficult because of the mountainous terrain and wildly indented coastline. Roads to the impoverished coastal villages either do not exist, or they are badly maintained and little used by vehicles. Poor transportation is linked to the fact that except for sea-salt production through evaporation and motorized fishing from some of the larger ports, there is practically no industry in the coastal region.

Sŏkp'o is easily accessible by sea, however, and since it has an excellent harbor of refuge, fishing boats from the major ports of Inchŏn and Kunsan occasionally stop by. If headed for port, they can usually be prevailed on to take passengers and baggage, particularly if, as is often the case, a member of the crew is a native or a kinsman of someone from the village. Frequently my trips to the city were decided on at the spur of the moment in order to take advantage of such opportunities. Otherwise, a two-hour walk is necessary in order to reach the nearest bus line, a ramshackle affair that offers regular transportation over narrow dirt roads to the town of T'aean and the nearby county seat, Sŏsan. From there another two hours by bus and four by train will get one to Seoul (see Map 2).

Villagers in Sŏkp'o are engaged about equally in farming and fishing. Most possess some skill in both occupations, although every family and individual has at a given moment a predominant orientation towards one or the other. At one end of the scale there are five well-to-do families who do no fishing

**Map 1. South Korea**

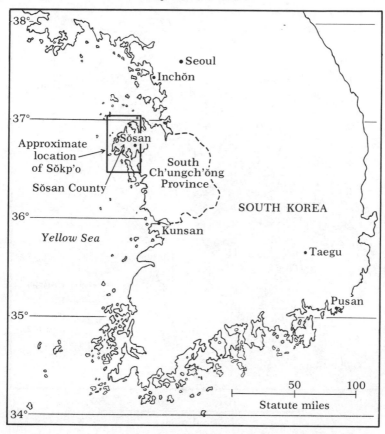

at all, and at the other there are several landless ones who are almost entirely dependent on fishing and the gathering of shellfish. In most families there are some members who fish and some who farm, the cycle of their activities changing with the seasons. Often parental pressure or the force of economic necessity determines what kind of work a young man will do, but personal desires and aptitudes also influence his choice, the higher prestige of farming being offset in terms of appeal to youth by the more adventurous and speculative nature of fishing.

3

Map 2. Sŏsan County

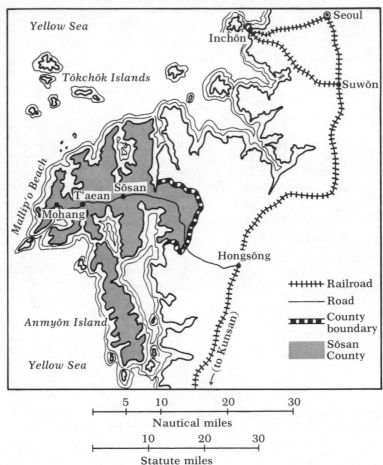

My reasons for choosing a research site on the coast of South Ch'ungch'ŏng Province were varied. The province, despite its lack of development today, has been for five hundred years a core area where many of the dominant aristocratic elite maintained their estates and ancestral tombs. Most Koreans consider that the mainstream of traditional, conservative culture is more thoroughly represented and more faithfully preserved there than in other parts of the country. Also, since one purpose of the study was to delineate a sociological reference point from which subsequent change could be observed and gauged, I was looking for a village far enough off the beaten track so that traditional forms of social organization and ideology would still be relatively intact.

In addition to geographic remoteness, I hoped to find a small community with an approximate balance between farmers and fishermen—in particular, one where deep-sea fishing was practiced. In this part of the Yellow Sea the tidal range is so great that many coastal villages are separated from deep water by miles of mudflats at low tide; as a result, fishing in sailboats is pretty much restricted to shallow tidal bays and estuaries. At Sŏkp'o and the neighboring villages, however, boats of fairly deep draft can anchor just off the beach, and even at low tide the open sea is readily accessible. Thus small isolated communities can combine farming and deep-sea fishing.

Before finally settling on one place, I spent many days hiking along the coast. The foreigner who travels in rural Korea on foot without introductions, schedules, or local knowledge invariably meets all sorts of minor adventures that provide strongly mixed impressions. In some villages where GI's with their cornucopias of candy, cigarettes, and chewing gum have passed through or are located nearby, the children crowd around shouting "hello!" and holding out their hands. In others they will run and hide or just stand silently enthralled by the unusual spectacle. In most places unmarried girls quickly disappear, and invariably there is at least one uniformed high school student, who rises eagerly to the occasion in order to practice or demonstrate his English.

Often farmers will stare with a quietly impassive dignity that outsiders sometimes mistake for hostility, but as soon as the visitor nods, smiles, and mumbles a greeting—no matter how bad his Korean—the mood abruptly changes. Everyone is curious (novel sources of entertainment are rare in the countryside), and a small crowd usually gathers. Mature men in a place where foreigners are seldom seen will probably be concerned most about etiquette: can a proper place be found with suitable food and drink to entertain the guest? If the village is poor, this may be a major source of embarrassment. Who should sit with him, and to what degree of respect is he entitled? Younger men with army service or experience in the city are likely to be much more casual, while an old man with a wispy beard and a long pipe, fascinated by blond sunburned hair on the westerner's forearm, may approach and tug at it gently. Then a child will follow suit, and another, and another.

The traveler is bewildered by his conflicting impressions and emotions. The hair pulling or clothes tugging may provoke indignation and a feeling of having penetrated to the midst of some primitive tribe. The young man who pushes forward eagerly with a parody of GI slang can be either welcome or distasteful, while demands for candy or gum by children are often insistent. Some of the people who crowd around are anxious to make contact, some discuss the stranger among themselves with extreme candor, and others merely stare. Is he being welcomed, derided, or exploited? The visitor stands there feeling isolated and helpless, probably grinning foolishly in an effort to please, and misinterpreting all the cues.

Eventually, after there has been enough conversation to find out how old he is, a person of influence who is approximately the same age (or sometimes the high school boy if his father is well off) will probably rescue him. Although they may be appalled at the stranger's lack of pride, dignity, and knowledge of the most elementary rules of social behavior, Korean villagers are almost invariably compelled by the pressing obligations of hospitality and the ubiquitous mood of tolerance to provide some sort of welcome. If it is mealtime, the stranger will be fed, and if it is night, he will be given a place to sleep. There will be a great deal of lamentation concerning the "miserable fare and unsuitable accommodations" but probably no mention whatever of payment, either then or the next morning.

After experiencing numerous variations on this theme, I stumbled one day onto Sŏkp'o. The high pass that separates the village from the outside world looks down across the scattered house clusters and rice fields to the rocks and beaches where land ends. Beyond is the sea and its islands.

In this village the smaller children at first ran behind their houses and peeked out at me furtively. The greeting of adult males was grave and formal, while women hastily skittered out of the path. I was impressed by the calm self-assurance and air of consistent propriety. Here I seemed to escape the obsequious respect and noisy importunity, as well as the kind of indifference that can make a foreigner feel somewhat less than human. That was in December 1965, and it was ethnographic love at first sight. During the following year I was to find out that great variation and considerable tension actually existed beneath this tranquil exterior, but each time that I have subsequently returned to the village my initial impression has been in some measure renewed.

## RURAL KOREA: HOMOGENEITY AND CONTRAST

Most foreign observers have commented on Korea's cultural homogeneity. With regard to language, food, architecture, family organization, folklore, technology, and clothes, one village seems very much like another. Probably the efficiency with which Japanese educational and agricultural extension programs were carried out also reinforced the extent of uniformity.

Nevertheless strong regional feeling persists, and Koreans themselves insist on the importance of provincial and local differences in customs, attitudes, and personality. The divisive effect of local loyalties has been apparent throughout much of Korean history, and today it is often decisive in determining the formation of cliques within the army, political parties, and business. Even the clustering of rural migrants in the Seoul slums is usually on a regional basis.

But a more fundamental kind of contrast and diversity exists within this context of regional variation. As a result neighboring villages may be distinctive not only in obvious aspects of social organization such as the composition of kinship groups, but also in more intangible ways that might be summed up with some such phrase as "collective mood." Abstractions such as community solidarity or cohesion, social harmony and cooperation, receptivity to innovation, and territorial pride as well as their opposites are difficult to pin down, yet it is often in this area that differences between rural com-

7

munities are most pronounced, with profound implications for the direction and rate of social change.

While a few Korean sociologists have emphasized the variety and importance of clan composition for village organization, most observers have tended to draw major distinctions between rural communities on the basis of geographic and economic criteria. Thus, farming–fishing, mountain–lowland, irrigated rice–upland (or dry) crops, single crop–double crop, and well-off–poor are some of the natural criteria that are frequently used for description. Some of these attributes tend to cluster together, and this kind of ecological approach can be useful, particularly with regard to practical studies and programs aimed at increasing productivity. I am mainly concerned here, however, with more intangible variables that are associated with the quality of interpersonal relations.

It should further be emphasized that this study is about one single community, and the extent to which it is representative of Korea as a whole varies greatly depending on the focus of inquiry and the kinds of abstractions involved. While all Korean villages share many obvious characteristics, it is also true that the kinds of striking differences in social organization and mood that distinguish Sŏkp'o from some neighboring communities seem to reappear consistently in other parts of the peninsula as well. When enough detailed ethnographic studies are available, it should be possible to work out a useful typology based on sound comparative criteria. In the meantime I can only claim to have examined in some detail one particular community.

Although it is too early to attempt a definitive assessment of Korean rural society, some effort should be made to provide a broader context for Sŏkp'o by suggesting something of the range of variation that exists in rural social organization. The village studies described below, while differing greatly in methodology, intensity of investigation, and overall quality, were selected because they provide some data permitting structural comparisons.

In North Kyŏngsang Province the village of Hahoe Dong has been carefully studied by Professor Kim Taik Kyoo (Kim 1964).

Hahoe Dong is the traditional ritual center of the Yu lineage. which claims numerous ancestors in high official positions during the Yi dynasty. While 58 percent of the 166 village households are members of this lineage, the extent of "clan" domination is more strikingly emphasized by the fact that its members control 87 percent of the village land, even after land reform. Discrimination along traditional class lines is still strong; intermarriage between descendants of the Yu aristocrats and commoner residents of the village never occurs, and members of this kinship group retain a monopoly of prestige, wealth, and power.

In addition to the sharp horizontal stratification, however, there are vertical divisions among the various branches or *p'a* of the lineage. Conflicts over property, ritual precedence, and (after the liberation) political ideology have exacerbated such divisions, which constantly threaten overall lineage solidarity. Because of this friction there was little cooperation, and group efforts to promote economic development did not exist. At the same time concern with family ritual remained a major preoccupation, and each branch of the lineage continued to carry out costly ceremonials to honor its ancestors and promote the prestige of the living. Professor Kim implies that in Hahoe Dong the deteriorating economic situation and declining population (a result of emigration) are related to the conservative bias of village social organization.

Professor Lee Man Gap in his invaluable study of six communities, entitled *The Social Structure of Korean Villages*, writes: "Outwardly it may appear that each village is the same —but each village is distinctively different in its human relations." He distinguishes three broad categories of village organization that are associated with these differences: (1) villages where a formerly aristocratic (*yangban*) lineage is predominant, (2) those where a commoner lineage is predominant, and (3) those where power and wealth are divided. On the basis of extensive interviews and observations, he concludes that "kinship solidarity and the discrimination of feudal status are factors that strongly operate in determining the structure of leadership in the village" (Lee 1960:23).

A still more complex distinction between modes of village organization emerges from another major contribution to the understanding of Korean rural society, *Three Clan Villages in Korea* by Ki Hyuk Pak and Seung Yun Lee. In two of the villages in this study, aristocratic or *yangban* lineages were predominant (62 percent of the population in each case), while in the third, members of a commoner lineage made up an overwhelming majority of the total population (74 percent).

In one case where a former *yangban* lineage had successfully maintained its near-monopoly of wealth and power, there was still a "sharp cleavage" between lineage members and former commoners. Every effort was being made to promote "clan unity" and "retain social prestige" through utilization of a clan hall where memorial services to the ancestors, study of the Confucian classics, and other clan business was carried out (Pak and Lee 1963:37). The strong traditional bias and relatively authoritarian leadership of the community was exercised in the interests of the predominant lineage.

In the other community where former *yangban* were numerically predominant, there had been a "loss of clan loyalty and consciousness" since the land reform, accompanied by a decline in social discrimination. Commoners had "equivalent social status" with the former aristocrats, and cooperation with other members of the community outside lineage boundaries had markedly increased. Associations between former landlords and their tenants were not only frequent but took place on an egalitarian basis (*Ibid.*:191).

In the village dominated by commoners, clan cohesion (which actually amounted to community solidarity) was more marked than in either of the *yangban* villages (*Ibid.*:200). And this sentiment was expressed in terms of egalitarian cooperation, mutual assistance, and programs for economic improvement rather than concern for the preservation of a glorious past or the maintenance of social prestige. This village, the most prosperous of those studied, was also the most successful in adopting technological innovations.

A survey of four villages in 1957 (Mills 1960) that was followed up after a ten-year interval (Lee 1969) provides some conflicting evidence with regard to technological innovation and community development. In the two villages where cohesive *yangban* lineages were still paramount, the original study described conditions somewhat similar to those in Hahoe Dong—for example, conservative leadership based on traditional class distinctions, concern with elaborate family ritual, relatively undeveloped village-wide cooperation, a high concentration of wealth despite the land reform, and the persistence of authoritarian attitudes.

The brief follow-up by a prominent Korean sociologist in 1967 places great emphasis on the "human factor" of strong and competent leadership as an essential condition for constructive change (Lee 1969:14). While admitting that authoritarian leadership based on traditional ideology is likely to be "backward," this report points out that where a "progressive," competent, and influential individual was also the representative of a powerful lineage, he was in a good position to make a positive contribution. On the other hand, a much more egalitarian village without effective leaders was less successful in adjusting to the changing economic conditions, in spite of its greater potential for cooperative effort (Pak and Lee 1963:13, 57, 59).

## VILLAGERS AND THE NATION

This book concentrates almost exclusively on interpersonal relations within the village, and a reader who is familiar with other peasant* communities may object that an important di-

*By "peasant" I mean a permanent resident of a small village economically based primarily on subsistence agriculture, but including also fishermen and anyone else who considers himself to be and is accepted as a full member of the community. The emphasis here is not so much on agriculture as on a small face-to-face community that is relatively self-contained in the sense that the focus of village life might be called inward rather than outward. Of course, some villages have always been much more isolated, both economically and socially, than others. Perhaps a whole generation of scholars has been misled by Robert Redfield's graceful prose, and the term "peasant" is merely an extension of a European mental category without much comparative significance for anthropology (Redfield 1960).

11

mension of social life, namely contacts outside the village, has received insufficient attention. He may be right. But in spite of the importance of personal ties with other communities and the increasing geographic and social restiveness, my impression was that the village of Sŏkp'o itself is still overwhelmingly important as the focus of the residents' lives in terms of loyalties, work, and social activity—including recreation.

It is true that certain individuals at any given time may be very much involved with outsiders. For example, a loan from someone in town to buy a fishing boat, or a love affair with a girl on the other side of the bay, can absorb most of a person's anxieties or energies for a while, but such commitments are nearly always temporary. Most attachments, values, religious beliefs, and behavioral norms exist and operate primarily within the context of village organization. Sŏkp'o's self-sufficiency in this regard is being steadily undermined, and probably at a quickening pace; still the situation is radically different from that described for China by G. William Skinner, who assigned great cultural importance to the much wider local market area as the "effective social field of the peasant" (Skinner 1964).

Sŏkp'o is more remote than most places, but remote is a relative term and the two-hour walk that separates Sŏkp'o from the nearest regular bus line certainly does not amount to isolation. Villagers are physically tough and used to walking, and the lack of a precise conception of time calculated in terms of the value of hours and minutes means that slowness of travel has not really amounted to a major barrier. Nevertheless, interest in the world outside the village is increasing, and women in particular do complain about the difficulty of getting to market or of visiting relatives in their native villages. Village leaders are increasingly concerned with improved transportation as a means of promoting economic development.

Administrative control of the village by the national government is neither continuous nor pervasive. Visits to Sŏkp'o by illustrious officials of the *myŏn* (subcounty) and *gun* (county) levels are rare, and most contacts with authority are through the village head (*ijang*) as intermediary (see Chapter 6). The legacy of traditional Chinese administrative practice whereby the central government showed little concern with village affairs as long as taxes were paid and there was no rebellion, lingers on in the attitudes of local officials even though economic planners in Seoul see things from a quite different perspective.

The village head functions as administrator, tax collector, agricultural extension agent, public health official, and guardian of law and order. He reports events in the village to the *myŏn* office as he sees fit, and when he returns to the village he is supposed to carry out the instructions received from above. These may deal with subjects as varied as the use of plant insecticides, tax collection, illegal wood cutting, the mobilization of local labor for work on roads, or the settlement of a drunken fight between a fisherman and a soldier in the coastal defense force. In Sŏkp'o at least, the village head has not been a forceful agent of change and government programs, already well diluted by the time they reach the local administrative level, usually are further dissipated in an atmosphere of apathy or opposition within the village itself.

There is also a cognitive component that has tended to reinforce the separation of Sŏkp'o from more developed centers of provincial society. Villagers, particularly older men, still fear and distrust outside authority in any form. Historical tradition as well as personal experiences with Japanese, American, South Korean, and North Korean administrators in the recent past have not convincingly demonstrated to villagers that their own interests coincide with those of the holders of power in Seoul, the provincial capital, or at the county and subcounty levels. The distrust is mixed with awe and respect, and any largesse from above in such forms as cheap, subsidized chemical fertilizer, school construction, or agricultural credit is of course welcomed. It is also rare.

Perhaps there has been a growing sense of indentification with the national government during the last four or five years and some sympathy for administrative efforts to promote economic development. Villagers certainly recognize their dependence on outside forces if "progress" is to be achieved, but it is a fragile sort of confidence that can be easily weakened by the whimsical and opportunistic way in which national policies are often administered locally or the cynical brutality with which local elections are "supervised" by the police. Places like Sŏkp'o are used to regulating their own affairs. Effective village institutions exist for reaching decisions, maintaining social control, and adjusting disputes. While no one today except perhaps a few old men would actually recommend total isolation as a preferred policy, the emotional antipathy to official interference is still strong.

Another intangible factor inhibiting the cultural integration of Sŏkp'o with more developed and prosperous communities in the region is the gap in social prestige that exists between townsmen and peasants, between the educated and the illiterate or less educated, and between residents of farming and of fishing communities. The people of Sŏkp'o are rated as inferior by their countrymen and feel themselves to be inferior on all three counts.

In addition to tax and corvée obligations, official agencies further affect the lives of villagers through the military service requirement and the fact that serious crimes require investigation by the police—unless they can be kept hidden from the authorities, a not-infrequent occurrence.

While I was in Sŏkp'o, a detachment (seven men) of the coastal defense force was first sent there to guard against the increased threat of raids by sea from North Korea. Since then this force has been increased, and its presence has also influenced local conditions to some extent.

A major development project in reclaiming tidal land for rice production has been financed and to a considerable extent directed by agents or subcontractors of the Korean government from outside the village. No benefits have yet been received from this scheme other than local wages paid in United States "Food for Peace" flour, but in time it will revolutionize village agriculture (see Chapter 7).

Individual, unofficial contacts with the world beyond the village boundaries are varied and numerous. Depending on the time of year (which determines leisure) and the availability of surplus products to sell and money to spend, anywhere from five to fifteen or twenty women and girls may attend the five-day markets held at the subcounty seat. This trip requires a short bus ride in addition to the long walk. Most of the women who marry into Sŏkp'o come from the immediate region, and a good deal of visiting back and forth takes place, usually combined with trips to market if the native village is along or near the main route. Husbands also visit their in-laws from time to time. Older people walk long distances to attend funerals or other important memorial ceremonies on behalf of relatives and friends in other villages. Koreans are renowned for their love of travel, and when time, money, and some semblance of an excuse permit, men will be found visiting the stores and often the wine shops of nearby provincial towns. But in the towns there always seemed to be far fewer of these pleasure seekers from Sŏkp'o than from the other villages that were more prosperous or closer to the bus line.

Several natives of Sŏkp'o work in nearby towns or in the big cities, and the number is now rapidly increasing. Although most of them do not return to the village more than once or twice a year, and often much less frequently, an expanding network exists that provides a temporary foothold and job information for persons migrating out of the village—particularly to the Seoul-Inchŏn area.

Villagers who work regularly on engine-powered boats based in a larger port naturally spend most of their free time there, and eventually they will marry and settle down away from home.

## CHANGE

In Sŏkp'o, despite some far-reaching changes that took place under the Japanese occupation and since the end of World War II, the traditional social system was still largely intact in 1966, and fundamental challenges to it were just beginning to arise. On the other hand, there were evident areas of tension in belief systems, codes of behavior, and basic economic relationships to indicate that some sort of structural change was

15

imminent. In the thirties under the Japanese, the acute land shortage that resulted from rapid population increases combined with work opportunities elsewhere to draw many young men away from Sŏkp'o. Again today economic development, particularly in the major metropolitan areas, is luring youth in ever larger numbers to the city, while the new ideology of modernization is just starting to penetrate village life.

In particular a relatively sudden revolution in the aspirations and outlook of young people was taking place; this can be attributed in large part to the influence of radio broadcasts from Seoul as well as to improved transportation. Even though there had as yet been little change in the status or roles assigned to youth, and conformity with most norms of behavior was still required of young people, they were restlessly questioning the validity of many values, and a minor revolution in premarital sexual customs had already started to take place (see Chapter 5).

Not only mature parents but men and women in their late twenties remarked on the sudden development of a new youth culture. In 1966 about one-fourth of all households in the village owned transistor radios, a luxury that reasonably well-off farming and fishing households had only recently been able to afford, thanks to rapid expansion of the South Korean electronics industry. Movies and magazines were still relatively inaccessible and had little effect on the youth of Sŏkp'o, but the constant expression on the radio of romantic love as an ideal through popular songs and radio dramas seemed to have substantially undermined the repressive force of Confucian puritanism and made a severe dent in parental authority within an extraordinarily short time. The influence of Seoul broadcasts was also evident in the outspoken determination of many young people to make their own decisions with regard to occupation, place of residence, and choice of spouse.

The growing importance of technological improvements in both fishing and agriculture seemed to predict that education, energy, and ability would be increasingly rewarded, while the slow erosion of the formal priority assigned to kinship values presaged perhaps a decrease in the support provided for im-

16

poverished or incompetent members of the community. The possibility also existed that community projects in both fishing and the reclamation of agricultural land could add substantially to the prosperity of everyone in the village.

The movement of people in and out of Sŏkp'o during and after the war, the influence of military service on most of the younger adult males, and a somewhat greater indulgence in travel by residents of all ages have been additional factors promoting change in recent years. But in 1966 it was the resistance to innovation combined with an air of old-fashioned, tranquil self-sufficiency that seemed most characteristic of the village, particularly in contrast to other communities located closer to main lines of communication.

An attempt has been made in Chapter 3 to indicate those aspects of village social organization that were particularly susceptible to outside influences. Despite some initiative within the village, the stimulus and resources for economic development have come mainly from outside. As development proceeds and increased productivity results, it will of course be accompanied by a tighter integration of the village economy with distant markets and a broadening of interpersonal contacts outside the community. It can be expected, however, that the process will be a differential one, the livelihood and attitudes of farmers being less profoundly altered than those of fishermen.

My general theoretical approach to the question of change is that in a given social context villagers share to a greater or lesser extent a common set of attitudes and knowledge of the rules that tells them what constitutes proper or normal expected behavior and tends to shape their choices of action both in routine and in new situations. At any one point in time the systems of ideas, institutions, and patterned behavior in the community coexist in some kind of temporary equilibrium, either relatively stable as in the past, or dynamic and subject to rapid change. In the latter case behavior is much less likely to be uniform and predictable. A shift in beliefs or values affects behavior, and this in turn can transform institutions; conversely, institutional change such as that from a

17

subsistence to a market economy is likely to exert a profound influence on ideology. It looks today as if the influence of ideas imported from abroad, public policy, and native cultural traditions are far more important in shaping the social changes that are taking place than those universal functional imperatives that some theoreticians have assumed must inevitably stem from the modernization process.

In Sŏkp'o the transition from a traditional, self-sufficient, relatively isolated community is just beginning. Economic development is only now getting under way with large-scale increases in productivity and communications still several years in the future. Profound ideological influences so far have been felt mainly by young people, who are leaving for the city in steadily increasing numbers, thereby lessening the impact on the village as a whole. The current generation of mature household heads and property owners differs from their fathers chiefly in possessing a much greater knowledge of the outside world and the importance there of money transactions and contractual relations. This knowledge had not yet transformed social and economic relations within the community, except that the new egalitarian political ideology (since liberation at the end of World War II) has rapidly eroded many vestiges of hereditary class status.

# 2

## PROBLEM AND THEORY

In undertaking this ethnographic study I had no particular theoretical allegiance and did not consider myself enrolled in any single school of anthropological thought. Instead of bringing along a hypothetical point of view for testing in the field, I was interested rather in some specific sociological problems.

Research dealing with rural Korea is still scarce, but some of the studies that have been made indicate the existence at the village level of the same sort of pervasive factionalism and interpersonal hostility that has plagued aristocratic society, and particularly the political elite, throughout much of the country's history.* I planned to examine in detail the nature of individual loyalties to kinship and other groupings and to determine the bearing that such allegiances would have on divisions and conflict within the village. Somewhat naively, perhaps, I assumed that the simplicity and relative homoge-

*Whether there has been more of this kind of internal division in Korea than in most other places is perhaps a controversial question. Certainly it has been conceptualized most specifically by Koreans themselves, who have a proverb to the effect that whenever three people are gathered together, there are at least two factions. And throughout long periods of Korean history the factional model has been used by native historians in interpreting and recording political events.

neity that has often been regarded as typical of village social organization would facilitate a systematic study of the bases of factional strife in Korea (Redfield 1941).

## ESTABLISHING THE PROBLEM

During my first six weeks in the village, I stayed in the guest room (*sarang pang*) of a prominent family that belonged to the formerly aristocratic (*yangban*) Yi lineage. My initial impression as a result of this experience was that social relations are dominated by considerations of kinship. The neighbors were mostly related households, and small children played with either siblings or cousins. Work groups in the fields and boat crews usually were composed of fathers, sons, uncles, and cousins, while the elderly men who often gathered in my room at night (I had usurped a favorite meeting place of the neighborhood) were mostly also kin.

My hosts and neighbors seemed preoccupied with family and clan affairs, and I thought I detected implications of contempt, ridicule, and economic jealousy in their comments about the rest of the village. The neighborhood was physically separated from the main sections of the village by a narrow sandspit, and when a visiting technician on a local dike project cautioned me against associating with "those low-class people across the bay," I was satisfied that the necessary ingredients for factional divisions were present.

The first inkling I had that something was wrong with these early efforts to categorize social relations in the village came with a roof raising that took place about 100 yards down the hill from my room. A few days previously when the main roof beam had been put in place, offerings were made to the spirit that would inhabit the house. At this ceremony only immediate neighbors and kin were present, and most of the food and drink was reserved for those who were more than about 55 years old;* younger spectators took only token amounts. The mood

*My "assimilated rank" was first established on this occasion at about 60 years of age (I was actually 42), and this lofty eminence on ritual occasions was repeated throughout my stay in the village.

*A ceremonial offering of food and drink is made when the roof beam is put in place. The house owner is on his knees after completing the ritual bows. Only relatives (and the author) are present.*

was restrained, and noisy children were cuffed into silence by their parents.

When the laborious business of actually putting on the roof began, some fifty people gathered of whom only about half were relatives of the house owner. Friends came from every section of the village in addition to all the close neighbors, and the work was accomplished during two days of intense activity in an atmosphere of great joviality and constant noise. As occasions like this were repeated at fairly frequent intervals, I gradually discovered that Sŏkp'o, contrary to my expectations, was a place where sociability, mutual tolerance, and cooperation among members of different lineages was a persistent feature of village life."

Starting with a description of the institutional and behavioral aspects of village life, I became increasingly aware that extensive diversity and contrast rather than homogeneity were characteristic of the community. A number of different kinds of complexity and opposition are involved, so that the

21

problem of finding an orderly interpretation of the behavioral data was a difficult one.

A certain kind of social complexity that exists in small face-to-face communities has been recently emphasized by anthropologists who are interested in the contrasts between village communities and urban agglomerations. The fact that "each individual is related to every other individual in his total network in several different ways" gives his social life "a complexity which his urban counterpart lacks." The resulting multiplicity of ties and the potential for conflicts of role behavior provide a constant source of tension (Frankenberg 1966:17).

Spatial contrasts are important in the sense that each neighborhood has a distinctive atmosphere made up of systematically related patterns of behavior. Similarly, certain contrasting forms of behavior are associated with the two major occupations, farming and fishing. A given individual may tend to remain within one environment, or he may shift back and forth with a change in roles or the social situation. Some village residents lead lives that are stable and predictable, while others seem to be constantly on the move and frequently act in different capacities. From a temporal point of view some of the variation in behavior can be seen as part of a long-term process, or as a function of changing economic and social status. Thus when a family improves its financial position and acquires more land, there are accompanying changes in attitudes and habitual actions. The growing influence of a new ideology of modernization and the accompanying economic pressures are, of course, also contributing a new and irreversible element of variation.

The following sets of contrasts, which represent several different kinds of analytical approaches, are particularly appropriate for a description of village life:*

| | |
|---|---|
| Kin | Community |
| Farming | Fishing |

*The contrast between collective participation and aggressive ego-orientation is a crucial one, but it cuts across the scheme of oppositions presented here.

| | |
|---|---|
| Hierarchical organization | Egalitarianism |
| Lineage rank | Personal charisma |
| Formal | Informal |
| Prestigious | Vulgar |
| Confucian family ritual | Shamanism and animism |
| Restraint | Unrestrained self-expression |

While not strictly comparable, the contrasts are interrelated in ways that reflect consistent patterns of behavior.

In analyzing the research data, I have been faced with the problem of reconciling the existence of sharp lines of division, notably those based on settlement patterns, lineage, age, hereditary status, and occupation with what seemed to me to be the prevailing mood of village-wide solidarity (see Chapter 6). There is a second and closely related problem: the formal system of ethics that reinforces distinctions based on lineage, age, and occupation is universally endorsed as the only correct model for actual behavior. Yet I found that patterns of behavior contradicting the formal values are often quite acceptable and may even be regarded as praiseworthy. And it is precisely this latter category of behavior that is most conducive to cooperation across kinship boundaries.

## THE CONCEPT OF STRUCTURE

The theoretical orientation of my thesis developed out of the effort to find a satisfactory interpretation in structural terms for these apparent inconsistencies. There has been so much variety and controversy in anthropological literature concerning the use of the term "social structure" that it is necessary at this point to state what I mean by a structural analysis. Structure refers to the interrelationship or arrangement among the parts of some whole. One school of thought regards social structure as "a property of empirical reality" or as "the social reality itself" (Nadel 1957:150). According to this approach, structural methodology consists in a description of social relations in terms of some prearranged scheme, most notably the delimitation of social groups and roles. An opposing point of view, that of Levi-Strauss, Leach, and others, regards social structure as having "nothing to do with empirical reality but with models which are built up after it" (Levi-Strauss 1953: 575). Or, "The structures which the anthropologist describes are models which exist only as logical constructions in his own mind" (Leach 1954:5).

I have adopted this latter concept of structure as formal hypotheses designed to help explain the workings of observed phenomena. In other words, structure is the anthropologist's explanatory construct; it is what he says it is and can be modified in accordance with the kind of data under consideration and the focus of his interest.

In recent years anthropologists with an ethnoscientific perspective have emphasized that in order to be valid such models must at some level of abstraction correspond to, or at least not contradict, the cognitive cultural code; that is, the shared "designs for living" that exist in the heads of members of any given society. But even while granting the theoretical importance of the concept of a shared code or "cultural grammar" as a determinant of behavior, we must also deal with a quite different and more complex body of ethnographic data.

In addition to linguistic texts, our concern is with the actual events of human interaction. The assumption that human acts are uniquely determined by the code often does not seem to fit the field situation. Contradictions, inconsistencies, and individual variation indicate that cognitive descriptions can provide only a partial explanation of behavior. Several alternatives may be culturally appropriate, and individual variation in unconscious drives or conscious motivation may be the determining factor. The pressure of institutional factors such as residence patterns, the variety and composition of lineage groups, or the distribution of wealth all have profound effects on social behavior so that it may not necessarily correspond to that prescribed by a set of rules for appropriate conduct.

Formal values concerning which there is widespread consensus are consistently violated, yet the contradictions are ignored or rationalized as individuals pursue their own interests, so that in the short run at least there is no abrupt change in general cognitive orientation. Ecological and economic forces can have a crucial influence on certain aspects of behavior that are not accounted for in strictly cultural terms. For example, the influence of an expanding national market will affect villagers' choices and actions in ways that might be predictable statistically but concerning which they themselves have no comprehension.

In devising a model that will contribute to an understanding of village diversity as well as cohesion, one must then consider institutionalized groups such as lineages, neighborhoods, work groups, and decision-making councils as well as beliefs and attitudes. In the ethnographic description I have tried to maintain a distinction between what Ward Goodenough calls the ideational and phenomenal orders (Goodenough 1964:11). On the one hand, an effort has been made to describe cognitive orientation on the basis of formal values, casual opinions or attitudes, and deductions made from observed behavior. On the other, the concrete situation "on the ground" as well as the events of human interaction has been taken into consideration.

## THE MODEL

In Sŏkp'o I found that related elements tend to cluster around two main focal points or fundamental themes, and in terms of ideology the model is therefore a dualistic one. I am postulating that two distinct ethical systems affect ordinary, everyday behavior. One is formal and explicit. It is largely lineage oriented and embodies a clearly structured hierarchical system of rank and authority that is closely linked with Korean aristocratic traditions, but that has a pervasive effect on village life as well, particularly with regard to kinship relations, personal status, and ceremonial activity.

On the other hand, what I have called the egalitarian community ethic is informal and has no codified set of moral principles, although many aspects of it are expressed in proverbs and homely aphorisms. Important values are mutual assistance and cooperation among neighbors, hospitality, generosity, and tolerance in dealing with both kin and nonkin.

25

Resistance to authoritarian leadership outside the family is combined with strong in-group solidarity for the natural community, defined as a society in which everyone knows everyone else, and where people interact more frequently with one another than with outsiders.

In this scheme a highly ranked, prestigious, formal ethic is confronted by a vulgar egalitarian tradition that embodies many features of what is often called tribalism. Both ideologies are an integral part of the cognitive orientation of each villager. A convenient analogy exists with the division of the population into farmers and fishermen. Men have skills and experience in both occupations, but at any given moment they can be regarded as practicing one or the other. And over a period of a year or so, a definite preponderance of one activity is evident for each individual. In the same way villagers can change from one ideological frame of reference to another in accordance with their participation in groups and their performance of roles that are appropriate to any given situation. But in the long run any given person seems to have a preference for one ethical point of view over the other, a preference that is determined by such factors as individual personality, lineage membership, residence, occupation, and education.

In Sŏkp'o many contradictions between the two value systems are reconciled or ignored. The importance of clan loyalty and obligation as a principle is unassailable, but in actual cases it is seldom pushed to the point where severe conflict with nonrelatives results. The communal ethic often takes precedence where an issue might provoke a genuine grievance. If settlement patterns, primary loyalty and obligation, competitive drives, ritual, and patterns of authority were all determined solely by considerations of kinship ideology, lineage boundaries would become overwhelmingly important and cooperation within the larger community more difficult to achieve. This is just what seems to have happened in some Korean "clan" villages where the overall sense of community has not been strong enough to challenge the moral emphasis on clan loyalty and authoritarian control by ranking members of the lineage. In much of traditional rural Korea the *yangban* probably felt a greater affinity for kin and other members of their own class in neighboring villages or towns than they did for the commoners next door. Without a strong sense of community, conflict between kinship groups and after World War II, tension between the *yangban* and commoner classes and among political factions were all readily expressed in strife within such villages.

Other places have been relatively free of such conflict, however, and Sŏkp'o is one of them. It was pointed out in Chapter 1 that the scanty evidence from sociological studies of other Korean villages suggests that harmony and a willingness to cooperate in everyday activities seems to be more likely where the village is not dominated by one or more *yangban* lineages (Lee 1960; Pak 1963; Kim 1964).

Many anthropologists have analyzed opposing or contradictory forms of behavior in terms of the extent to which people's acts conform to a single value system, defined as a more or less explicit set of rules for proper conduct in various situations. Behavior that does not conform is then called aberrant or deviant. The people of Sŏkp'o look at their own way of life in much the same way. There is one legitimate, universally recognized, and formally codified system of morality—that of traditional Confucian ethics. Almost anyone in the village can list its basic principles: filial piety, respect for elders, and lineage loyalty and continuity. Proper behavior in specified dyadic relationships, particularly those of deference and obligation to kinsmen, is stressed. Another fundamental tenet is that the path to excellence is through education, and that the virtuous (or educated) man should have authority. Most conscious moral instruction, both at home and more formally in the classroom, is still based on the Confucian code, and villagers will almost invariably sermonize in textbook terms if asked to give an opinion about what is right or wrong in any particular instance.

In actual daily interpersonal relations, however, they often do not act in accordance with established ideology. Some actions are indeed deviant or antisocial and are universally condemned. Still, there is a large area of acceptable and sometimes required behavior in which egalitarianism and the demands for cooperation and conviviality on a community-wide basis take precedence over formal clan ideology. Villagers say they have a clear idea of what constitutes correct or moral behavior, and most people will assert that what they do both as individuals and as members of groups conforms closely to the ideal. When confronted with examples where the official values are contradicted, however, they dismiss them as exceptional cases.

What I have tried to demonstrate is that this interpretation of the villagers is not always correct, and that "exceptional" cases are often really artifacts of a separate ideological system. It sometimes seems that the sanctions for enforcing communal behavior are somehow embedded in the structure of the village itself and operate at a different level of consciousness.

Contradictory forms of behavior are found in all cultures, but they seem to have been more dramatically expressed in Korea than in some other parts of the world. The opposition that exists between rigid puritanism and sensuality, between restraint and excess, or between serene tranquility as exemplified by the dignified scholar and the violent emotionally charged activity of the ecstatic shaman or *mudang* (a female shamanistic practitioner) is a constantly recurring theme of Korean history, folklore, and literature. Such contrasts as these are readily apparent in the context of village life, and they are linked in ways that support the definition of two separate systems of values.

The dualistic ideological model presented here is based on a community that in 1966 was in many ways still traditional, but the rapid tempo of both technological and social change will cause the model to become increasingly obsolete. It has a static quality that makes it inadequate as a tool for interpreting radical innovation. To be of value in explaining the social organization of modern Korean villages in a period of rapid transformation, it will have to be modified to take account of the powerful ideological forces implicit in the process of modernization. In spite of the changes that were steadily taking place in the late 1960's, however, young men and women who hoped to realize the new ideals through their own personal experience still felt obliged to leave the village. The old concept of "proper behavior" (*parŭn haengdong*), which covers the entire spectrum of social acts, still represented the thinking of the vast majority of household heads, and social censure plus parental and economic control provided effective sanctions to back up the standards of ethics and etiquette.

## SOME THEORETICAL COMPARISONS IN SOCIAL ANTHROPOLOGY

The idea of unity and harmony emerging out of mutually interdependent, ranked oppositions is a fundamental one in Chinese philosophy (Bodde 1953:19), and its influence on ethics as well as on bureaucratic efforts to establish an ideal society has been profound in the East Asian culture area. In recent years many prominent anthropologists as well as other scholars have devoted their attention to the analysis of social reality as an expression of ideological systems. While no real attempt has been made to develop such an argument here, it is tempting to speculate about parallels between the traditional Chinese world view (or rather, the Sŏkp'o version of it) and the hierarchically ordered sociological dualism that I have described for one village.

There is increasing ethnographic evidence of the universality of dualistic phenomena in human thought and social organization. In his brilliant book, *The Ritual Process*, Victor Turner has delineated in great detail an opposition between structure and *communitas* that shows striking parallels with the distinction drawn here between lineage ideology and community ethic. He describes the opposition "as though there are here two major models for human interrelatedness, juxtaposed and alternating" (Turner 1969:96).

By structure, Turner means the formal, fixed, well-defined, and hierarchical elements of social organization involving rank, property, ascriptive status, and behavioral norms, including such particularistic factors as kinship rights and obligations. Opposed to this is an ambiguous "modelessness" where equality, humility, low status, and a sense of common brotherhood prevail. The essence of *communitas* is that it is a "blend of lowliness and sacredness," of the spontaneous, immediate, and concrete (*Ibid.*: 96,127).

Turner develops his theme as a way of interpreting certain ritual customs and symbols in Africa that mark crises and transition periods in the lives of individuals, and he sees social life as "a type of process that involves successive experience of high and low, *communitas* and structure, homogeneity and differentiation, equality and inequality." Each individual undergoes "alternating exposure to structure and *communitas*" (*Ibid.*: 97).

Subsequently these concepts are generalized into a broader duality that pervades all societies at all times and places (*Ibid.*: 129), and that develops in a fashion strongly resembling the sequence of stages postulated by Anthony Wallace for revitalization movements (Wallace 1970: 191-196).

In spite of the many convergences, which apparently indicate that Turner, the classical Chinese philosophers, and the inhabitants of Sŏkp'o are all grappling with similar problems of human nature and social organization, a major contrast between the interpretation offered here and Turner's theoretical perspective is indicated by the different uses of the term "structure." By narrowly restricting its meaning to "relationships between statuses, roles, and offices," Turner deprives himself of an essential analytic concept for integrating what he calls "structure and antistructure" into a well-defined, manageable, and coherent synthesis. While any society must comprise both, according to Turner, they are absolutely different in kind: structure can be defined in relatively precise and abstract terms, while antistructure is ambiguous, spontaneous, and apparently somewhat mystical in nature.

But surely *communitas* also has structure, even in the narrow restricted sense favored by Turner. The reversal of status still entails status. A change of roles does not mean that roles no longer exist. When the jester mocks the king, the social context and order of events can still be defined, and the participants as well as the spectators are not acting with random abandon but rather in accordance with patterns that everyone comprehends. As a matter of fact, Turner probably would be the first to label his approach to the study of African ritual as a "structural analysis." The essence of revitalization movements is the extraordinary authority exercised by a charismatic leader, and although the initiates or followers are leveled by comparison with their former roles, new patterns of authority are quickly established.

Actually the situation is more complex, and it becomes necessary to distinguish between established hierarchical organization, temporary role reversal, and "antistructure."

It seems methodologically more useful therefore to expand the theoretical compass of "structure" to include all patterned relations between different classes of symbols or acts. At this higher level of abstraction, social structure constitutes the anthropologist's hypothesis regarding the articulation of these relations within a cultural whole. Turner sees order, logical definition, and rational function as exclusive to one side of the dichotomy while antistructure, although functionally important, is modeless and expresses itself in mythology, literature, the arts, philosophy, and protest movements. It seems to me that this may constitute yet another example of the time-honored confusion between an observer's hypothesis and what exists in the minds of those actually participating in a culture. Native cognitive models certainly exist for behavior that fits the *communitas* pattern, and native systems of classification are applied to both the symbols and the acts in this mode as in the other (Turner 1969:9).

So we are led to ask, From whose point of view is *communitas* ambiguous? Who is it that has trouble defining it? Is this elusiveness and subversiveness an inherent attribute of a given society, or is it a function of the anthropologist's theoretical bias? The predilection for an explicit, neatly ordered explanation of how an on-going society maintains itself still underlies a great deal of anthropological thinking in spite of the recent emphasis on conflict, deviance, and change. If this is the point of departure, then one is led inevitably to see social phenomena in terms of the extent to which they reinforce or challenge established institutions and patterns of authority.

The student of cultures can label his overall integrating construct anything he pleases, since it is his own artificial creation. But no matter whether it is developed in terms of yin and yang, structure and antistructure, or lineage and community, it still constitutes a model of how society is supposed to work and therefore represents an effort to impose order or structure on a mass of data concerning human relations and ideas.

My point of view in this book is similar to Turner's in emphasizing the contrast between established order and ideology on the one hand and a less prestigious informal egalitarianism on the other. But we are still dealing mainly with problems involving rank, authority, and clusters of values on both sides of an arbitrary dividing line, and as such they are equally susceptible to structural analysis. The Chinese notion of yin and yang as comprising complementary oppositions within an all-encompassing whole fits the situation better than a concept of absolute contrasts. To identify the communal concept with an intangible, emotional, ecstatic, and revolutionary force to be conceived of as a completely different order of human association appears to be too drastic a theoretical tactic for coping with the data on egalitarian communalism, much of which has a routine, ordinary, everyday quality. None of this is to deny the existence of the kind of "direct immediate and total confrontation of human identities" that Turner is interested in (Turner 1969:132). But it seems evident that this is merely the extreme case in what amounts to a continuum and involves special psychological factors of a temporary nature.

The model developed here contrasts with Robert Redfield's view of folk and peasant society in that it emphasizes opposition and diversity in a small, isolated community rather than homogeneity (Redfield 1953:13).

Nevertheless it is undeniable that solidarity in Sŏkp'o, as in Redfield's folk society, depends at least partially on a considerable degree of consensus regarding the moral order. There is extensive agreement on what constitutes both ideal and acceptable forms of behavior. It is in the interpretation of particularistic factors affecting specific situations that differences arise. In other words, everyone talks the same moral and ritual language, while there is usually considerable tolerance and understanding of the various pressures and motives that drive individuals to perform controversial or even antisocial acts.

A certain parallel does exist between the two systems of values distinguished in this work and Redfield's use of the terms "great" and "little tradition" (1960:41). He sees the two traditions, which are alternatively labeled "hierarchic" and "lay cultures," as interdependent and interacting in village life (1960: 50, 146). But in Redfield's scheme the "little tradition" is always described as a kind of degenerate or dependent offshoot of higher, urban culture, simpler in content and later in time. It has no independent intellectual or social coherence of its own.

Because he is attempting to handle both the synchronic and diachronic dimensions of the problem simultaneously, Redfield makes no clear analytic distinction between the contrasting characteristics and mode of relationships in peasant villages and cities at a given moment and the ways in which such elements change through time. This confusion of spatial and temporal distance is particularly misleading if applied to traditional East Asian societies, because of Redfield's persistent tendency to interpret the urban end of his folk-urban continuum in terms of social factors that are typical only of a certain kind of modern industrial environment. Primacy of the technical order, social disorganization, secularization, heterogeneity, impersonal or contractual human relations, and cosmopolitanism have not always been characteristic of urban society. Nor is there any necessary connection between them and the "great tradition." In Imperial China and in Korea as well, the "great" and "little traditions" existed together in cities, towns, and villages. Men of letters moved back and forth frequently from urban to rural settings, while classical learning, the arts, religion, and philosophy flourished under thatched roofs as well as behind city walls.

To a much greater extent than in China, however, a single metropolis seems to have dominated Korean intellectual and social life and to have acted as a focal point for aspirations and resources. But this city derived its prestige and preeminence from bureaucratic rather than cultural factors. The concentration of material luxury and the struggle for self aggrandizement that were an integral part of aristocratic city life in Korea amounted more to a corruption or distortion of the "great tradition" than an expression of it. Thus although a striking rural –urban gap has always existed in terms of standards and styles of living, the kind of sharp cultural discontinuity between village and city that Redfield emphasizes does not seem to be really applicable to premodern Korean society. With the adoption of a progress- and change-oriented ideology during the last fifty years or so under Japanese and American influence, contrasts between rural and urban "designs for living" have, however, been intensified.

George Foster's concept of peasant society as one in which individuals see themselves "in a perpetual and unrelenting struggle with each other" (1967:134), with the result that "extreme individualism" (1967:301) prevails, directly contradicts the ethnographic data and conclusions presented here. Perhaps it is the general typological validity of the category "peasant" that is on trial, however. Foster's model is discussed further in Chapters 3 and 7.

An alternative theoretical approach to the problem of relating actual behavior to conflicting norms or contrasting clusters of values is represented by what has been called the "extended case method" or "situational analysis" (Gluckman 1961; van Velsen 1964). Here the emphasis is on determining through the study of actual cases how individuals manipulate conflicting norms in trying to achieve their goals. In other words, the element of personal choice among various types of socially acceptable behavior is stressed. This form of analysis has much to recommend it as a way of accounting for frequent "exceptions," and for tying in structural interpretations with problems of variation, change, and conflict.

The basic assumption that people are always and everywhere manipulating the system through their conscious choices needs to be examined closely. While obviously true to a certain extent, it is equally obviously a matter of degree and interpretation. Many students of social change have, in fact, used this variable as one way of distinguishing between simpler and more complex, transitional societies. The choices open to a peasant in a traditional small subsistence community are extremely limited, but as villages become more closely integrated with national political and economic networks, the numbers and kinds of available alternatives rapidly expand (Halpern 1967:123).

Premodern societies also differ markedly in the strictness with which social rules are observed and the kinds of alternatives available. Values, and to a considerable extent behavioral norms as well, usually have strong emotional associations—a kind of visceral component—and often it seems more realistic to regard the individual as being manipulated by ideology rather than the reverse. Probably "situational analysis" is a more useful tool when dealing with "loosely structured" or "achievement-oriented" societies than it is for rural Korea. In Sŏkp'o too aggressive and open a pursuit of self-interest is not really a socially acceptable alternative, so that investigation along the lines of "situational analysis" usually leads the anthropologist to a description of deviant behavior in the sense that it is generally censured by the community. Such "deviant" acts occur, of course, and indeed they do lead to conflict (see Chapter 7). But rewards for this kind of behavior are still low, since the individual's personal reputation and effective relations with kin and neighbors are bound to suffer.

In any society, certain crucial problem areas exist where important choices are in fact open, and where this kind of analysis is fruitful. The discussion later on of marriage choices and neighborhood loyalties in Sŏkp'o represents a modest effort in this direction. Certainly the new option open to youth of leaving the village entirely to seek opportunity in the city is proving to be a fundamental force for change. This alternative is now acceptable in the sense that parents have been forced to acquiesce, whether or not they approve.

The general theoretical point of view presented here has

much in common with that presented by E. R. Leach in *Political Systems of Highland Burma*. He uses as the articulating principle for his structural analysis "ideas about the distribution of power" (Leach 1954:4) and distinguishes two polar ideal types of political organization that are associated with different "esteem systems." Individuals in their search for power "may belong to more than one esteem system, and these systems may not be consistent" (*Ibid.*:10).

Leach is concerned with the structural contrasts that exist among separate communities and he postulates a range of variation between two ideal forms of political organization, *gumlao* and *shan* (*Ibid.*:9). The political situation of each village is regarded as an unstable combination or compromise between elements of these opposed principles.

What I have attempted to do is define opposing ideologies, not so much in terms of authority and status but as systems of ethics. Then, instead of comparing communities, I have described for a single village the way a reconciliation is achieved between the two contrasting ideal systems. Korean villages show great structural variation, however, and a comparative study placing them along a continuum between egalitarianism and hierarchy in a manner somewhat analogous to Leach's model would also be possible. As in Leach's theoretical scheme, the ideal abstractions exist in static equilibrium, but any specific community can be viewed as at a more or less stable point somewhere between the two polar opposites.

In villages where strong *yangban* lineages are overwhelmingly dominant, the community ethic is likely to be suppressed and ideals of cooperation and egalitarianism may be subordinated to lineage ideology. The opposite situation exists when a village is composed entirely of commoner clans. In the latter case, although considerations of kinship are still strong, collective solidarity across lineage boundaries should be well developed. Within this conceptual scheme Sŏkp'o falls into place considerably closer to the egalitarian end of the spectrum.

# 3

---

# ENVIRONMENT
# AND
# ECONOMY

The only historical reference to Sŏkp'o that I could discover describes it as the northern end of a projected canal across the peninsula on which work was carried out intermittently from 1395, at the start of the Yi dynasty, until 1669 (Lee 1963:99–133). The objective was to provide a safe route for vessels carrying rice from the Cholla provinces to Seoul, since each year many ships were wrecked along this stretch of the coast on their way north. The canal was finally completed in 1669, according to official dynastic records, but could never be used because of the great difference in tidal heights at its termini.

Old men remember accounts of a rich herring fishery that was said to have existed in the Yellow Sea until about one hundred and fifty years ago. Both branches of the Kimhae Kim sib reportedly migrated to Sŏkp'o at different times from South Kyŏngsang Province, attracted by the large catches of herring that could be taken in tidal stone traps or in nets close to shore. Today herring are no longer caught in the Yellow Sea.

The lineage of the Yi dynasty kings is called Chŏnju Yi. It is still the most influential kinship organization in South Ch'ungch'ŏng Province, and regional wealth and political power remain largely in the hands of persons bearing this name. The Sŏkp'o branch traces its descent from the twelfth son of King

T'aejong (1400–1418), one of whose descendants, a former county magistrate in North Chŏlla, moved to the village in 1649. It is possible that he had some supervisory function in connection with the canal. Or perhaps he was exiled with his entire family as a result of factional struggles in Seoul. There is no mention of any such banishment in the historical record, but it seems inconceivable that a high official world voluntarily settle in such a remote area.

South Ch'ungch'ŏng Province is renowned in Korea as the core area of the Yi dynasty (1392–1910) landed aristocracy. Its inhabitants are popularly characterized both in folklore and in contemporary cartoons as slow and gentle compared with the more volatile Korean norm. There has been little economic development, and the popular Seoul stereotype of Ch'ungch'ŏng people as extremely conservative and relatively deficient in energy and ambition may not be entirely unfounded. The Chinese (Confucian) ethical tradition has been particularly strong in this region where a classical education and good manners were valued above most other personal qualities.

In 1950 a thoroughgoing land-reform law undermined the economic base of the former aristocracy; as a result the province is still littered with the impoverished remnants of an elite that had been brought up to lead a life of leisure on the basis of rent from hereditary lands. Today many of these people seem to be sustained largely by an ingrained, unshakable conviction of their own moral superiority over anyone who works with his hands. None of the permanent residents of Sŏkp'o belonged to this category, but some visitors and a couple of parasitic temporary residents were assiduous in their efforts to exploit local farmers without working themselves.

Fifty years ago in the village of Sŏkp'o there were only forty households, thinly distributed among the same three neighborhoods as today. The old men in their sixties and seventies who were my informants concerning the past guessed that the population had been fairly stable prior to the Japanese annexation in 1910. According to local genealogies, ancestors of the four major kinship groups that predominate in the present-day village arrived between 1649 and 1710. Oral tradition tells of three ancient clans of Chinese origin named Ko, Nam, and Tan, who were displaced or "died out" after the arrival of the present inhabitants' forefathers. There are no residents with these names today, and no record of them could be found in the village or at the county seat.

## RESIDENCE PATTERNS

Although the sound of waves is nearly always clearly heard, and the ocean is visible from every bit of high ground, the village seems to have turned its back on the sea and looks out over the bay and mountains that extend eastward. The natural village contains 108 households with a population of just under 700. Administratively it is part of a unit with the cumbersome title of Sŏkp'o Village, Second Section. This includes another twenty-two houses, but since they are separated from the rest of the village by a good-sized mountain and a thirty-five minute walk, all but two have been excluded from this study. These two households are closely related (younger sons) to families in the main village and are well integrated with it in terms of both daily interaction and conceptual orientation.

For administrative purposes Sŏkp'o is divided into six hamlets, but the actual settlement pattern consists of three clearly defined major neighborhoods separated by topographic features of the terrain. It takes about half an hour to walk from one end of the village to the other, the closest neighborhoods being only about five minutes apart. The smallest, that of the formerly aristocratic Yi lineage, has twenty-nine households, while the largest has forty-six and is called the Big Hamlet (k'ŭn maŭl). This is the geographic and social center of the village and adjoins the harbor. The other clusters of houses are strung out wherever the wooded hills provide shelter from the sea wind. There are also a few relatively isolated houses along the connecting paths (see Map 3).

Within a cluster, houses are usually 20 to 50 feet apart depending on the terrain. As new houses are built to accommodate the expanding population, they tend to be farther away from the traditional nuclei and higher up on the hills where land is less valuable.

Because of the steep slopes and narrow valleys there is not

**Map 3. Sŏkp'o**

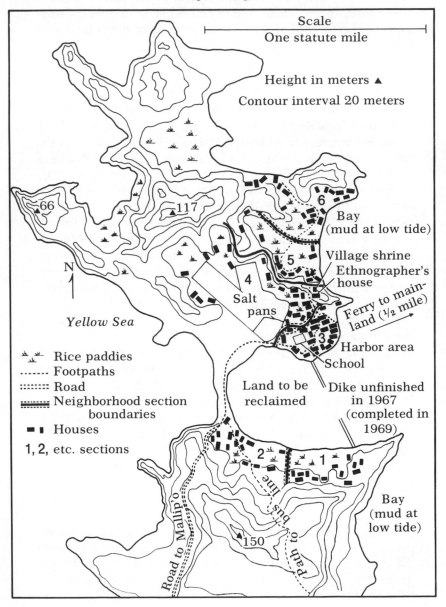

Scale
One statute mile

Height in meters ▲

Contour interval 20 meters

▲66

▲117

6

Bay
(mud at low tide)

5

Village shrine

Ethnographer's
house

4

Salt
pans

N

Yellow Sea

Ferry to main-
land (½ mile)

3

Harbor area

School

Dike unfinished
in 1967
(completed in
1969)

Land to be
reclaimed

ᨕᨕ Rice paddies
······ Footpaths
∷∷∷∷ Road
▰▰▰ Neighborhood section
        boundaries
■ ▮ Houses
**1, 2,** etc. sections

2

1

Road to Mallip'o

Path to bus line

▲150

Bay
(mud at
low tide)

much level land suitable for irrigated rice cultivation. The complex coastline and extreme tidal range make it possible, however, to reclaim mudflats wherever a dike can be thrown across a sheltered inlet to keep out the sea. The narrowest coves were converted into rice land during the Japanese occupation, so that today quite extensive dikes—400 or 500 yards long—must be built in order to reclaim additional land. At present the population-land ratio is high, and land hunger is extreme. However, if the proposed reclamation projects in this region are successful, local farmers will be much better off than the national average.

About three miles to the south a neighboring village has an entirely different topographic layout. There, a fairly high ridge divides the village so that half the houses face the ocean and a small harbor with boats, while the rest on the other side are enclosed in a valley descending towards the interior. Houses are quite widely and evenly dispersed in both sections, and physical clusters or neighborhoods are difficult to discern. The geographic separation between predominantly farming and fishing communities is much sharper than at Sŏkp'o, where no house is able to disassociate itself entirely from the maritime environment. The next village along this coast is another four miles to the south and has a still different spatial arrangement. Nearly three hundred houses constitute a single, continuous, somewhat dispersed community on a broad, gentle slope facing a bay to the east. On the western side behind the village, high ground drops away steeply to a narrow ocean cove with a small breakwater where boats are moored. Evidently the form that fishing-farming villages take in this region is determined by a variety of factors with no single pattern predominating. Topography, as well as land ownership and use, occupations, lineage organization, tradition, and personal preference, all affect settlement patterns.

## RESOURCES

### Land

Excellent crops are grown in the alluvial soils of this region if they are adequately irrigated and fertilized. Drainage is a problem for low-lying rice fields, particularly in the case of reclaimed tidal flats. After a dike is completed, it takes five years before enough of the salts are drained off to permit even fair rice harvests.

Villagers claim their soil is inferior to that farther inland for the cultivation of rice and barley, and in fact a good deal of salt and sand is blown onto the fields by ocean winds that also can directly damage crops. Nonetheless the best yields seem to be comparable with those of other areas. Some extremely sandy soils are cultivated, as well as an increasing amount of hill land that formerly was forested.

Most of the land is steep hillside, more or less well covered with pine. The slopes close to the village are privately owned, and the half-acre or so of such forest that most families own is exploited economically in a number of ways, although it does not provide any real income. Branches and pine needles are the only fuel available for cooking and heating, so that households without forest land must "contract" to gather this essential commodity on the property of others. A wide variety of wild plants are gathered in the spring and used as vegetables.

The cutting of timber for house and boat building is rigidly controlled by the *myŏn* authorities, ostensibly in the interests of conservation. Actually, the peasant must pay for permits to cut his own trees or do it clandestinely at the risk of confiscation and fines. But public and private interests outside the village combined to violate conservation regulations in the spring of 1966 with impunity when about six hundred acres of *myŏn* land adjoining the village were sold to a large Seoul paper company. This was one of the finest stands of big trees in South Korea, and in two months the area was totally stripped. Several officials reaped large rewards, and a sizable kitty was established for progovernment electoral campaigning before the 1967 elections.

## The Sea

Although the village is almost entirely surrounded by water, local inhabitants do not have a long seafaring tradition. Before the arrival of the Japanese, they did not even use sailboats, so that fishing was restricted to the bays or the water just off the coast. Tidal areas are an important source of octopus, clams, and small fish, while the coastal waters out to about five miles are intensively fished with techniques learned from the Japanese. The Yellow Sea fisheries are not particularly rich, however, and in recent years catches of many varieties of fish in the immediate coastal waters have been decreasing. Rocks that are uncovered at low tide provide extensive oyster beds. Harvesting these is an important and growing part of the village economy.

Potentially the ocean can provide direct, fast, and cheap transportation linking remote places like Sŏkp'o with larger ports. In this region coastal shipping today is less well developed than it was under Japanese rule, a reflection of provincial as well as national government prejudices.

## Climate

This part of Korea has a temperate climate with certain monsoon and continental features that make it quite distinctive. Winters are cold and dry, while summers are hot and moist. The mean annual precipitation varies from about 35 to 40 inches; less than 10 percent falls in the winter, while particularly heavy rains usually come in July and August. Thus the distribution of rainfall is erratic, so that droughts and floods are frequent. The average temperature is about 26°F in January, and about 79°F in July. Strong winds are frequent throughout the year, blowing mostly from the north or northwest in winter and from the southwest in summer, although gales from other directions also occur. In spite of the fairly cold winter temperatures, a long growing season permits double cropping, but the area is limited because of the difficulty in draining rice fields so that other crops can be planted.

## Population

In 1966 there were 689 persons living in the 108 households that comprise the natural community of Sŏkp'o. Table 1 summarizes the statistical information available from past years. The sex ratio of 106 males to 100 females has been fairly con-

TABLE 1.   POPULATION AND NUMBER OF HOUSEHOLDS IN SŎKP'O
IN FOUR DIFFERENT YEARS.

|  | *1957* | *1964* | *1965* | *1966* |
|---|---|---|---|---|
| Total population | 559 | 652 | 660 | 689 |
| Number of households | 75 | 100 | 103 | 108 |
| Average number of persons per household | 7.5 | 6.5 | 6.4 | 6.4 |

stant in recent years. As shown in Table 2, females outnumber males in the age categories below 20 and over 60, but there are far more males between 20 and 30 and to a lesser extent between 30 and 40 as well. This probably reflects both the difficulty that young men have in attracting brides and the eagerness with which daughters are married out of the village.

TABLE 2.   AGE AND SEX DISTRIBUTION OF SŎKP'O
POPULATION, 1966.

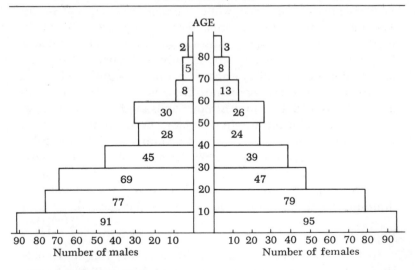

Totals:   355 males
              334 females
Sex ratio:   106 males
    to 100 females

TABLE 3. SIZE OF SŎKP'O HOUSEHOLDS BY NEIGHBORHOOD, 1966.

| Number of persons in family: | Neighborhood and residence section | | | | | |
| | Yangban | | Big Hamlet | | "Over There" | |
| | 1 | 2 | 3 | 4 | 5 | 6 |
|---|---|---|---|---|---|---|
| 1 to 3 | 1 | 0 | 3 | 2 | 1 | 2 |
| 4 to 6 | 6 | 7 | 10 | 11 | 5 | 6 |
| 7 to 9 | 5 | 4 | 6 | 8 | 7 | 7 |
| 10 or more | 3 | 3 | 4 | 2 | 2 | 3 |

The average number of persons in a household has decreased substantially in the last ten years, from 7.5 to 6.4. Large families of ten or twelve persons are usually fairly well off, with household heads who have high lineage rank or influence or both. But some notable exceptions exist, especially in the case of formerly prosperous households that have gone down hill or poor families with lots of children. The data on household size according to neighborhood are summarized in Table 3.

## NEIGHBORHOODS

Each of the three major groups of houses that comprise the village has a distinct character. In a general way and with varying exceptions and complications, the major lineages can be identified with certain neighborhoods (see Table 4). Also,

TABLE 4. NUMBER OF SŎKP'O HOUSEHOLDS IN EACH LINEAGE BY NEIGHBORHOODS AND SECTIONS, 1966.

| | Neighborhood and residence section | | | |
| | Yangban (1 & 2) | Big Hamlet (3 & 4) | "Over There" (5 & 6) | Totals |
|---|---|---|---|---|
| Lineage | | | | |
| Chonju Yi | 22 | | 1 | 23 |
| Kimhae Kim | | 23 | 30 | 53 |
| Naju Kim | | 1 | | 1 |
| Other Kim | 4 | 1 | | 5 |
| Mun | | 13 | 1 | 14 |
| Pak | 2 | 1 | 1 | 4 |
| Cho | 1 | | | 1 |
| Song | | 1 | | 1 |
| Kang | | 3 | | 3 |
| Sin | | 2 | | 2 |
| Yun | | 1 | | 1 |
| | | | | 108 |

the administrative division into six sections does in fact correspond to certain social and geographic distinctions within the bigger clusters.

From the vantage point of the Big Hamlet (sections 3 and 4) the other areas are usually referred to as "over across there": in one case across a tidal bay connected to the Big Hamlet by a sandspit, and in the other direction to the north of a wooded ridge that makes an equally sharp line of demarcation (see Map 3).

## The Yangban Neighborhood

Sections 1 and 2 across the bay are inhabited overwhelmingly by the Yi lineage. One Cho, two Pak, and four Kim families are scattered among the twenty-nine households of this neighborhood, but all except one are affinal relatives (or their descendants) of the Yi. This neighborhood is predominantly agricultural. Houses are spread out somewhat more than in the Big Hamlet, but the most striking contrast lies in the air of quiet industriousness that prevails. Women remain mostly inside their own homes, or if they go outside on errands to the well, the fields, or to other houses, they rarely loiter along the paths to gossip. One almost never sees them in conversation with men.

The steep mountain barrier that divides Sŏkp'o from the rest of the world rises just back of this area. In clearings on the wooded slopes are ancestral tombs, some of which are still marked by the crumbling stone monuments of an ancient aristocracy.

## The Big Hamlet

If the "upper-class" neighborhood of Yangban is marked by bucolic tranquility and dignified respectability, the Big Hamlet is quite the reverse. Here just above where the boats are moored are the wine shops, the one village store, and many of the houses of the poorest fisherman. The nucleus of this neighborhood consists of about thirty houses grouped closely together, so that the area between them is used mainly for kitchen vegetable gardens rather than for planting grain.

*The girl is carrying about 90 pounds of water up a steep hill to the author's house. Behind her can be seen part of the Big Hamlet and the partially completed dike. Since it is almost low tide, rows of stones placed to form oyster beds are visible.*

Throughout much of the year groups of men or boys gather in a few favorite spots near the beach for idle conversation. Women and girls are more in evidence than they are among the Yi households, although considerable variation exists among the families. There is more coming and going of people and a far greater incidence of noisy discussion and quarreling than in the other hamlets.

This is the village meeting place. Men from other neighborhoods as well as fishermen and merchants from out of town gather here to see friends, hear the news, drink, and gamble. The primary school, where town meetings are held, is nearby.

Many residents have spare time because they own so little land, while fishermen often have nothing to do when the weather is bad or the season unsuitable. So even though the ranks of the idlers are swelled by visitors from other neighborhoods, this most populous nucleus of the village has its own special air of impoverished leisure. Extremely crude language is used without restraint, and women join in some of the discussions, talking back to men in a way that is seldom heard across the bay or over the ridge.

My house looked down on this section; I could see everyone's comings and goings (including the movement of boats) and hear their shouts and quarrels. Breakfast fires were lit everywhere in the village at about the same time, but none of the residents of the Big Hamlet bothered to get up early and work outdoors for an hour before eating as was customary in the other neighborhoods.

A few households in this area have fairly substantial land holdings or good-sized investments in fishing gear and boats, but the average annual income here is considerably less than in the rest of the village. Among the four newcomers to the Big Hamlet since the Korean War two are poor affinal relatives of established Kim households, while the other two are impoverished couples who provide a dramatic illustration of the tragic fate traditionally reserved in Korea for those who marry for love against their family's wishes.

One lineage of the Kimhae Kim sib predominates; the other, somewhat more prosperous, has its ancestral tombs and most of its land across the ridge ("over there"). A good deal of crossing back and forth has taken place, however, so that the neighborhood and lineage boundaries correspond only approximately Table 4 shows the number of households that belong to the different kinship groups in each neighborhood.

## "Over There"

The fifth and sixth administrative sections are somewhat cut off from the other parts of the village by the ridge on which my house was built. Although a few boats were habitually moored off the "over there" beach, the atmosphere was predominantly agricultural, showing many similarities to the Yi stronghold (sections 1 and 2) across the bay. Land holdings are larger than in the Big Hamlet, and most fishermen own their own boats, although a few men from the poorer familes do crew for others. In this neighborhood, although all but three of a total of thirty-three households are Kims, the houses are widely separated into six clusters, only two of which are composed predominantly of close relatives. In both of these a well-to-do landowner forms the core, and he directs the collective agricultural labor of his kin. In the larger of the two clusters, the landowner is one of the four most influential persons in the village, and the eight nearby related families clearly look to him for leadership. The senior line of this lineage has occupied the same spot for more than two hundred years.

The other four house clusters are somewhat less cohesive from the point of view of mutual obligation and common productive activity, since they have closer kinship ties elsewhere in the neighborhood or across the ridge (in one case among the Yi households across the bay). Possibly a greater degree of informal conviviality prevails in these small subneighborhoods than in the two kinship-oriented house clusters where a kind of dependent unity has been established around a dominant individual.

Despite these differences there is a sense of joint identity on the far side of the ridge that received its most notorious expression at the time of the Communist occupation in 1950, when the inhabitants of this area generally collaborated with the North Koreans. A somewhat less intense aura of family pride and cohesion and a subtle, intangible, but still perceptible coarseness of manner among the residents contrast with the aristocratic neighborhoods. Village gossip emphasizes the aloofness and stinginess of several of the larger landowners.

The wide dispersal of close kin can be explained partly by the fact that younger sons often build a new house near the most distant of the family fields when they marry. Or if the father's house is small or in bad repair, he may leave.it to a son and build himself a new one in a different neighborhood.

## AGRICULTURE

Although farming is becoming more diversified all over South Korea, wet rice agriculture is still overwhelmingly important in terms of land use, proportion of total production, and the provision of food for local consumption. Attitudes and values among farmers in Sŏkp'o focus primarily on rice, so that possession of paddy land, work connected with rice agriculture, and the grain itself are all far more prestigious than the equivalents for other crops. In spite of the importance of fishing, the possession of fields (particularly paddy fields) is still so crucial as an indication of success and status, as a necessary qualification for playing an influential role, and for economic security, that sooner or later most economic resources are invested in land.

Land and to a lesser extent oxen are used in place of a bank. Excess capital invested in land provides security, income, and additional prestige. There is also great personal satisfaction, since increasing the family's holdings constitutes the greatest single criterion of successful fulfillment of the responsibilities of a family head. Because of the constant demand, either land or oxen can be converted into cash on short notice.

On the average, Sŏkp'o families have 0.93 acre of irrigated rice land per household, compared to 0.98 acre for the entire country. The amount of unirrigated or dry fields per household is less than half the national average, however.

There are 66 acres of unirrigated fields, most of which are planted with barley, although many other crops are also grown. In approximate order of importance these are: Chinese cabbage, sweet potatoes, beans, peanuts, wheat, garlic, red pepper, turnip, cucumbers, sesame, flax, corn, *kaoliang*, various spinach-like greens, eggplant, and squash. Nearly all are for home consumption although small surpluses of peanuts, pepper, sweet potatoes, and garlic are sometimes taken to the market town. The rice and barley are practically all eaten in the village; although a few households have a surplus, some of which goes to market, the village normally has a net grain deficit. In the past this has meant that the fifteen or twenty poorest families with almost no rice land at all have had to restrict their consumption to the barest minimum necessary for survival. In the spring, after winter food stocks are exhausted and before the barley harvest in late May and June, such people usually suffer from severe malnutrition for a month or six weeks. If the crop was poor during the previous year, the number in this category reportedly rises to more than half the total population, while conversely the number is reduced after a bumper crop.

During my stay in the village, large amounts of flour sent to Korea under the U.S. Government "Food for Peace" program were brought in. This flour was paid out at the rate of 3.7 kilograms per day for labor on a dike that was being built to create new rice land out of tidal mudflats. Although the villagers are not particularly fond of flour and often sell it in order to buy rice, the effect of the program was to eliminate hunger in 1966 and subsequent years.

According to local accounts, poor people in other years have been obliged to subsist in the spring on what they could gather along the seashore and in the mountains. Some members of the family may visit relatives in nearby villages to ask for help, while feelings of reciprocity and mutual obligation among relatives and neighbors within the village are exploited to the limit. I was told that the most unfortunate were reduced to an annual period of wandering about the region begging for food, while unmarried sons and daughters were sometimes urged to leave home and try their fortunes in the city.

Such accounts of spring "starvation" have been widespread all over Korea during the recent historical period. It is extremely difficult to assess the numbers affected and the severity because of the farmer's traditional propensity for exaggerating his poverty and that of his village in order to escape the rapacity of landlords and tax collectors. In recent years the government has also tended to exaggerate food shortages in order to obtain as much relief grain as possible from abroad.

In this particular village, however, the basic situation with regard to the consumption of agricultural foodstuffs seems clear. Practically everything grown in the village is eaten locally, and there is a substantial grain deficit that is met by reduced consumption, the sale of fishery products, loans, and various forms of relief.

## Rights in Land

Arable land—primarily irrigated rice fields and to a lesser extent dry fields used for other crops—is still the most important scarce good in the village, although younger men and fishermen increasingly tend to think in terms of money capital and alternative kinds of investment. Title to land is held by the head of the household, who has the legal right to dispose of it as he pleases. But land is generally regarded as the corporate property of one or more households, and the residual right of each member to a share of its product and a say in its disposition is usually recognized.

Despite these powerful limits on arbitrary action by the household head, he can and occasionally does assert his right to make unilateral decisions regarding the disposal of land. Thus the customary rights of family members are not always strong enough to withstand the despotic authority of a household head when he chooses to exercise it forcefully. There seems to be no legal check on such authority. A number of examples came to my attention.

In one case, the largest land holder in the village had died suddenly several years previously without making any specific provision for the division of his land between two sons, one of whom was still unmarried. The elder brother became head of the household and assumed control of the land. Later when his younger brother married and established a separate household, everyone expected that the older man would give him about one-third of the property, a customary division in such cases. The elder brother turned out to be greedy, however, and gave less than 10 percent of the patrimony to his brother. He is constantly criticized for this behind his back, and his reputation and influence in the village suffer as a result. His younger brother, who is competent and conscientious, does not have enough to support his family and is forced into economic dependence on his brother's household. Relations between the brothers are bad, and the younger frequently talks about leaving the village, although he is a section chief (*panjang*) and respected by his neighbors. The wealthy brother seems to be oblivious to what people think and devotes his time to acquiring more property. In spite of the loss of prestige he still exerts some influence in the community simply because of his wealth.

A somewhat different situation arises occasionally when a

man who has contracted personal debts sells land in spite of the protests of his relatives in order to satisfy the creditors. In one extreme case that occurred several years ago, a piece of land was jointly "owned" by a lineage, the income being used for ceremonial expenses. However, the land was registered in the name of the genealogically highest-ranking member of the lineage, who sold it to pay off a rich creditor from another lineage. Despite outraged feeling at the sacrilege there was no legal redress, and eventually money had to be collected among all the kinsmen in order to buy back the property. The offender's position as an influential leader in his lineage was irreparably damaged, and his sons and grandsons are still regarded as not quite respectable.

## Land Holdings and Classification of Economic Status

There has not been a particularly heavy concentration of land ownership in the village in recent times. According to the accounts of men in their seventies who are able to remember conditions at the close of the Yi dynasty when there were only forty households, a rather egalitarian situation prevailed then just as it does today. Certain family segments have had their economic ups and downs, but from all accounts there has been much more continuity and consequently less social mobility than seems to have existed in traditional rural China. Despite the sharp class differences and high social prestige enjoyed fifty years ago by the *yangban* Yi lineage, members of this line reportedly possessed less rice land per capita than the most prosperous commoner lineage. They did hold most of the mountain land, and as a result Yi families have been able to expand their holdings through the construction of terraced rice fields and the conversion of forest land into unirrigated plots. Today they have a very slight edge over the other lineages.

The range of individual holdings of paddy land is from nothing to almost 7000 *pyong*, or about 6 acres; but only two persons own more than 5 acres (see Table 5). The value of good rice land in Sŏkp'o is about $1100 per acre, although there is considerable variation depending on the quality of the soil and access to water. The value of the grain produced on an acre of

TABLE 5. AMOUNT OF ARABLE LAND PER HOUSEHOLD IN SŎKP'O, THE COUNTY, THE PROVINCE, AND THE NATION, 1966.

| | Sŏkp'o | | Sŏsan County | | South Ch'ungch'ŏng Province | | South Korea | |
|---|---|---|---|---|---|---|---|---|
| | No. of households | Percent | Thousands of households | Percent | Thousands of households | Percent | Thousands of households | Percent |
| Less than 1/4 acre | 12 | 11.5 | 0.8 | 2.3 | 8 | 2.5 | 73 | 0.3 |
| 1/4 to 3/4 acre | 30 | 28 | 3.6 | 10.2 | 40 | 13 | 358 | 14 |
| 3/4 to 1 1/4 acres | 19 | 17.6 | 5.4 | 15.5 | 52 | 17 | 464 | 18 |
| 1 1/4 to 2 1/2 acres | 26 | 24 | 11.8 | 34 | 104 | 33.5 | 818 | 32 |
| 2 1/2 to 5 acres | 19 | 18 | 10.5 | 30 | 85 | 26.5 | 657 | 30 |
| 5 to 8 acres | 2 | 0.9 | 2.3 | 6.5 | 18 | 5.8 | 137 | 5 |
| More than 8 acres | 0 | 0 | 0.6 | 1.5 | 6 | 1.9 | 35 | 1.4 |
| Total | 108 | | 35 | | 313 | | 2542 | |

NOTE: The great difference in percentages between Sŏkp'o and the larger territorial entities reflect not only the relative poverty of the village, but also the fact that the vast majority of households included in the county, province, and national statistics are in farm villages where fishing does not exist as an alternative or supplementary occupation.

good paddy land in an average year is approximately $300. Rice land in Sŏkp'o seems to be somewhat higher priced than in many other villages, even though most of it is of inferior quality. Population pressures are particularly acute, with little migration out of the village and fairly rigid topographic limits on the expansion of arable land. Also, commercial fishing operations bring substantial quantities of cash into the village at certain seasons, and much of this is invested in land.

Before the land reform one absentee landowner possessed about 25 acres of good paddy land that he had acquired during the Japanese occupation by damming a narrow inlet and reclaiming the tidal mudflats. Under Japanese rule tenants paid 50 percent or more of their crop in rent and had no security of tenure. By taking advantage of the ignorance of the villagers following passage of the 1950 Land Reform Law, the absentee landowner was able to dispossess nearly all his tenants and convert more than 15 acres into salt pans. Consequently, land reform in this village constituted an economic disaster for some forty-five tenant families, many of whom lost their means of livelihood and were forced to move away. In 1966 the price of salt was so low that the owner stopped all production, thus eliminating approximately one-sixth of the village's most productive area from any use whatever.

The land reform law does work to the advantage of the few tenants who rented terraced fields that were not incorporated in the salt pans, however. They now pay only one-third of the crop as rent and their use right to the land is guaranteed. There is little tenancy in the village except for this one area. Low rents and guaranteed tenure make tenancy an unattractive proposition for a landowner, who usually prefers to use hired agricultural labor if he is not able to farm all his land himself. Furthermore, tenancy is now repugnant to the villagers because it implies a lower social status; and as a result of the furor over land reform and intensive indoctrination under the Communists it is vaguely felt to be illegal. Some concealed tenancy exists, particularly among relatives, but also among some of the poor families who have moved into outlying areas of the village in recent years. It probably will increase as more efficient farmers prosper and gain control of more land, and as the population continues to grow. On the other hand, reclamation projects, if successful, will substantially increase the land holdings of nearly every inhabitant in the village.

Fishing exists as an alternative means of livelihood for those with insufficient land, and this probably helps prevent the growth of a rural proletariat utterly dependent on landowners and therefore forced to acquiesce in the kind of circumvention of land reform laws that is taking place elsewhere in Korea (Parsons 1965:11).

In Sŏkp'o the size of land holdings, agricultural productivity, and standards of living are all low compared to national and provincial averages (see Table 5). Still, the existence of fishing as an alternative occupation and the fact that there are so few large landowners mean that the gap between rich and poor is substantially less than in many nearby villages. Geographic remoteness and the consequent isolation from commercial markets and radical technological innovation have so far insulated this relative economic equality from violent dislocations. At the same time the loss of aristocratic privilege and the spread of democratic ideology has greatly diminished the social distance that existed fifty years ago between aristocrat and commoner.

The detailed analysis of land holdings given in Table 5 shows that in 1966 twelve households possessed less than 300 *pyong* (¼ acre) of arable land. Ten of these have been classified in Table 6 as "impoverished."

An examination of how such landless families exist is in-

TABLE 6. ECONOMIC CLASSIFICATION OF SŎKP'O HOUSEHOLDS (INCLUDING FACTORS IN ADDITION TO LAND).

|  | *No. of households* | *Percent* |
|---|---|---|
| Impoverished | 10 | 9.3 |
| Poor | 35 | 32.3 |
| Middle: |  |  |
| Lower | 18 | 16.7 |
| Upper | 24 | 22.2 |
| Well off | 19 | 17.6 |
| Rich | 2 | 1.9 |
| TOTAL | 108 | 100.0 |

structive. One man who suffered a fishing disaster is now getting help from his Yi clan relatives for whom he provides agricultural labor. In addition, he owns a stone fish trap and distributes the catch to all who have assisted him. There are two cripples, both of whom were set up with wine shops by their relatives. One of the village's three shamanistic practitioners also falls in this category. Although he is popular, and his services much in demand, he and his sons are alcoholics and have sold off most of their land. Two families are poor affinal relatives of well-off households. In both cases they have moved to Sŏkp'o since 1945, and the men work for their in-laws either in the fields or as members of boat crews. The younger brother of the largest landowner in the village has so little land that he must also be placed in this category, although his actual position is more secure than the others. A recent migrant to the village has no land but manages to live by netting fish with techniques not used by the other residents. One family of a very small lineage (two households) that has nevertheless been in Sŏkp'o a long time has considerable forest land, and firewood is gathered for distribution in the village. The heads of two more families fish on other people's boats, while the most truly impoverished household is that of a widow with children who has no close relatives in the village. Her neighbors, who are also poor, provide some help—but grudgingly and in small amounts.

Thirty families own or farm as tenants between ¼ and ¾ acre of land. Such people are also very poor, especially if there are numerous children or if other unproductive relatives are living under the same roof. However, some young couples in this group, who have only one or two infant children, live in reasonable security, since they are just barely self-sufficient in rice and can supplement their meager agricultural production with income from oystering and fishing. Landholdings of this size provide only a marginal subsistence, but where good management, extra skills, and conscientious frugality exist, "poor" households are hard to distinguish from many "middle farmers" of the next higher category. Conversely, a heavy drinker, an incompetent wife, or lazy sons bring the standard of living of some "middle" farmers down to that of the "poor."

The middle category has been divided into lower and upper sections. Most of those in the lower middle group, with from ¾ to 1¼ acres, also live a precarious existence with little margin for luxuries. They are not able to send their children to school beyond the sixth grade, but usually food, shelter, and clothing are minimally adequate. Some families in the upper middle group possess radios and foot-operated sewing machines. Ceremonial obligations are faithfully carried out but as cheaply as possible, usually with the aid of other lineage members and neighbors. In a family with land holdings as small as this, there is nearly always excess underemployed labor except at times of peak agricultural activity, and a youth who joins a fishing crew and brings home 20,000 *wŏn* (about $75) during the season provides a considerable extra margin of security. This middle group, comprising forty-two households, is the largest in the village and is increasing in size.

Some nineteen farmers own between 2½ and 5 acres and can be called relatively well off. They are not worried about the prospect of hunger and can dress decently. Ceremonial obligations are fulfilled scrupulously, and visitors and guests are given copious amounts to eat and drink. Families in this group all had transistor radios, and adult males usually wore wristwatches.

Finally there were two households with more than 5 acres; these constituted a separate group, *hors de classe*, in the economic ranking used by villagers. Sick members of these families went to see the doctor in town, and an education through high school or even beyond was conceivable for talented children. The heads of these two families had the capacity to make small capital investments in new productive facilities. One of them, who represented a prominent branch of the former *yangban* lineage, possessed a strong sense of social responsibility, and was anxious to promote innovations in agriculture and fishing. The other, already referred to as a miser, was extremely conservative and devoted his energies to acquiring more land.

The economic gradation described above in terms of ownership of land is subject to considerable modification, both because of the variation in family size and in terms of additional possessions such as forest land, boats, or other fishing equipment. Some adjustment to account for these factors has been attempted in Table 6.

There is a sharp contrast between the situation at Sŏkp'o and at Yi Gong Ri, an entirely agricultural inland village about twelve miles away. There anyone with less than an acre of land is considered poor, while the average farmer possesses between 1 and 2½ acres. With more than this a man is considered "well off," and "rich" if he has 4 acres or more. Not only are the average holdings considerably larger, yields are a good deal higher as well.

## Oxen

Oxen are an important and scarce economic resource. Only twelve households out of 108 possess full-grown animals, although they are essential for agricultural work. While the risk (from injury or disease) is greater than with land, advantages (both economic and psychological) are commensurate. Oxen are loaned to neighbors, relatives, and friends in exchange for agricultural labor at the rate of two man days for one ox day, so a man with more land than he can farm finds it extremely useful to have an ox. Actual land holdings are so small that a day or so of ploughing suffices for most farmers, and the oxen are traded around busily at the peak seasons.

They require or at least are believed to require a great deal of care. They are groomed frequently, and twice a day they are fed a hot mush made of grain and certain grasses. The ox's stall is an integral part of the house structure and opens into the central courtyard.

Owning an ox in Sŏkp'o means more than just security and respectability. It stands for success, and men who are predominantly farmers take nearly as much interest in oxen as Americans do in cars. People say there is a special feeling towards the ox as part of the family, with a kind of mutual understanding that develops after years of working together. The value of a full-grown working animal is 60,000 *wŏn* ($200) or about the same as the cost of constructing a medium-sized house.

In nearby villages that are entirely agricultural the importance of oxen as a focus of men's achievement drives is more
marked than in Sŏkp'o. The buying and selling of animals at
five-day markets or through itinerant cattle brokers is of obsessive interest to mature farmers. In these villages where
average land holdings and income are greater than at Sŏkp'o, a
higher percentage of the households own oxen. On the other
hand, there is a greater concentration of wealth, with sharper
contrasts in living standards between well-to-do and poor
peasants.

## FISHING

Until the arrival of the Japanese in 1910 (their direct influence was not really felt in the village until four or five years later) Sŏkp'o had no sailboats, and fishing with hook and line and
with nets was carried out near the coast at a relatively primitive technological level. All equipment was manufactured locally including hooks, although iron of course was obtained
elsewhere.

Large stone fish traps built where sandy beaches adjoin rock
outcroppings take advantage of the great tidal range. They have
been there as long as anyone can remember and have been
handed down in a few families as an important source of food.
In recent years the runs of mullet, shad, and corvenia along the
coast that used to fill the traps periodically have dropped off
sharply and some are no longer maintained. A good deal of
work is required to put the stones back in place after a storm,
and management and maintenance of the traps is now mainly
done by the poor and the old who have no other work.

Occasionally the traps still fill up with fish, and an excited
crowd quickly gathers as the desperate fish begin to mill around
more and more frantically. Many of the spectators help gather
the fish as the tide goes out. Any fish that jumps over the stone
wall or finds a gap in the rocks belongs to whoever catches it.
The owner usually distributes a good portion to relatives and
others to whom he may owe favors. If the catch is unusually
large, he will use part of it to pay off obligations on the spot,

keep a considerable portion for himself, and turn the rest over to the village.

The inhabitants of Sŏkp'o bartered some of their fish during the late Yi dynasty period for food and a few manufactured goods that were brought to the coast by people from inland towns and villages. Under Japanese direction a revolution took place in fishing. A different kind of boat with sails was introduced and the villagers learned much more efficient "long line" techniques for catching ray, eel, corvenia, and croaker. They also learned various kinds of netting techniques from the Japanese, who supplied the fishermen with the necessary gear. The Japanese, in addition to building roads and a rail network, established coastal passenger and freight shipping service on a regular basis. Large city fish markets and canneries were built to handle the increased fish production. Sŏkp'o was too isolated to profit much from the expanded national market for fish, but trading with the immediate hinterland increased substantially.

New methods of fishing are being introduced again today, and boats are going farther offshore as the immediate coastal fisheries become progressively depleted. A much higher investment of capital in larger boats, nets, and engines is required, but the rewards for successful crews are greater. A variety of new technological skills as well as experience offshore is necessary, which explains why the efforts so far in Sŏkp'o have not been particularly successful. A new kind of inshore fishing with nets for anchovy, which are then boiled and dried on the beach, was introduced five years ago and has brought quick profits, however. Eight boats each with a crew of four were at work in this particular fishery in 1966, with more scheduled to be in the water soon. The introduction of engine-powered boats in 1967 permitted direct transportation of some of the fish catch and the oyster harvest to the big Inchŏn wholesale market for the first time.

Fishmongers, both men and women, have always come to Sŏkp'o from the nearby town of Wŏnbuk (a walk of about five miles plus a ferry ride) to obtain fish. The existence of this commercial outlet, small as it is, has meant that fishermen, unlike farmers, have participated in some sort of competitive market.

*The net, representing an investment of about $500, is several hundred yards long. Two groups of five or six men each pull at opposite ends of the horseshoe beach.*

When there are big catches, a certain amount of money can be made. Often, however, fishermen have been obliged to borrow from the dealers so that even when their luck is good, it means an easing of indebtedness rather than a quick profit.

In contrast to farming, fishing is regarded as highly speculative, and investment, profit, and losses are often spoken of in terms similar to those used for gambling.

A significant change has been taking place during the last few years as increased population and an expanding national economy put more pressure on available fish resources. Fish prices have gone up, and the dealers, who take away their stock in baskets on their heads or backs, now compete with each other for the catch. When a fishing boat (sail) returns with the day's catch, half or more may be sold to these buyers who wait on the beach. They try to establish special relations with individual boat owners because there is always a shortage of fish, and the buyers want to be assured of a source of supply. The surest way to do this is by lending money to hard-up fishermen who must then pay it back, along with 60 percent annual interest, in fish. While most fishermen have some sort of agreement with a buyer, they try to maintain a degree of independence in disposing of their catch. Occasionally someone in the fisherman's family (usually a woman) will carry the fish six kilometers to market in an effort to squeeze every bit of income out of the catch. But it is extremely onerous work carrying heavy loads over rough ground, and there is a certain hesitancy about usurping the professionals' function.

Fish are an important medium of exchange in many social transactions within the village. "Gifts" of fish expressing the fulfillment of various obligations or an attempt to gain favors are frequent. Sŏkp'o fishermen resort to considerable subterfuge in order to safeguard this traditional outlet for their catch from the demands of buyers. On four occasions I spent the entire day out fishing, each time on a different sailing junk. In three cases the boat owner put more than half of the choicest fish in a relatively inaccessible compartment on top of which lines and other heavy gear were piled as we approached the beach. Then when the buyer (or buyers) came scrambling aboard, the owner and crew, bewailing their small catch, showed them only the remainder of the fish that had actually been caught. Not until the dealers had been ferried off to the other shore were the rest brought out. Some were divided among the crew, and I was always given one. The rest was either distributed on the spot to villagers who had been alerted by some mysterious communications network that I never understood, or they were delivered by members of the boat owner's family directly to certain houses. Invariably the supply seemed insufficient to satisfy the demand.

At certain times of the year the boat owner would keep his entire catch for salting and drying. The cash value of croakers was so great, however, that except for important ceremonial occasions they were rarely consumed in the village. Information concerning the actual disposition of the fish was difficult to obtain, even when I joined the crew. Fishermen almost invariably underestimated their catch not only to dealers from out of town but also in talking to fellow villagers. The best explanation that I could devise was that the owner used the fish to pay off various kinds of obligations, to barter for agricultural prod-

*The fish have been taken from the boat to the owner's courtyard, where they are being distributed to relatives.*

ucts, and as presents, both ceremonial and coercive. Since his estimate of priorities might frequently be at odds with that of creditors who were anxious to obtain fish, he attempted to conceal the amount of his total catch as well as how much he had given to whom.

The contrast between farming and fishing as a way of life is a theme throughout this monograph. Differences in attitudes towards work as well as in the actual cycles and patterns of activity are profound. Yet most men in the village divide their time between the two areas of economic activity and possess considerable skill in both.

Many of the fishermen are poor with very small plots of land, and farming activity takes up only a small part of their time. The slack seasons for fishing (in general, winter) last longer than for farming. In addition there are more or less extended periods of bad weather when no boats go out, so that those men who are predominantly oriented towards fishing have more leisure and keep more irregular hours than farmers. Much of the leisure is spent with other men either outdoors by the boats or in wine shops. The company of fishermen is more exclusively a man's society than agriculture, where women share much of the work.

A certain amount of subsistence fishing—to provide food for the household, relatives, and neighbors—is carried out in routine fashion with skills learned in childhood and a minimum of equipment. Most of the poorest men in the village probably would continue to operate in this manner if left undisturbed.

Another aspect of the contrast between fishing and farming is the fact that fishing has been traditionally a despised occupation. This has meant lower standards of living, less education, and lower social status for households composed mainly of fishermen. In spite of the village-wide consensus with regard to core values, there is considerable difference between farmers and fishermen in their personal conduct. Idleness (often enforced), drunkenness, its behavioral corollary quarreling, and adultery all are more prevalent in the neighborhoods where fishermen are preponderant.

To the extent that fishermen tend to identify themselves less with the traditional, conservative, and agricultural way of life, they are probably more receptive to change and development, both technological and social. Also, fishing as an occupation is steadily being upgraded as the prospect of cash profits excites the imagination of "boat people" and farmers alike. A new kind of selective process is beginning to operate, since personal qualities such as ambition, individual intitiative, originality, and technical ability that have not been highly valued in the agricultural and collective milieu of the past, now are important for successful fishing operations.

In recent years the relative prosperity and social status of fishermen in some of the offshore islands and in the larger ports has improved significantly. In Sŏkp'o, although a handful of capable men seem to have the potential to take advantage of new fishing opportunities, most fishermen have neither the necessary education nor the social competence and self-confidence that goes with it. The irregular cycles of activity and the speculative economic attitudes have conditioned most of them to dislike the farmer's steady, conscientious approach to work. Increasingly a distinction is developing between those who ride the boats and those who finance them and gain the profits.

Both technology and the general economic environment of the fishing industry are subject to more rapid and more fundamental change than agriculture. Men who have never sailed out of sight of land are being confronted with the problems of offshore navigation and the location of schools of fish. Fishery entrepreneurs are concerned not only with price changes in the big city markets but also with the international market for exports. They are dependent on Inchŏn for fuel oil, ice, and operating capital, a radical change from the situation two years ago when sailboats were built and operated entirely with village resources.

## OTHER ECONOMIC FACTORS

### The Labor Supply and Family Size

The village during all but two or three weeks of the year has a large supply of excess labor, although there is a chronic shortage in some families where the adult male is sick or an older boy has been drafted. Idleness is much more apparent among men than women, who seem to be constantly busy at household tasks, gathering shellfish, or agriculture.

Lack of work is more evident in the two poorest neighborhoods where fishermen predominate; since my house was located between them, I may have received an exaggerated impression of underemployment for the village as a whole. But this area, particularly along the beach where boats are pulled up, is actually the central meeting place of the village, and the groups of men sitting in wine shops or in front of the store include many from the other more agricultural neighborhoods as well. Bands of youths usually are excluded from the company of older men and often can be seen wandering about except during the short anchovy fishing seasons or the times when every hand is needed for transplanting, harvesting, or thrashing.

There is a good deal of variation in the ratio of work to available labor among different households depending on the size of the family, the amount of land, and whether the primary orientation is towards fishing or farming. In nearly every case my informants were curiously reluctant to recognize the fact that there was not enough work to keep people busy. Comments on the labor situation nearly always were phrased in terms of the need for additional help during the most hectic periods.

It is estimated that one competent, hard-working adult can farm about an acre of paddy field and an acre of barley, but only about one-third of the households in Sŏkp'o have this much land. Since there is usually more than one and often three or four able-bodied males in a family, the basis of underemployment is obvious. Until six years ago when there were thirty sailboats fishing a six-month season, there was much more pressure on the labor supply. Today there are less than half this many boats, most of which fish a much shorter season. According to the accounts of old men, everyone was much busier fifty years ago.

With much of the leisure enforced and additional opportunities to work scarce, one sign of affluence is industrious activity.

This does not mean, however, that leisure is not desirable and enjoyed, or that work is highly valued for its own sake. Men and women are proud of their skills, but work itself does not seem to constitute a positive value in the puritanical sense. Although inevitable and necessary, the less there is the better, would seem to sum up the outlook of most villagers. Storekeepers in towns and cities are widely envied and admired, because they sit all day earning a good living without doing any hard work.

Nevertheless most people work hard and efficiently. Although there is no urgent sense of a deadline and there are plenty of pauses for eating, drinking, and chatting with passers by, the job is finished as quickly as techniques and equipment permit. Some farmers, particularly older conservative men with a solid reputation to uphold, seemed to be unhappy unless they were busy with agricultural jobs and rarely showed up in the casual men's groups of the Big Hamlet. Their visits to other neighborhoods were mainly restricted to ceremonial and political occasions or errands connected with work.

My informants often mentioned the advantage of having many children around the house so that they can start doing small jobs and running errands from the age of 8 to 10, although they are not usually expected to work full time until they are 15 or 16. Villagers are conscious of the pressure that each extra mouth to feed puts on family grain resources, but there seems to be a general reluctance to face the problem of economic costs involved in raising children. Having lots of children about (especially boys) is agreeable for the grandparents and a matter of pride for the father, while the burden of work and worry falls chiefly on the mother—who predictably has been most receptive to propaganda concerning family planning. But the status of a wife is low until she has one and preferably two sons, so that she is just as eager as anyone else to see children born during the early years of a marriage. Also, household work is greatly eased by the help of a competent daughter from about the age of 11 or 12, so the mother is not content with only sons.

Another important economic factor reinforces these built-in pressures to expand the population. In the short run a man is, in fact, better off if he has three or four able-bodied sons. Between the end of primary school and marriage—a period of about ten years—sons constitute by far the cheapest, most efficient, and most docile labor. In addition to helping with the work at home, they can join boat crews either in the village or in Inchŏn and bring home cash income that would never be available otherwise. Public works projects, such as the dike, that require unskilled labor give families with young men a clear economic advantage. The advantage is based chiefly, of course, on the fact that these sons bring their wages home and subordinate their own wish to buy clothes, watches, or radios to the needs of their families. Some times there is a degree of conflict, but in the great majority of cases, both young and old take pride in observing traditional norms of filial piety and family solidarity.

In case of sickness or the inevitable military service, a man with two sons is far better off. The same principle operates if a youth shows promise and is sent to middle and high school. Such a boy not only does not contribute his labor at home but constitutes a severe economic drain on family resources. In most cases he will learn to despise village life and will settle down in some minor clerical or commercial job in town, where his expectations and desires are out of all proportion to his meager salary. His family derives great satisfaction and a certain amount of prestige from having an educated son living in town, but no return on a very sizable investment. If there is no second son, the head of the house faces a bleak old age.

So, in assessing the economic context of birth control programs, it is necessary to consider also the narrow perspective of an individual head of household. But if his sons are numerous, their situation after the land is divided will be more precarious, and unless there is another occupation or an increase in arable land acreage (through tidal reclamation) their poverty is usually assured. Villagers explicitly recognize this as a cause of poverty in making economic rankings. A household with several sons is described as much less well off than one with the same amount of land but where an only son will keep the property intact. This is the static traditional view, and it is still prevalent. On the other hand, if the outside earnings of a son or sons permit the family to buy more land, the usual process may be arrested or even reversed for a time.

## Cooperation and Labor Exchange

Cooperative effort (*ture*) and the exchange of labor (*p'umasi*) without payment in money or kind is an important factor in village economic activity. Everyone takes the obligation to help on certain occasions seriously, and if for any reason a person cannot participate, he is expected to send someone else from the household. Cooperative labor is customary for house building, transplanting rice, threshing grain, moving, hauling boats, and on ceremonial occasions such as weddings, funerals, and death anniversaries. Cooperation is also general in time of any emergency such as fire or storm. Occasionally additional labor required at the season of peak activity is paid for with grain after the harvest, a transaction that is called *p'umsak*.

There is a series of overlapping groups that habitually get together, although the members may be different for different functions. For example, the core of a roof raising group norm-

*A cooperative work group of relatives, friends, and neighbors put on a roof.*

ally will be residents of the same neighborhood, but relatives and friends from other parts of the village also play a prominent role, some because they have special skills or are indebted for past favors, and others simply because they have a tradition of working together. By contrast, ceremonial occasions primarily require the cooperation of kin with the important addition of help from immediate neighbors. No exact accounting is kept of the amount of labor contributed in terms of time or skills or effort. The important thing is to participate, and help is given ungrudgingly and for many hours or even days at a stretch.

People enjoy working together at such times in an atmosphere of collective euphoria, fueled in the case of the men by considerable drinking. There is a continual hubbub with much joking and horseplay, but since everyone has the necessary skills and is used to working together, a great deal of effective work is accomplished. Leadership in the sense of a recognized locus of responsibility and a definite chain of command does not appear to exist, although orders (often contradictory) may be constantly shouted by several of the participants. Possibly the best description would be to say that morale is invariably high when voluntary cooperative work is in progress, and everyone has a good time. Despite the fact that no one is paid, the "host" must supply plenty of food and drink, and his kitchen swarms with women shouting, laughing, and cursing as they dish up prodigious meals for the workers.

In this area of traditional village cooperation, neighborhood ties play just as important a role as those of kinship. Often the neighbors will be kin, but where they are not, the obligation to help is just as strong. In the few cases where kin do not exist or do not have the resources or the desire to help, neighbors invariably take on the burden.

By way of contrast to this somewhat idyliic description, it should be pointed out that the villagers did not work well together on a reclamation project for wages. The problem, resulting from a combination of disciplined regulation and a more subtle morale factor, is further discussed in Chapter 7.

When fishing with nets, an individual's desire for material gain is reinforced by the sense of joint cooperative effort, and both incentives sustain men during long periods of extremely hard labor. Chanting, mutual shouts of encouragement, and the mounting excitement as nets are drawn closer to the beach or boat are all characteristic of Sŏkp'o fishing, just as they are of many other fishing societies. If the catch is good, each man can estimate his own share in exact monetary terms. When transplanting rice together, on the other hand, there is no such immediate profit incentive and the atmosphere of diffused optimism reflects instead group solidarity and the promotion of a generalized collective welfare.

Many other forms of cooperative labor exist on a smaller scale without the same festival atmosphere described above. Groups of kin, usually all male or all female, habitually perform certain specific agricultural tasks together. Such a work group, formed of representatives from each of several related and usually neighboring households, works on the land of each family in turn.

Labor exchange has already been mentioned in connection with the lending of oxen. Less formal exchanges take place frequently when someone who has helped a friend or neighbor asks for assistance in return. If the job is bigger and several people participate, it is difficult for an outsider to draw a distinction between cooperative work and labor exchange, but villagers seem to have a clear idea of which principle they are operating under—either that of direct reciprocity for specific services rendered, or as participants in a socially sanctioned joint enterprise.

Differences in wealth have an effect on the patterns of work cooperation. A wealthy man with more land than most needs much more labor. Wages are not paid for agricultural work, but he is in a position to reward people in various ways with food, drink, seeds, agricultural implements, or small loans. Or he can permit the cutting of wood for fuel on his forest land. In a time of family crisis, the help of such a person can be crucial. As a result something resembling a patron-client economic relation exists between some well-to-do farmers and their poorer neighbors. Any blatant overt assertion of the "patron's" higher status would, however, be criticized and resented.

Poor households, particularly those belonging to smaller and less influential lineages, are always assiduous in helping their neighbors. The women can be counted on to assist in the kitchen if a wedding or other ceremony takes place, and the men are sure to be at the core of any cooperative work party. Such people have plenty of leisure as a rule, and the rice, drink, and other delicacies that are always served on these occasions represent a significant economic incentive. Above all, it is the poor who stand to benefit most from the system of collective responsibility. They must often depend on the good will and help of their neighbors, while the well-to-do farmer can maintain himself independently. The system acts ultimately as a form of welfare insurance providing some protection for economically marginal members of the commuity.

## Debt

About 60 percent of the villagers have substantial debts (Table 7), and many other minor loans are made that were not recorded. Getting a loan even with high interest rates and excellent collateral is usually a problem. Some people said they were reluctant to borrow from relatives, since an unpaid loan can disturb family solidarity. Usually kin are easier to approach, more disposed to understand and sympathize with one's economic troubles, feel an obligation to help, and are less likely to be obnoxiously insistent about repayment. Out of fifty-four persons with whom this problem was discussed, twenty-six said they would first ask relatives for money, thirteen preferred unrelated neighbors, and ten said they would approach friends. The remaining five respondents, all of whom were poor risks, said they would go outside the village to obtain money. Such answers undoubtedly reflect the variability of personal circumstances and personality. A few households are on bad terms with their relatives; in other cases where neighbors are preferred, it may be because the borrower lives in a neighborhood where there are no related households.

Pressures for repayment are great, and there were numerous cases of forced land sales to pay off debts. Villagers feel strongly about this. The sanction is not legal action but social

TABLE 7. ANALYSIS OF INDEBTEDNESS OF CERTAIN VILLAGERS IN
SŎKP'O BY NEIGHBORHOOD, WITH REASONS GIVEN FOR
GOING INTO DEBT.

| | *Yangban* | *Big Hamlet* | *"Over There"* |
|---|---|---|---|
| Number of households in sample | 19 | 28 | 12 |
| Number with debts | 7(37%) | 21(75%) | 6(50%) |
| Average amount of debt (in *wŏn*) | 4,000 | 15,000 | 10,000 |
| Reasons given for indebtedness: Consumption of funds for— | | | |
| food | 2 | 12 | |
| medicine | 3 | 1 | |
| ceremonial expenses | 3 | 3 | |
| other living expenses | | 3 | 1 |
| Investment in— | | | |
| agriculture | | 3 | 3 |
| fishing | | 5 | 1 |
| education | 2 | | 1 |
| Number of indebted households in "poor" or "impoverished" categories (from Table 6) | 2 | 14 | 0 |

NOTES:
1. Some informants gave more than one reason for going into debt.
2. One is tempted to predict increased prosperity for the residents of "Over There" on the basis of the investment figures.
3. Some informants in the Big Hamlet probably exaggerated the amount of indebtedness, but the general picture is accurate.

pressure. A man's reputation suffers heavily if he cannot repay. In one case where heavy debts to outsiders were paid by relatives in order to protect the family name, the debtor found himself slipping into a kind of dependent status with the relatives who had bailed him out. Occasionally he would try to reassert himself, and since he was in his late fifties and of a fairly high rank genealogically, the situation was difficult, with clan cohesion showing some strain.

The sanctions enforcing fiscal responsibility are only fully effective within the village. An alternative to repayment is simply moving out. Contractual obligations with people in town depend almost entirely on personal relations, since the villager would never think of recourse to law.

## Attitudes towards Production and Wealth

The fundamental analytical assumptions of economics—that there is a scarcity of goods and resources relative to wants, and that individuals make choices in using available resources in order to maximize their satisfactions—can, of course, also be applied to the study of a farming-fishing community in Korea.

George Foster makes a similar assumption when he defines the "Image of Limited Good" as follows: "Peasants view their total environment as one in which all the desired things in life . . . exist in finite quantity and are always in short supply, as far as the peasant is concerned," so that "an individual or a family can improve a position only at the expense of others" (1965:296–297). He supports his view of the peasants cognitive orientation by stating that "in the average village there *is* only a finite amount of wealth produced, and no amount of extra hard work will significantly change the figure." Or further on, "The average peasant sees little or no relationship between work and production techniques on the one hand and the acquisition of wealth on the other" (*Ibid.*:298).

These are profound insights that apply also to the situation in Sŏkp'o. Foster, however, goes on to make generalized inferences from his assumptions as follows: "Peoples who see themselves in threatened circumstances which the Image of Limited Good implies react normally in one of two ways: 1) maximum cooperation and sometimes communism, burying individual differences and placing sanctions against individualism; or 2) extreme individualism. Peasant societies seem always to choose the second alternative" (*Ibid.*: 301).

In direct contradiction to Foster's view, one of the major purposes of this book is to describe and document the manner in which the people of Sŏkp'o have "chosen" the first alternative. "Burying individual differences and placing sanctions against individualism" is an excellent description of an important, consciously held social value that infuses more or less successfully almost every aspect of village behavior.

Foster's model is unrealistic in implying that two mutually exclusive categories, an extreme form of cooperation or an extreme individualism, exist as behavioral norms or as unconscious cognitive orientations. Peasant society or any other society will always show a give-and-take between both. What makes Foster's conclusion concerning peasant societies throughout the world surprising is that ethnographic accounts of East Asian peasants have repeatedly emphasized the cooperative and communal nature of much of economic and social activity.

The idea of a limit on total wealth and resources relative to a fixed or expanding population is crucial, however, and does correspond to the attitude of most of the inhabitants of Sŏkp'o. The contrast in outlook between peasants whose thinking is dominated by this assumption and our concept of the productive, innovative activist exploiting his environment deserves great emphasis, but the inferences that can be made from it in Korea are diametrically opposed to Foster's interpretation.

In Sŏkp'o and the surrounding villages cooperation and egalitarianism have been important elements in traditional village life. The divisive effects of economic and class differences, rival kinship loyalties, and personal hostility have been managed within an ideological and social environment that emphasizes subordination of individual to group interests, scrupulous maintenance of correct personal relations, and the preservation of social harmony within the face-to-face community. The statement that "peasant societies seem always to choose the . . . alternative [of extreme individualism]" just does not apply.

The typical villager cannot be seen simply as an individual competing with his neighbors in order to maximize material possessions, or any other egoistic satisfaction for that matter. The traditional ideological system imposes many limitations on what might be called rational economic motives. In Sŏkp'o people dwell constantly on the extent of their poverty, but in actuality they are far less preoccupied with acquiring material goods than their cousins in the city. The subordination of individual goals and satisfactions to those of the collectivity—family, lineage, neighborhood, or village—is nearly automatic, while excessive individualism stands out and is likely to be criticized.

If it is combined with personal aggrandizement, social censure is bound to be severe.

Under cover of apparent conformity with collective norms most individuals are constantly promoting their own interests, and the prevailing tolerance permits someone who is both ruthless and thick-skinned to do some outrageous things. But there is a limit beyond which a man cannot go and still participate fully in village social life. The amassing of personal wealth in itself, particularly if it appears to be at the expense of one's fellow villagers, does not bring rewards in terms of higher status. On the contrary, it can lead to suspicion, censure, and even isolation. As in so many primitive or underdeveloped societies, it is the redistribution of wealth in certain prescribed ways that adds to a man's prestige. Demands for hospitality, generosity, the proper observance of ceremonial obligations to kin, and assistance to neighbors still usually have precedence over the profit motive in determining behavior.

This situation seems to prevail only as long as there is participation in the social collectivity, where traditional mechanisms of social control are able to function. When villagers migrate to the town or city, restraints on egoistic, acquisitive behavior no longer operate to the same extent (except among close kin), and there is a reorganization of values. This is even true for temporary excursions. For example, a village housewife may follow a different normative code when she travels to the market town to buy or sell goods. While some permanent market relations do exist on the basis of mutual confidence, they often end disastrously and bitterly. Transactions with outsiders are much more competitive and insecure than those within the village.

Many fishing and commercial ventures end abruptly with one partner taking all the available funds and absconding. I heard the same story again and again in Sŏkp'o and neighboring villages. A trusted friend, almost always from outside the village, suddenly disappears with the proceeds of a particularly large fish catch or with money destined for payment to a crew, leaving his partner with heavy debts and no funds. The result is usually sale of the boat or the last remaining quarter-acre of rice land.

Although villagers are extremely suspicious of financial

arrangements with outsiders, there are always those who seem unable to resist. The desire for speculative profits combined with considerable naïveté concerning financial pitfalls in the world beyond Sŏkp'o plays into the hands of the "confidence man" type of entrepreneur. He will move on and can ignore the economic wreckage and outraged feelings left behind. The villager, on the other hand, is obliged to go on living surrounded by the same people, where everything he does is known and talked about.

"Suckers" are beguiled by more than just desire for economic gain. The prospect of being the center of bustling activity connected with fishing or commerce is a glamorous one that provides immediate short-run social rewards. If a large new net is being prepared for use, or a recently acquired boat with an engine is being outfitted for sea, a crowd is attracted and many who start as spectators join in the work. The owner's wife brings food and drink, and he himself becomes the focal point for pleasant excitement while his generosity stimulates respect and gratitude. The opportunity to play such a role is sometimes irresistible.

In contrast to the dangers involved in dealings with outsiders, there is within the village an endless (both in space and time) network of reciprocal obligations. Every transaction—gift, loan, barter, or sale—is carried out within this framework. Occasionally there is dissatisfaction and argument when the participants take a different view of the record to date, but in most cases there is not only consensus but a delicate sensitivity to the other person's situation, so that the rule of reciprocity can be stretched to avoid embarrassment or hardship.

From the point of view of cognitive orientation, a major point to be stressed in contrasting a Sŏkp'o villager with western economic man is his conception of productivity: the cause-and-effect relations between human effort and the creation of new wealth. Conscientious hard work and skill in agriculture are valued, but there seems to be some resistance to the idea that yields will be substantially altered by increased individual effort or through innovative practices. Agricultural techniques in Sŏkp'o are significantly more conservative and less productive than those of neighboring villages. When pressed on the subject, residents tend to blame poor soil, lack of capital, the short-age of credit, an insufficiency of technological and financial aid from government agencies, and poor communications; but mostly they ignore the problem. Men are proud of their agricultural skill and resent the implication that their farming methods are inadequate. When farmers discuss specific crops, there is inevitably a return to the conclusion that yields are determined by the soil and the weather.

Yet everyone knows that agricultural practices introduced by the Japanese resulted in vastly improved yields, and everyone also knows that crops are better in other villages where new methods and improved irrigation systems are used. I got the impression that most farmers lacked confidence in their own ability to increase productivity by altering or controlling the effects of weather or the composition of soils. Rather than accept responsibility for undertaking controversial innovations, they usually stress their own lack of knowledge and ability with a kind of formalized humility. There is then a retreat to the fatalistic proposition that crop yields are determined by outside forces beyond the individual's control. A decision to invest scarce family resources, both money and labor, in new agricultural practices is a difficult one for the head of a household to make. The speculative attitude that exists with regard to fishing and commerce does not seem to apply to rice agriculture. Landowners are not conditioned to regard their fields as a proper area for individual initiative and experimentation.

The reluctance to seek new solutions for agricultural problems and to promote change does not imply a conscious resistance to the notion of economic progress itself, which has in fact acquired almost the same pseudo-mystical aura in Korea as in the West: that of being able to solve all problems and fulfill all desires. From the villagers' point of view, faith in progress has nothing to do with individual initiative and achievement. Progress is bestowed. It is an entity, not a process. It can be forced on the village as during the Japanese occupation, or it can be granted by a generous America as when Eighth Army bulldozers suddenly appear to build a dike and reclaim land from the sea. But it is not primarily associated with efforts by the individual to manipulate the environment for his own ends.

Progress is a blessing to be accepted passively. Where individual struggle is involved, it is in the effort to make sure that one's own village, or lineage, or family is not left out by the whimsically unpredictable administrative machinery through which the benefits of progress trickle down.

To state the proposition in somewhat different terms, Koreans (with particular emphasis on the traditional elite) are accustomed to expressing competitive energy and achievement drives in the manipulation of personal relations and social situations rather than in efforts to dominate the natural environment. As the United States has found to its consternation, skill in sophisticated negotiation comes to them naturally.

In naming poor communications as a cause of low agricultural productivity, the villager is usually thinking of the inaccessibility of markets and the problems involved in obtaining low-interest loans from the Agricultural Cooperative. But there is a much more basic, although indirect, sense in which the remoteness affects productivity. The village is geographically at the end of the line, and as a result attitudes towards agriculture are still subsistence oriented. Participation in a competitive agricultural market system would not have any immediate, important economic effect on the vast majority of Sŏkp'o's farmers, because surpluses where they exist are too small. Still, the fact of competition with, or at least exposure to, more efficient producers in a market place seems to have provided in other villages the jolt necessary to transform passive fatalism into a more rational consideration of ends and means. A new way of thinking about agriculture is spread about: the realization that individual initiative has something to do with improving crop yields.

Some examples may be useful in order to point out contrasts between traditional village thinking and what seems so inescapably and rationally obvious to a western observer. Most wealth is still calculated in terms of rice—a commodity that is, of course, readily transformable into other forms of property. Thus everyone wants more land so as to increase his production of rice and add to his wealth. More production not only means immediately satisfying the desire for larger portions of rice at mealtime, but it also means that debts can be paid off, children sent to school, medicines bought, and favorite fishing and commercial schemes capitalized. With rice land absolutely limited and population increasing rapidly, concentration on improving rice yields would appear to be the obvious and only means available for achieving desired goals. Yet farmers are often indifferent to the fundamental changes necessary in order to increase yields and ensure against crop damage by unfavorable weather.

Small-scale water storage, irrigation, and fertilization projects would require a heavy investment of labor, which is plentiful, and some use of scarce capital. But they would not necessarily exceed the resources of a middle-grade farmer with one to two acres of rice land. The fact that such projects are needed and would raise yields is grudgingly admitted, and the construction techniques are known. The reluctance to undertake them is mystifying, and I spent a lot of time trying to decipher basic attitudes. There seemed to be a factor of pure prejudice based on professional distaste for innovations.

On further examination this "distaste" turned out to be rather complicated. It is reinforced by unpleasant memories of the Japanese occupation, when many similar projects were undertaken under coercive pressures. There are examples from all over Korea of how farmers expressed their new freedom at the time of the liberation in 1945 by rejecting and even destroying recent Japanese technological innovations in agriculture, while those that had become part of the accepted way of farming through many years of use were retained. It should be remembered that Japanese controls over the farm economy were so tight that increased productivity, large as it was, did not usually lead to greater income for the farmers, most of whom were tenants paying high rents and subject to other confiscatory practices.

Other values as well are in conflict with sound agricultural practices. The value attached to land itself quite apart from crop yields can be obstructive. In fact, part of the trouble seems to lie in a failure to make an analytical distinction between land area, value, and productivity. Since tiny terraced rice fields, often of marginal economic value, have been pushed up every water course as far as possible, there is no place left to build reservoirs without destroying a certain amount of arable land. Small ponds dug in the corner of a paddy field are a familiar sight only a few miles farther inland on the road to the county seat, but in Sŏkp'o they are rare, and despite the failure of the rains to come on time during three of the last five years, none are being dug. A great deal of conversation finally revealed that farmers begrudge the loss of 150 to 200 square feet of precious rice land. A simple calculation showing that the amount of crop loss for that field alone due to lack of rain in a single year was greater than the value of the land removed from use failed to impress anyone. Another factor is that the owners of reservoirs and ponds are obliged to provide water for all the fields below the source of water, regardless of whose fields they are. That such arrangements lead to conflict when water is scarce is a truism; therefore, according to some informants, they are not worth the trouble.

Other considerations are still harder to pin down. Rice land is an essential element in the moral order of the farmer's universe. There is a fatalistic optimism in the beneficent quality of natural processes—provided man, heaven, and earth maintain properly harmonious relations. Digging up paddy fields destroys something of moral worth on the one hand, while constructing a reservoir can be construed as an expression of doubt in the normal working of the cosmos on the other. Such notions, ultimately derived from Chinese philosophic concepts, are still widespread among the older generation. Although probably no farmer today has enough classical education to give a coherent statement of them, the superstitious implications are widely felt.

It is necessary to give point to these generalizations by some consideration of the diverse elements within the farming population. About half of all irrigated rice land is owned by men over 50 who are not only conservative but insist strongly on their authoritarian prerogatives, both in determining land use and in controlling the actions of their sons. Another significant portion (about 15 percent) is owned by poor farmers whose subsistence is so marginal that the idea of making a current investment in productivity for future consumption is out of the question. Still another group with little interest in agricultural innovation is composed of those who are primarily fishermen, but own small plots as well. They own another 15 to 20 percent of the total paddy land. Such men work in the fields when there is no fishing, but usually it is their women and children who till the soil. Thus, less than 20 percent of the village rice fields belong to younger men with enough resources to think about increasing productivity.

At present, by what appears to be pure coincidence, only one of the three or four men with intelligence, ability, and an action-oriented desire for change—those who might be labeled potential innovators—is concerned with agricultural development. A good deal of talk goes on about the advantages of various methods and crops, but Sŏkp'o is not a place where one urges someone else to try out an innovation without attempting it oneself, except as a joke.

One exception to the prevailing conservatism deserves mention. Some of the poorest familes, who possessed small plots of extremely sandy soil that was relatively unproductive when planted with traditional crops, have grown peanuts during the last few years with considerable success. Success is a relative term, which in this context means that their poverty has been somewhat alleviated. These families, with very little to lose, followed the lead of others in neighboring villages.

## Economic Development

Fundamental economic changes are taking place among the coastal villages of Sŏsan County, both in the area of technical innovation and with regard to the nature of transactional relations. Village economic life is increasingly and inexorably (although at widely different rates and in different sectors) being transformed by and integrated with the growing national economy.

In Sŏkp'o the process is just beginning. For the first time men with ambition, aggressive energy, and a readiness to accept innovation have a decisive advantage over their fellow villagers, and shifts in the division of wealth similar to those that have been taking place in other villages can be expected.

Lucky or more competent individuals will find they can do better on their own and desert collective institutions for individual entrepreneurship. The system of collective responsibility that guarantees everyone a certain minimum standard of subsistence then no longer operates so effectively, and the range of village living standards widens. In the area that I studied where there are gradations of geographic inaccessibility from village to village, the differential nature of this process is evident. The breakdown of traditional institutions often is accompanied by an increase in competition, envy, and hostility among individuals and groups.

Foster's model of peasant cognitive orientation might be useful for the study of change in Korean villages if it were radically altered as follows: In a community where the Image of Limited Good is widely held as an unconscious assumption, and traditional institutions are being undermined by economic change and development, there is liable to be an increase in mutual distrust and unrestrained acquisitive individualism.

The hypothesis that economic development in different sectors has a differential effect on social structure and values, depending on whether it reinforces traditional practices or transforms them (Epstein 1962) is generally supported by the situation in Sŏkp'o. Fishery development is tending to integrate a portion of the village economy with national markets, while travel and the exigencies of competition are changing the attitudes, beliefs, and expectations of fishermen. Agricultural development, on the other hand, reinforces many traditional customs and values. Of course, successful land reclamation and irrigation projects, by increasing living standards, permit more travel for everyone and higher education for many children. But the consequent process of change is far more gradual than among fishermen, particularly since the more prosperous farmers tend to revive traditional prestige-enhancing practices such as elaborate ancestor rituals, the study of Confucian classics, geomantic investigations, and the maintenance of a large extended family in one household.

The distinction between fishermen and farmers is not so sharp as the preceding discussion implies. As I have indicated earlier, all fishermen do some farming, and many predominantly farming families have at least one member who fishes regularly. Nevertheless, there is a distinct contrast between households and neighborhoods that are primarily oriented towards fishing and those that regard themselves as farmers. In contrast to the farmers, many fishermen are concerned about the backward nature of their equipment and skills and they are relatively eager to adopt new techniques. Only lack of capital prevents them from buying 60-foot draggers with all the latest electronic equipment.

Fishermen, and to a lesser extent farmers as well, are likely to be impatient with progress or production increases that occur in small increments. There is little faith in the cumulative effect of minor improvements, and the need to practice planned, sustained austerity in the present as a means of forming capital for future investment is not widely recognized. Enthusiasm is easily aroused by the prospect of dramatic and glamorous economic changes that will abruptly solve current problems, but so far it has been necessary to import most of the ideas, technology, capital, and leadership. Villagers have little confidence in their own capacity to effect substantial changes, and gradual improvements do not have much appeal.

Koreans themselves point to historical reasons for their impatience with conscientious, dogged, hard work and austerity as an expression of achievement drives and as the approved path to success. A long history of warfare, invasion, pillaging, and destruction is supposed to have conditioned the populace to such a degree of economic uncertainty that only a bonanza or immediate windfall profits have any appeal. It is certainly true that much Korean economic activity has a speculative aspect that seems closer to outright gambling than to productive enterprise.

Another historical reason is sometimes given to explain economic behavior: exploitation of the peasant by aristocratic landowners and administrative officials consistently deprived him of the rewards of his labor and condemned him to a marginal existence. Even today government policy provides few incentives for the farmer. Low rice prices are maintained in order to placate the more politically active city dwellers, and most productive investment is in industry.

Something of a paradox exists, in that while economic development in a place like Sŏkp'o seems to require a release of individual energies and ambitions as a means of challenging tradition, the continuation of cooperative work habits and group solidarity is also essential.

Conservative attitudes towards agricultural productivity are linked to village traditions of cooperation and egalitarianism. The underlying conception of a fixed economic "pie" supports collective opposition to anyone who threatens to obtain a disproportionate share of power, prestige, and wealth, and individual aspirations are subordinated to collective interests. More diffuse objectives such as the esteem of one's fellow villagers or the desire to play an influential role in village affairs take precedence over acquisitive drives, and competition is expressed more between groups than among individuals.

Moreover, because of the fragmented land holdings and lack of other resources, cooperation among individual farmers is a necessary condition for successful development projects at the village level. Utilization of the tradition of collective responsibility and interdependence has proved to be a crucial factor in mobilizing rural energies and resources. In particular it must compensate for deficiencies of local administrative agencies and for the natural resistance of farmers to outside leadership when officials do attempt to exert it. Various degrees of compromise between aggressive individual initiative and cooperation presumably will have to emerge.

The kind of coercive leadership exercised by the Japanese regime in order to achieve innovation in farming and fishing is almost unthinkable today in South Korea, but strong and effective direction is needed. A gradual reconcentration of land ownership is taking place in most areas, while the landless rural proletariat is rapidly increasing in number. This partial and clandestine return to a landlord-tenant system as an alternative to the ideal of small owner-farmers might not necessarily impede the advance of agricultural productivity, but the social cost to South Korea probably would be prohibitive, given the harsh competition that exists between the two Koreas in all areas of social and economic development.

Another difficulty lies in the fact that until recently nearly all the stimulus for progress has come in the form of outside assistance. Material aid has been readily absorbed, while proposals for radical change that conflicted with local practice have been ignored. As a result a continuing process of "structural change" usually has not been generated in spite of the vast aid and development programs that have been carried out. Personnel in the American and Korean agencies in Seoul that are concerned with the problem are fond of saying that unless farmers invest some of their own resources, a development project amounts only to a temporary handout and has no permanent effect.

A kind of converse is also true, however. Farmers will not invest anything in a new scheme unless they are convinced beyond any doubt that it will work. The problem lies in stimulating one or a few respected men in the village to undertake model innovations, but they must have the ability and resources to make success a certainty. Only then will others follow. Failures (and there have been many) reinforce conservatism and inertia.

The approach of the commercial market means, of course, that in a village like Sŏkp'o a new kind of incentive—cash income—will reinforce pressures for increased production. This process is obstructed by government policy, which in order to limit urban unrest keeps rice prices artificially low. A more realistic price would provide higher standards of rural consumption and nutrition and would enable many more farmers to make productive investments in their land.

Migration from the countryside is another problem related to economic development. The city attracts not only the landless poor in enormous numbers but also the ambitious and relatively well educated sons of well-to-do farmers. Capital is transferred out of the village to finance their education, or to set up small businesses in town once the learning process is over; the community thereby is constantly losing crucial material and human resources.

Nevertheless, in Sŏkp'o at least, the economic situation is slowly improving. Agricultural productivity is staying ahead of population growth, and most people say they are somewhat better off than they were ten years ago.

# 4

## CLASS, STATUS, AND MOBILITY

Although nearly all accounts of premodern Korea have stressed the pervasiveness of various forms of social stratification, recent efforts to define class boundaries and determine precisely the criteria for membership have stimulated a good deal of scholarly controversy. In the previous chapter variations in atmosphere and custom among the neighborhoods of Sŏkp'o were attributed largely to class differences. A comparison of status and class distinctions half a century ago with those of the present will serve to introduce a more detailed discussion of this complex subject.

### FIFTY YEARS AGO

Class divisions in Sŏkp'o were far more distinct and rigid fifty years ago than they are today. According to the accounts of men in their seventies who were young adults before the effects of Japanese rule had penetrated to the village, the Yi or former *yangban* lineage* maintained its formal status superi-

---

*In a formal, technical sense farmers such as the Yi of Sŏkp'o were not even *toban* or country gentry, let alone true aristocrats. They worked with their hands, at least as hard as other villagers, and their living standard was not noticeably different. In traditional

ority over other kinship groups and its geographic separation from them. My informants agreed that deferential forms of address and behavior were used by other villagers in dealing with *yangban*. For example, commoners did not smoke or drink in their presence. Also, the aristocrat-commoner distinction was reflected in the dress of both men and women.

There was a good deal less unanimity with regard to class differences in values and ethical behavior, however. One Yi elder maintained that the distinction was quite simple: members of his lineage did not steal or lie and observed "correct behavior" (*parŭn haengdong*), while the rest of the village did the reverse. He was sharply contradicted by another kinsman of approximately the same age who maintained that cooperation, mutual understanding, and respect across clan lines were as prevalent fifty years ago as they are today. Others acknowledged that "customs" (*sŭpkwan*) were different, but refused to attribute moral inferiority to the other lineages. I was not really able to determine whether this attitude reflected recent ideological indoctrination and an effort to present the best possible image of the village to an outsider, or if it represented traditional communal notions of cohesion and tolerance. It seemed evident from the attitudes of my elderly *yangban* informants, as well as from their accounts of former practices, that depending on the individuals concerned, everyday interaction with commoners varied from expressions of arrogance or noblesse oblige to friendly, informal association.

Old men from the commoner lineages verified the existence fifty years ago of deferential behavior and forms of address as well as distinctive clothing. They also acknowledged that the Chŏnju Yi had a more illustrious history during the last five

---

Korea the *yangban* class constituted a sizable proportion of the population. Probably the stereotype—a person with wealth, education, and recognized social status who did no manual work but concerned himself mainly with political affairs or literary studies—actually comprised a minority. In any case, the Yi of Sŏkp'o were *yangban* in that they incontestably traced their ancestry from the twelfth son of King T'aejong, and because of the fact that they considered themselves as *yangban*, a claim that was recognized by their fellow villagers.

hundred years than their own families, although a member of the Kimhae Kim sib stressed the familiar theme of his ancestors' descent from royal blood at a much earlier period.

Even before the end of the dynastic system, however, a number of other factors cut across this hereditary stratification, so that the problem of individual and family status is less simple than the traditional class division would indicate. One complicating element is the marked difference in status and wealth that existed within each lineage. It is difficult to determine the extent to which poor members of low-ranked Yi lineage segments actually were included in the category of *yangban*. On the other hand, influential, well-to-do men in the commoner lineages had a prestige that could not be ignored by *yangban* leaders. Thus the hierarchy of status within each kinship grouping seems to have offset to some extent the division between aristocrats and commoners. Nevertheless high-ranking members of the Yi lineage had more prestige in the village than anyone else. The village head, who reportedly had more authority than he does today, was always from a prominent Yi family.

A cultural factor that further mitigated the severity of class differences was the importance of education as a means of acquiring prestige. Schoolmasters were mostly outsiders who settled temporarily in the village, and their services were available to anyone who paid the fees. If the Yi clan monopolized a teacher, there was nothing to prevent the other clans from attracting a teacher of their own. Such itinerant purveyors of Chinese classical learning appear to have been plentiful, and I heard of many who spent a few years in Sŏkp'o and then moved on. Someone who could read and write, and who had spent three or four years (rarely more) grappling with the basic texts that set forth Confucian morality, acquired a special aura quite apart from family origins. Such people had access to the only source of wisdom and ethics, and their opinions on all aspects of village affairs could not be ignored. What distinguished *yangban* lineages was the importance that members attached to education, and Sŏkp'o was no exception. Although well-off commoner families did educate some children, this occurred less often than among the Yi.

Wealth in the village, particularly good rice land, was relatively equally divided among the four large kinship groups. *Yangban* did not engage in fishing or shellfish gathering, a prejudice that put them at something of an economic disadvantage compared to the commoners, but this was partly offset by their possession of stone fish traps which, according to all my informants, were far more productive fifty years ago than they are today. The Yi households did have a disproportionate share of mountain land and were able to trade firewood and timber for fish and other necessities, but by the end of the Yi dynasty their forests were almost completely cut down.

Thus although the *yangban* maintained their traditions, and an approximation of an "aristocratic" style of life continued to exist in certain households, actual living standards in terms of nutrition, clothing, and housing did not vary greatly within the village. Such variation in wealth as did exist was more on the basis of land holdings than of hereditary social status.

## THE CONTEMPORARY SCENE

Egalitarian pressures during the intervening years have erased most overt expressions of superiority or inferiority in personal relations between members of different kinship groups. People seem both puzzled and embarrassed by a discussion of who is better or who ranks higher than anyone else, and their train of thought constantly shifts to questions of age, reputation, education, and property rather than family background as a source of prestige.

I was unable to detect any class feeling whatsoever among children. At school there are no groups or cliques along kinship lines, and most strong friendships are with children from a different neighborhood. During the ten years that the school has been in existence it has probably helped promote intimacy and cooperation outside neighborhood and lineage boundaries.

But all mature adults are conscious of the *yangban* and commoner traditions and, as pointed out earlier, evidence in terms of neighborhood atmosphere and etiquette is not lacking. When some older men from the Yi clan visited the Big Hamlet, it seemed to me that they were accorded a special degree of deference and most people were at least temporarily on their good behavior. But this kind of respect was given only to certain individuals in accordance with their personal reputation and lineage rank. Their behavior in turn was somewhat more imposing than that of others—an almost patrician combination of dignity and authority.

Visitors from other locations within the province seemed to be much more concerned with class distinctions than were the villagers themselves. I was warned a number of times against the dangers of associating too much with "low-born uncultivated" persons, and one man from Sŏsan twice expressed regret that I had built my house in the wrong neighborhood.

A certain degree of lingering class consciousness was expressed by some informants when discussing desirable qualifications for a prospective son- or daughter-in-law. "Good family background" *(choŭn kamŭn,)* is clearly distinguished from wealth or personal characteristics, but only the elderly and a small conservative minority considered it to be more important. Younger and middle-aged married persons, both men and women, emphasized the importance of money and ability, while the unmarried were more concerned with physical attraction. Most people in discussing marriage choices said that it was as important to avoid an alliance by marriage with a family of much higher status and standard of living as it was with one of bad reputation, since in the former case exchanges of gifts and visits would cause unnecessary embarrassment and expense.

Parents are particularly concerned with marrying a daughter into a family where she will be well treated, because they have little opportunity or right to intervene on her behalf after she leaves her own household and enters another lineage. A girl who marries into a much wealthier family would almost certainly be looked down on by her in-laws, particularly her new female relatives.

Today, despite some remnants of hereditary class division, the concept of class does not fit well with the actual system of status relationships. The esteem in which a man is held by his fellow villagers is determined mainly by his personal reputation, occupation, age, and wealth. These criteria cut sharply across traditional class boundaries, since each lineage has rich and poor, educated and ignorant, farming and fishing, and respected and tolerated households.

## Age Grading

An informal and flexible sort of age grading is an important element of contemporary village social organization. A variety of terms exist for the various stages in a man's life, and conceptions regarding the boundaries of such stages in terms of age are fairly uniform from person to person. The chart below represents an amalgamation of the ideas of several informants with regard to social status:

| Age | Category | Description |
| --- | --- | --- |
| 0 to 7 | Infants | Useless toys; irresponsible; not really human |
| 8 to 14 | School children | Useful for errands, messages |
| 15 to 25 | Youth | Full-time workers; frivolous and irresponsible; docile labor |
| 25 to 30 | Mature youth or young married man | Begin to assert selves; still little influence or respect |
| 30 to 35 | Young head of household with children | More dignified; but real status and respect only in exceptional cases |
| 35 to 40 | Young mature adults | Begin to be solid citizens |
| 40 to 55 | Men of influence | Authority, leadership, respect |
| 55 to 60 | Young old | Less heavy work; lose some of authority |
| Over 60 | Old | Mostly respect |

At important events where many people are present, several different age groups invariably form. In looking over hundreds of photographs that I took in the village with quite different objectives in mind, I later discovered that in an overwhelming majority the men included at random in any one picture were within a few years of each other. On the other hand, women's work groups, whether washing at the well, gathering oysters, or gardening, include people of all ages. Similarly, in domestic household work grandmother, daughter-in-law, and granddaughter all work together in the kitchen or courtyard.

Two related factors seem to be involved in determining age groups; on many occasions, both ritual and otherwise, protocol is quite explicit, and a man's assigned physical position places him with age mates. In less formal situations, boys and men naturally seek the company of those who are near their own age through long familiarity, and because they can relax without having to worry about proper behavior and circumspect speech.

Formal respect and authority are not synonymous. With age, a man continues to acquire formal status that demands increasing deference. But as his physical and mental powers wane, the respect becomes more perfunctory, turning into a kind of etiquette that is also important as an indication of good manners on the part of the younger person. Although there is considerable variation among the different neighborhoods and households in the degree of respect accorded old men, the ideal itself is universally recognized and people condemn any blatant violation of it.

Fifty years ago men over 55 tended to monopolize both authority and high status in village councils as well as in family and clan matters. The practice still exists in a few households where men in their sixties and even seventies continue to exercise control over mature sons and full-grown grandsons. Some of the problems that arise when an old man does not retire gracefully are discussed in connection with kinship. Older men still predominate in lineage councils where the chief concern is with ritual matters, the control of improper behavior, and the reputation and well-being of the clan. But with regard to village affairs the real men of authority and influence (*sillyŏkcha*) are between 40 and 55. Older men are not equipped by experience and education to understand and deal with the kind of technological and political problems that have confronted the village in recent years.*

*One source of difficulty that has been reported in "clan" villages with a dominant *yangban* linage is that the emphasis on an age-based status hierarchy has resulted in an extremely conservative leadership opposed to most forms of innovation (Pak 1963:142).

## Personal Status

Education is an important formal determinant of social status today. Study beyond primary school gives an individual added prestige within his family as well as throughout the village, and where a younger son had received more schooling than his elder brother, the resulting tension was not resolved until one or the other moved out and set up a separate household.

Compared to many villages Sŏkp'o's educational standards are low, because it is so remote. In 1966 there were only five or six students out of about ninety in the eligible age category who were attending junior high school and high school. All were from well-to-do families that had relatives in town where the children could board. In villages that were located within easy walking or bus-riding distance of the Sŏsan schools, between one- and two-thirds of all eligible children studied beyond the sixth grade.

The great ideological emphasis on education as a criterion of human worth gives villagers a profound sense of inferiority amounting almost to a crisis of confidence in their dealings with outsiders. In this sense the contempt of educated townsmen for country people is shared by the peasants themselves.

If asked what contributes most to high prestige and social rank, most villagers without hesitation will cite education. At this ideational level education has almost ritual efficacy. It really does not matter whether the person in question has studied the Chinese classics or has attended the regular public schools; his moral worth has been augmented. Only men with an education are qualified to direct others. This traditional ethical principle is not restricted to old people, since informants in their twenties also tended to rank people by degree of schooling. The fact that so few people in Sŏkp'o have studied beyond primary school may be a factor contributing to the lack of authoritarian and hierarchical leadership.

When asked about ultimate goals if the village became really prosperous, most people gave priority to higher education for their children. The reverse of this obsessive or mystical attitude towards education is that boys faced with the realization that they will never study beyond the sixth grade, and that nearly all their ambitions must be renounced, feel stifled (*taptap hada*) in the village environment.

It was difficult to shake this faith in education by pointing to contradictions in the village and in Korean society. Only one of the ten most influential leaders of the village had a high school education, and of the five most prosperous farmers only one had been to middle school. Facts such as these were dismissed as temporary aberrations due to historical accident.

On the other hand, when discussing improved technology for farming and fishing, the inadequacy of the normal educational process was freely criticized. The need for practical training and experience in addition to classroom exercises, if practical results are to be achieved, is recognized. Two older boys are attending trade schools in Inchŏn; one is at a fisheries school and the other is taking an electronics course. Although they are greatly envied by the other youth, their parents consider this a poor substitute for the real thing—that is, a conventional high school.

A child who goes to middle school and high school is irrevocably separated from his village and age mates by years of different experience and training and by his changed status when he comes home. He has been transformed into something too precious to waste on ordinary manual labor. Somehow he has been exempted from the bitter struggle for subsistence and reserved for finer things more suitable to his superior talent and virtue. Such a person often becomes a costly ornament decorating a hard-pressed family. The fact that his family takes great pride in having a son wander idly through the village, perhaps graciously lending a hand at harvest time, is undeniable. He wears clean clothes and usually manages to provide himself with a watch, dark glasses, and if the family is well off, a transistor radio. But within the village only the headman, his recording clerk, the schoolteacher, and possibly the storekeeper can earn a meager living on the basis of middle and high school learning. The others must either adjust to a far more difficult life or leave for the city when the support of their parents ends. In 1966 there were two "educated," idle young men from the Yi clan and two from the rest of the village. The latter worked a good deal more than the two from the *yangban* neighborhood.

Women who come into the village as brides often have a middle school education, which gives them added luster but creates some resentment as well. There seems to be a tendency for informal cliques based on this distinction to form among women.

In recent years there has been a large surplus of widows as a result of the Korean War, and three refugee women from the north have married into the village, two of them bringing children by previous marriages. These two were forced to take poor widowers in order to obtain husbands, while the third, rumored to have been a former *kisaeng* (professional entertainer) in North Korea, had beguiled a young and handsome fisherman away from his family in Tangjin, a good-sized port some thirty miles up the coast. All three were better educated, more energetic in their manner, and possessed more varied skills than most of the other village women. There seemed to be no strong regional prejudice against them, although all were involved in fairly frequent disputes, probably because of their more overt egocentric behavior. One in particular, a notorious trouble-maker, was often criticized, but in fact they all enjoyed a certain prestige because of their wider experience and education.

A number of other factors of a less formal nature contribute to a person's status and popularity. The harmonious ordering of family affairs is an important condition for retaining the esteem of one's neighbors. A normal amount of domestic friction is regarded tolerantly, but where prolonged and intense conflict exists between brothers, husband and wife, or (most importantly) son and parents, the reputation of the entire household and particularly its head will suffer. It is a truism to insist that everyone knows all about everyone else's affairs, and that indiscreet gossip is a continuous part of village life. Any notable breach of filial piety causes a scandal that severely damages a man's personal prestige.

Generosity and hospitality are important in establishing a reputation for good character. A rich man can exert significant influence through his economic power alone, but if he is stingy or excessively sharp in economic transactions, he will not be respected. Without general respect he can not exert real influence, either as an arbitrator mediating quarrels and conflicts of interest or as a promoter of joint constructive effort on a village-wide basis. These more general, diffuse functions are the ones that a truly successful man in village affairs aspires to. To play such a role requires a reasonably secure economic base—specifically, the possession of enough irrigated rice land to support an extended family plus a large enough surplus for ceremonial obligations, the requirements of hospitality, and a certain amount of assistance (usually to poor relatives).

Fishing entrepreneurs without a secure base in land are not yet influential in village affairs. This situation may be changing, since the two men who have sold nearly all their land and have fairly large investments in boats and nets are still in their thirties. Both are elder sons—vigorous, ambitious, and eager to assert themselves politically—but their financial ups and downs during the last two years well illustrate the speculative risks involved. Other, more subtle limitations on their aspirations exist as well. One has quarreled with his father and lives separately, while the other has no education, drinks heavily, and pays little attention to etiquette. The more respectable, conservative farming element of the village finds it natural in private to link such moral defects with the fishing profession, and these men are faced with real obstacles in their efforts to establish themselves as men of influence. Widespread popular sentiment favoring the traditional definition of "correct behavior" is still combined with a disparaging view of fishing in terms of social prestige that is shared by most fishermen themselves.

Other relatively young men (in their late thirties) of some competence and popularity recently have been appointed to such positions as local head of the fisheries cooperative or supervisor of a dike building project. Although they do not possess enough land to be potential village leaders in accordance with the qualifications established above, they are pointed to with pride by their fellow clansmen. Jobs such as these, although temporary, have a bureaucratic aura that carries considerable prestige.

Inevitably as the pace of economic change picks up, there is a shift in attitudes regarding the qualities that are most desirable and regarding what constitutes success. But it is still true today in Sŏkp'o and in provincial towns as well that the preferred path to success and wealth is appointment (or election) to administrative and political office. This is the ultimate ambition of most villagers for their children. The possibility of success is exceedingly remote, of course, and the nearest available alternative is some degree of education beyond primary school.

On the other hand, a secret poll of schoolboy ambitions in the sixth grade showed that their preferred occupation (55 percent) was captain of a fishing boat (engine powered); this was followed by farmer (20 percent), and then teacher, soldier, and merchant. This probably reflects the glamor for boys of engines, travel, and what appears to be an adventurous life, but it is also true that larger-scale fishing operations involving modern technology are becoming more respectable.

A more intangible quality affecting prestige is the role of individual popularity in interpersonal relations. If an air of quiet dignity and calm measured self-expression is most admired and most influential in formal councils, this is usually not the case in the everyday casual groups where men gather to pass a good deal of their time. Ribald jokes and the noisy vehement expression of ideas are more normal in such gatherings, although there are variations according to neighborhood and situation in the kind of behavior that is considered appropriate. What often happens is that men gravitate to the group they find most congenial. In this sense different kinds of charisma are effective within the village, and influential men draw followers, usually of approximately the same age, from other neighborhoods and other clans.

## MOBILITY

When asked about the rise and fall of families economically during the past fifty years, villagers assured me that the most prominent lineage segments had maintained a dominant posi-

tion for long periods. The highest ranking households genealogically in each lineage were not the wealthiest, but in every
case they were relatively well off and had been for as long as
anyone could remember.

One striking result of the modified form of primogeniture
practiced in the village is the fate of a younger son. Unless he
leaves the village, his subordinate and dependent ties with his
elder brother persist even after he marries and sets up a separate household. His land holdings will be small and his standard
of living lower than in the "big house" (if it is a prosperous one)
in which he was raised. Unless he has exceptional qualities, an
education, or access to an unusual source of cash income, he
is relegated to an inferior position both socially and economically. He will depend on his older brother in many ways, and the
result is often a kind of uneasy patron-client relation that must
in the interest of respectable morality be presented as one
of constant harmony. Collateral branches of even well-to-do
lineages can therefore fall rather quickly in both economic and
social rank.

Most families (60 percent) reported a slight improvement in
economic conditions over a ten-year period, with the last five
years being regarded as particularly favorable. Another 20 percent said there had been no change, but several members of this
group were probably motivated by typical peasant caution. As a
rule, credit was given to the Park Chung Hee regime for the
change, although some informants talked in general terms of
improved agricultural technology, and one even stressed personal effort.

In those families where fortunes declined during the same
period (20 percent), a variety of reasons were given that, when
compared with the comments of more fortunate villagers, sometimes appeared to be excuses—a recitation of misfortune and
grievance—rather than rational attempts to understand what
had really caused the trouble. It was only through conversations
with neighbors that I learned of such factors as persistent
drinking and gambling, a disastrous commercial or fishing part-
nership, frequent unnecessary trips to town, or fines for illegal
wood cutting. A failure to have sons and the consequent neces-

sity to adopt a relative was cited as the reason for one family's decline. Sometimes gradual impoverishment was attributed to illness and a consequent shortage of labor, while other men blamed the large size of their families. Bad fishing luck and the shortage of water for crops were also frequently cited as occasions for going into debt.

The previous chapter contrasted the desire for many children and the advantages to a family in the short run of abundant labor with the related impoverishment of succeeding generations. This kind of built-in impasse is an important long-run factor in the declining fortunes of some households.

Farming is a respectable way of life but not a means of achieving prosperity. Without some sort of radical innovation such as a new cash crop combined with access to markets or a revolutionary change in agricultural technology, it is impossible for the average farmer or even the reasonably well-off farmer in Sŏkp'o to improve his economic status by agriculture alone. In other words, no amount of diligent hard work is going to permit a family to increase its land holdings when the capital resources consist of only one and a half (or less) acres of irrigated rice land. Actually, the situation of most people is so precarious that illness, a crop failure, extravagant ceremonial and educational expenditures, or the loss of fishing gear in a storm can lead to indebtedness and a downward spiral resulting in the gradual sale of land. Cash is required to avert such a disaster, and agriculture does not provide it.

Although "wealthy" farmers with more than three acres can live reasonably well by village standards, conservative farming practices and the remoteness of markets also effectively prevent them from increasing their real wealth. If one examines the annual budget of a household that is getting more prosperous, it is invariably as a result of cash income in addition to subsistence farming activities. New opportunities that do bring in cash are becoming available. Markets for fish and shellfish are steadily growing and becoming more accessible. Young men who are strong and willing to work hard have opportunities to earn from 15,000 to 30,000 wŏn ($50 to $100) for three months work either at Sŏkp'o or in the offshore islands. Oystering by

101

women has already been mentioned as a source of cash income. Soldiers in Vietnam (there are two from Sŏkp'o) receive double pay, and nearly all of it goes to their families. For a while there was also work on the dike being built to reclaim tidal mudflats for rice production; wages were paid in flour that could then be sold.

Households that retain their cohesiveness as a corporate group and have access to one or more of these sources of income are in a position to improve their economic situation. But young men and to a lesser extent girls are somewhat less docile about turning their earnings over to the family than they used to be. A transistor radio, dark glasses, new clothes, trips to town, and for some a guitar, have an immediate fascination that may conflict with the requirement that individual interests be subordinated to those of the family.

## HIERARCHY, LEADERSHIP, AND STATUS

Within the village a broad distinction can be made between authority based on formal, permanent hierarchical factors and the kind of direction that is usually exerted informally in an egalitarian context. Hierarchical concepts of authority ordinarily are associated with lineage structure—specifically, genealogical rank, age, and reputation. Bureaucratic authority, also hierarchical in nature, is only an occasional phenomenon in village affairs. Ideally it depends on moral superiority attained through education. Outside the context of lineage and formal bureaucracy strong leadership has no legitimation, and in fact villagers are opposed to it, both in theory and in practice.

Traditionally, notions of hierarchical leadership are associated with philosophy and ethics rather than with the accomplishment of practical goals. Hierarchy in Sŏkp'o is the ranking of persons in terms of moral worth rather than a chain of command for the exercise of authority. In this regard village ideology faithfully mirrors Chinese social ethics. According to the doctrine, social harmony can only be achieved through the establishment of correct human relations, and for this goal relative status must be clearly expressed. Villagers regard high-ranking persons as responsible for ethical and ceremonial leadership, not the direction of everyday activities, and this is true of the county magistrate as well as of the clan elders.

Several informants specifically praised the village head because he did not try to impose his ideas too forcefully. He has enormous prestige in the village for his moderation, honesty, and concern for proper behavior, but he uses his influence in an indirect manner. He is a moderator rather than a leader and is careful not to risk his popularity by driving too hard to achieve specific goals that would excite immediate and strong opposition. The county magistrate came to Sŏkp'o only twice during a period of more than a year, and each time his mission was purely ceremonial—once to console the widows of men lost at sea, and the second time to speak at a ceremony honoring the foreign resident.

The great importance of values connected with a hierarchy of age, lineage rank, and education would seem at first to put everyone in a clearly defined subordinate or superior relationship to everyone else. Within the extended family and its offshoots this is clearly the case, and the head of the household has very real authority over all activities of the members. Within the clan and *p'a*, or major lineage segment, ranking elders have considerable personal status, control over ritual, and a far from negligible role in matters of social control, that is to say, the determination of what constitutes seriously immoral behavior by their kinsmen (particularly youth) and the decisions that should be taken in any particular instance. In 1966 there was a certain amount of grumbling when household heads of the Yi lineage were assessed for the upkeep of ancestral tombs. A group of younger men had protested that the money would be better spent on daily consumption needs. One member of the lineage, in explaining the matter to me, said, "Of course they wouldn't listen to anyone who is near their own age, so pressure to fall in line had to come from an old man."

Nonetheless, the authority of such elders does not go much further, except within their own households, and the process of decision making involved in many other aspects of village life (that is to say, the way in which things actually get done) seems to operate largely outside this formal system of rank. Where people of approximately the same generation and age are engaged in some common activity, it is hard to discern clear lines of authority and responsibility, even though the boat owner, for example, in the case of a fishing crew, or the farmer whose grain is being thrashed, may be present. When a decision is required, there is a lot of noise and nearly everyone makes repeated vehement suggestions, but no one person consistently imposes his will through what might be called an agreed-upon chain of command.

An example from my field notes illustrates the situation on one boat:

It was four o'clock in the morning, and we went a couple of miles across the bay to pick up a friend of the captain's before leaving for Inchŏn. The coastline was dark with no easily distinguishable features, and there was neither light nor voice to guide us. Soon we were aground in the mud. There was a lot of poling and shouting from the bow and a great deal of starting, stopping, and reversing of the propeller as we hunted for a channel that would take us right up to the rocks. Changes of course, plan, and even helmsman took place rapidly without any apparent coordination, all accompanied by a constant stream of shouted warnings from the bow and insistent suggestions from everyone else. Judged by New England standards the atmosphere on the boat was one of chaotic excitement bordering on panic.

Throughout the episode, however, nothing occurred that really upset the skipper or crew, or that even seemed noteworthy enough for them to talk about afterwards. No serious mistake in seamanship was made, and the boat was worked reasonably effectively. There was no visible evidence of the captain being in command except that he held the tiller more than anyone else. Everyone seemed to operate independently according to his own whim, and yet it all fit together somehow to produce the desired result. When we finally did get near the rocks and located our passenger, the boat handling was impressive. Considerable surge of the sea and jagged half-submerged rocks made it a nasty spot. I still don't know if the captain's impassivity amidst pandemonium was fatalism or expert knowledge of the "landing."

Ordinarily members of a fishing crew all address one another as equals in informal blunt language, the only exception being that if one person is younger and does menial jobs such as cooking, the manner and language of the rest of the crew towards him is much more peremptory. One time on a sailboat in a strong breeze the owner was holding the tiller, while the rest of us were enjoying the fast ride. One of the crew shouted that we were headed for a shoal and would soon hit, but the captain paid no attention. The crew member insisted, finally resorting to blunt commands and an actual effort to take hold of the tiller. The captain wrested it away from him, we did not change course or strike anything, and the incident was immediately forgotten. The contrast with western concepts of shipboard discipline was breathtaking.

Of course, men of higher personal reputation or demonstrated skill have more influence in such situations, but everyone has his say and the process of reaching a consensus is often not only noisy but subtle and time consuming as well. An authoritative tone of command concerning work in progress as a rule is just an assertion of personal status. If it is legitimate, the other person will ordinarily defer. If not, it will be countered by an equally positive and usually contradictory statement. In neither case does the barking of orders seem to have much to do with how the job is eventually accomplished. In the absence of clear leadership responsibility, aggressive confident individuals are constantly asserting themselves and just as constantly canceling each other out.

Owners of boats and net crews or landowners who hire agricultural labor sometimes complained that they could never delegate authority. If the owner does not constantly reassert his position and demonstrate that he is actually in charge, some of the men working for him will ignore orders and take things into their own hands. It is significant that when larger work groups are formed to carry out new development projects, the members belong to an approximate peer group that traditionally operates in this loosely structured manner and leadership is often a problem. Although a man will accept the authority of his father, older brother, or uncle without question, he tends to resist efforts by almost anyone else to exercise continuing and consistent control over his activities. Conflicts seem inevitably to arise when villagers participate in joint enterprises such as the operation of large deep-sea vessels or construction of a dike where prolonged responsible leadership is necessary.

On the other hand, when people gather in the village in considerable numbers to work together transplanting rice, putting on a roof, hauling nets, or threshing grain, they all possess the necessary skills and are accustomed to working together. As a result, a great deal of work gets done without strong leadership being necessary. But enthusiasm for sustained hard work is quickly dissipated in an atmosphere of disciplined regulation where the element of traditional egalitarian sociability is missing.

## DISCUSSION

Within the village two kinds of personal status can be discerned that correspond in a general way to the dichotomy drawn earlier between different ethical systems.

At the ideational level, there is the concept of the morally superior man combined with that of the venerable kinsman as an authority figure. Opposed to this is the far less prestigious but somehow more vital image of the doer, the popular man who creates an atmosphere of excitement. In terms of traditional, explicit values, however, the man of action who achieves a degree of dominance through force of personality gets little recognition. His appeal is twofold, on the one hand pragmatic and on the other emotional, but in either case it is outside the formal legitimate ideology of lineage and etiquette.

In terms of behavior, the contrast is between a sober restrained dignity and a sort of energetic bullying combined with humorous comraderie. The formal hierarchical system permits a man without either brains or ability to play the role of village sage by combining a sedate air with a firm veto against change, and it is usually possible for such a man to discredit the innovator as soon as anything new fails to live up to expectations.

The contrast here is between a person who has prestige because of the kind of man he is (in both an ascriptive sense and in terms of individual personality) and the person whose prestige is the result of the commotion he causes. This more dynamic status lacks the supporting strength of kinship groups and the legitimation of a system of ethics. It requires constant effort and results if it is to be maintained.

No one in Sŏkp'o really controlled both sources of personal status. A man whose prestige rests on lineage rank, age, and a reputation for moral behavior is relatively secure from threats to his position. Still, his influence is waning in a changing world where individual energy and initiative are becoming essential for success. The position of an activist, while more precarious, is being gradually favored by new economic imperatives.

Many observers have noted that attempts at strong decisive leadership in Korea usually produce equally strong opposition. In the same way, hard-driving villagers who consistently try to mobilize and direct others inevitably run into opposition, regardless of whether or not their goals are selfish.

# 5

## LINEAGE AND HOUSEHOLD

The argument of this book stresses the importance in Sŏkp'o of maintaining good interpersonal relations across kinship boundaries and describes the informal values and social mechanisms that contribute to village-wide solidarity. It does not, however, attempt to minimize the crucial nature of kinship as a basic feature of social organization. Behavior in the village can be neither described nor explained without a thorough understanding of kin relations, while the crux of formal ideology is the local patrilineage or clan. Religion, value systems, productive activity and economic transactions, personality development, authority structures, social control, and relations between villagers and the outside world are all inseparably entangled with kinship structures—either as they are conceptualized in ideal form or as they are manifested in actual institutions and behavioral situations. Loyalty to the kinship organization and obligations to relatives have priority in the formal value system over most other claims on a person's allegiance or resources.

### STRUCTURE OF THE SYSTEM

In its ideal form the Korean kinship system is integrated, coherent, and elaborately documented all the way from single households in the village to lineage organizations or sibs that exist on a national scale and can include more than a million members. Traditionally, the careful recording and preservation of genealogies was an exclusive prerogative of the aristocracy, but some commoner kinship groups evidently kept local genealogical records as well. Since restrictions on commoners were removed with the Japanese annexation in 1910, nearly everyone has found a way to fit himself into the system, and today in the cities most people seem to claim descent from *yangban*. But the major kinship organizations continue to publish genealogies (*chokpo*) keeping the record up to date, so that every member can find his exact position and claims to membership in any given group can easily be verified. The lineage is completely and strictly exogamous.

Because they are widely known and accepted, I have followed G. P. Murdock's usage of the terms "clan," "lineage," and "sib" in describing Korean kinship institutions (Murdock 1949:46–47,68). The traditional system as it exists in Sŏkp'o can be seen as embodying the structural principles of both lineage on the one hand and of clans on the other.

The lineage as a Korean cognitive category (*munjung; chongjok*) does in fact correspond to Murdock's description in that it is defined by unilinear descent from a common ancestor and by rules of exogamy. The Korean version is patrilineal. Because of the meticulous development of written genealogies, distant relationships can be accurately traced, and the membership of lineages is extremely large compared with most other societies.

Where a local lineage is fairly numerous, such as the Chŏnju Yi in Sŏkp'o with twenty-three households, it is usually divided into two or more segmentary lineages called *p'a*.

A women is legally and sociologically separated from her lineage at marriage. Her name appears in the *chokpo* of her lineage only after her marriage, and then it is her husband's name, not her own, that is recorded. Technically her lineage membership is permanent, as defined by the rule of exogamy, and the traditional prohibition against remarriage of widows makes it unlikely that the definition has to be made more than once.

All of Murdock's criteria for a clan, defined as a kin group based upon both a rule of residence and a rule of descent, are also met at the village level: (1) the central core of the group's members are unilineally related agnates; (2) the group has residential unity; (3) the group exhibits actual social integration (Murdock 1949:66,68). Analytically it is possible to distinguish three kinds of kinship groupings; clan, lineage, and for a minority of households a sort of truncated kindred, heavily weighted on the patrilateral side.

The clan exists as the largest localized unit for common ritual and as a focus for local feelings of kinship solidarity. Also, clan leaders have considerable authority with regard to ritual practice, etiquette, and other aspects of social control. Women are absolutely excluded, however, from all such activities, and the whole structure can also be regarded as a hierarchically interrelated set of lineages and lineage segments with wives added on in subordinate roles.

Within the boundaries of the village I have found it appropriate to use the word "clan" for each of the four major kinship groupings when it is necessary to emphasize the fact that members live together in the same community and possess a sense of mutual solidarity. Women who marry into it become part of the clan, but the structural model of kin relations that villagers presumably have in their heads focuses on agnatic, hierarchical, and genealogical links. The prefix *oe* (outside) is commonly used in referring to affinal and matrilateral relatives, while the contrasting prefixes *ch'in* (close, direct) or *chong* (ritual, religion, descent) normally are used as part of words that designate groups of agnatic relatives within the lineage.

Koreans do not ordinarily make a terminological distinction between clan and lineage. A large number of different terms are used in referring to relatives, but in most cases, the meanings overlap and a single term is often used with a variety of meanings in different contexts. On the other hand, the term most frequently used in the village for kin with whom there is frequent interaction is *chiban* (within the household), which has less of a lineal and purely agnatic connotation and refers rather to a collective group of relatives comprising one or several households that are coresident locally. Sometimes *chiban* is used in a more general sense for all fellow members of the same *p'a*. In Sŏkp'o the *p'a* is roughly congruent with the formal mourning group (*tangnae*, all members of which are patrilineal descendants of a common great-grandfather); *chiban* is sometimes used in this sense as well. Members of this group have certain specified ritual obligations in accordance with the lineage distance between them and the deceased.

In Korea every prominent lineage has a geographic core area or ritual base where the first ancestor from whom genealogies are reckoned established his household and where ideally a succession of eldest sons descended from the founding ancestor continues to live. All of the collateral branches or lineage segments, whether coresident or established in other communities, recognize the senior genealogical line of descent and the fact that it holds ritual authority for the entire lineage. Each branch in turn has its ranking line of descent and subordinate branches. When one branch of a true *yangban* lineage became dominate because its members held high office at the national level, there was a tendency for the center of gravity of the entire lineage— in terms of both the senior line of descent and the geographic base—to shift in its favor.

So far the description of Korean lineages has been one of an ideal system. In actual fact many of the former *yangban* kinship groups, through careful administration of their records and screening of membership claims, do approach closely to the ideal and may be termed true lineages. On the other hand, there is a large portion of the population that has in one way or another attached itself to one of the major descent groups. Such people do not have a recognized position in a legitimate lineage record or *chokpo,* and descent groups of this nature must be called sibs, since members acknowledge a common bond of descent but are unable to trace actual genealogical connections (Murdock 1949:47). The clan interpretation is perhaps more valid as an approximation of native concepts for the commoner groups, while descendants of the former aristocrats think of themselves as a lineage.

Many of the lineages or sibs have the same patronymic, although the place of origin is different. Thus a Korean will specify, in identifying himself, that he is a Chŏnju Yi or a Kimhae Kim in contradistinction to a Kwangju Yi or a Kyŏngju Kim.

In Sŏkp'o all four major descent groups can be termed local lineages, while the two branches of Kimhae Kim together constitute a sib (or subsib). While all have local genealogies, and one of the Kimhae Kim branches claims that its *chokpo* is genuine, only the Yi (who are of aristocratic origin) can accurately trace their ancestry, not only to the ex-country magistrate who first established himself in the village in 1649, but also through him to the twelfth son of King T'aejong (1400–1418). Their claim to descent from the Yi dynasty royal line is recognized by the lineage authorities at Chŏnju, and a representative from the village is invited to participate in the annual rites held there to honor illustrious ancestors.

Although genealogical connections often may not be traced between similarly named descent groups from different places of origin, and the rule of exogamy is not strictly applied, there is according to some Koreans a vague feeling of relatedness and considerable prejudice against intermarriage. Other Koreans, particularly those from Seoul with a modern point of view, deny any sense of common descent whatsoever and state that intermarriage is perfectly acceptable. In Sŏkp'o the idea of marriage between two people with the same family name is repugnant, even though they may be from different sibs or lineages.

## Descent and Inheritance

Senior ritual status, most of the property, and overwhelming authority within the immediate family group is handed down to the eldest son. The senior member genealogically of a lineage segment maintains his status position vis-à-vis collaterals even though he may be younger. Cases occur occasionally where members of the same generation are separated by twenty or thirty years, but careful records are kept so that there is never any ambiguity, even if a man of 50 is obliged to defer to a boy of 20 on matters involving lineage seniority. Such a situation is liable to entail some ambivalence in personal relations, however, since the principle of deference to age is so firmly established.

Ideally the eldest son continues to live with his parents after marriage while younger sons move out, usually at the time of their marriage. On the death or retirement of the father the eldest son will receive most of the property and thereafter will have considerable authority and economic control over the households of his younger brothers. His extended family household, consisting typically of parents (occasionally one or both grandparents as well), unmarried siblings, and his unmarried children, is called the "big house" (*k'ŭn chip*), while the homes of his married younger brothers are "small house" (*chagŭn chip*). Every household except those of recent settlers in the village fits into this system of hierarchical links. So, except for the senior ranking local household of the lineage, all extended family households that are "big house" to their offshoots have in turn a "big house" that is senior to them.

The eldest son inherits the responsibility for carrying out proper ceremonies and for maintaining the prosperity and good name of the lineage. The authority over younger brothers is of course balanced ideally by his obligation to assist them, and even though offshoots of the extended family may be established at some distance from the "big house," the cohesiveness that existed when everyone was under one roof does not disappear. Patrilineal descent in Sŏkp'o means that the eldest son inherits real political and economic authority along with his ritual seniority.

Although property, status, and obligations are usually handed down in accordance with these general principles, the right of the household head to dispose of his land and goods as he sees fit is also recognized. Wills specifying a particular division of property have a long tradition in Korea, in contrast to the situation that has existed in China and Japan. Parents may favor a second or third son over the first. In such cases the younger sons will probably get a somewhat larger share of the property than in a typical division, and the parents may even live with the son who is most congenial. On the other hand, the rule that the eldest son should get the largest share and that he should have authority over his brothers is not challenged. The only case I could discover of equal inheritance of land was one in which the eldest son had moved to town, where other sources of income permitted him to lead a much more luxurious life than that of his brother who continued to cultivate the rice fields.

### Adoption and Fictive Kinship

Because of the crucial importance of continuing the family line so that rituals on behalf of lineal antecedents can be properly carried out, adoption is fairly frequent. The blood line must be preserved through adoption of a close consanguineal relative in order to maintain continuity, both for the welfare of the ancestors' spirits and for the prosperity of their living descendants.

In actual practice the system does not work very well, and relations between an adopted son and his parents are often unsatisfactory. In fact, villagers recognized adoption as a contributing factor to the decline, both economic and social, of certain families. There were two particularly vivid examples in my neighborhood (the Big Hamlet) where expectations of a peaceful and contented old age had been shattered by the delinquent behavior of adopted sons. One trouble is that adoptions usually are not made until late in life when all hope of having a son is finally abandoned, and a man begins to be concerned about his approaching death. The nephew or other collateral relative who is adopted will in most cases be in his teens or older, and the psychological and emotional ties that reinforce filial values are not present. In Sŏkp'o the appearance of correct relations was better maintained among those Yi (*yangban*) families that had adopted sons.

Two kinds of institutionalized fictive kinship were fairly common in the village. In one the ideational rationale was somewhat similar to that of adoption in that it occurred when men with only one son or with a daughter and no sons were concerned lest proper rituals not be carried out after their death. In this case there was no question of continuity of the lineage; precautions were taken only for the well-being of one individual spirit. The custom is called sworn sibling (kyŏrŭi hyŏngje).

For example, the father of a girl with no brothers will provide her with a "sworn" older brother. There is no change in residence, but thereafter they will use the appropriate kin terms to each other, and marriage is unthinkable. The parent of the sworn brother or sister is called siyang abŏji or siyang ŏmŏni, and mourning rites will be performed for him or her just as if a real parent had died. I heard conflicting reports from different informants regarding the way such brothers were chosen. In some cases it was considered a reflection of close friendship between the fathers and a desire to bind their families together by institutional ties, while others insisted that divination based on dates of birth was the decisive factor.

A quite different form of fictive kinship attempts to deal with the problem of infant mortality. People believe that malevolent spirits are particularly dangerous to attractive children. In order to throw the demon off the track, a child, particularly in families that have lost previous children, will be "sold" to other parents who are referred to as "raising parents," the yang abŏji and the yang omŏni. Subsequently kin terms will be used, not only between the child in question and his artificial parents but also with their children.

Certain classificatory kin terms are used in Korea beyond the boundaries of kinship, so that frequently, both in Seoul and in Sŏkp'o, one hears "uncle" (ajŏssi) or "aunt" (ajumŏni) used in addressing unrelated persons.* A maid living with a family probably will use kin terms for everyone in the household.

## KINSHIP IDEOLOGY AND RITUAL

Chinese influence has been overwhelming in the development of Korean kinship organization and ideology. Throughout Korean history there has been a great deal of contact with China as a result of the travels in both directions by students,

---

*The English translations for Korean kin terms in this sentence refer, of course, to classificatory meanings, not to specific individual kin.

refugees, monks, traders, soldiers, and diplomats. It seems probable, however, that the decisive models for the development of Korean beliefs and institutions are formal, ideal versions embodied in classical Chinese literature and the writings of social philosophers rather than actually observed behavior patterns (Choi 1966:218).

Beginning with the establishment of a Confucian academy in the Silla period (682 A.D.), the content of education in Korea has consisted primarily in Chinese learning, and even during the periods of great Buddhist influence scholars were trained primarily in Confucian texts.

Almost without exception an indoctrination in Chinese ideology has been a basic influence in the formation of Korea's elite and has constituted an essential precondition for individual advancement and success. The Chinese conviction that only an educated man can achieve true virtue was wholeheartedly adopted in Korea, so that the principles of Confucian doctrine became synonymous with formal morality. The core value of this system, filial piety, was more than an ethical rule. It became a basic articulating principle of society. Definitions of morality in Korea were largely focused on maintaining proper relations within the family.

In China the strict application of Confucian principles to both private and public morality seems to have been somewhat tempered by the despotic, pragmatic, political tradition of the legalists on the one hand and the spiritualism and quietism of the Buddhists and Taoists on the other. In Korea, especially since the fifteenth century, the prestige of this essentially lineage-oriented ethic has been overwhelming. No other way of thought was allowed to challenge it, and the belief that moral leadership and virtuous example were enough to bring about good government and social harmony became the dominant ideology of politics.

In spite of profound ideological and structural similarities, the Korean kinship system has a number of features that distinguish it from the Chinese. In particular there is much greater emphasis on seniority both with regard to terminology and in terms of status and authority. Although the elder brother in

China did have some priority in ritual matters and for the "transmission of office and property" (Feng 1937:169), the ranking of siblings was not as crucial a principle as in Korea. Also the distinction between senior lineages and junior collateral segments ("big house" and "small house") is distinctively Korean and Japanese.

Because of the essential link with education, which in the past tended to be largely monopolized by the aristocracy, indoctrination in Confucian ethics and the practice of associated ritual and etiquette were far more widespread and intense among the elite than among commoners. But the prestige of this upper-class ideology was so great that it pervaded every level of society in some form or other. On the one hand, status emulation, or the attempt of ambitious elements at society's lower levels to pattern their behavior after that of the aristocrats, helped to spread Confucian ideas and ritual; on the other, rulers and *yangban* energetically propagated the principle of filial piety, both as a guide to personal ethics and as a way of ordering the state.

A great deal has been written about filial piety, particularly in the Chinese social context, and ideologically the doctrine in Sŏkp'o is a faithful copy. Respect, devotion, and proper submission to one's father is the fundamental principle of ethics. If the father dies, the eldest brother should take his place as the immediate focus of authority and deference. Also, there is a profoundly hierarchical attitude towards lineage continuity that demands special respect and deference for the senior line from a founding ancestor through eldest sons. But the primary sense of obligation is focused on one's own father and his immediate antecedents. A member of a collateral branch, then, should recognize two lines of descent as particularly worthy of respect. In addition a more generalized principle of seniority operates within the clan, so that deference is due all kinsmen who are older or who are members of a senior generation.

In ritual matters the principles of descent and generation have precedence over age in determining status and proper ritual behavior. In most other contexts the emphasis seems to be primarily on the importance of deference to elders. Thus at the

117

*This is the annual* sije *ceremony. Adult males of a commoner lineage are shown in ritual obeisance before ancient ancestral tombs.*

annual ceremony when distant ancestors are honored (*sije* or *sisa*), a young man whose father and grandfather are dead may be the central figure around whom a number of older men play a subordinate role. For example, they will pour wine for him to drink. However, the moment that formal ritual aspects of the ceremony are over, the youth will rejoin his own age group where it would seem preposterous to drink in the presence of older men.

Whenever formal protocol is involved, the principle of lineage rank tends to be reasserted. Once, after transplanting rice all day with members of the Yi (*yangban*) lineage, I was invited to a copious meal where men of all ages from four different households were present in groups of four around separate food trays. I sat with the household head, his elder brother, and his son, while two imposing, dignified men in their fifties were relegated to other groups, comprising mostly young men. These older men, although heads of their own households, were from inferior collateral branches, and it was possible subsequently to observe many other ways in which the status difference was observed within the context of lineage affairs. Seating arrangements in the guest room (*sarang pang*), the order in which drinks were served or pipes were lit, and the authority with which opinions were expressed all reflected the relative rank of individuals. This kind of formality was much less emphasized outside the *yangban* neighborhood, however, and where men of different lineages gather together (including members of the Yi), hierarchical rules were displaced by a much easier and more relaxed form of association on the basis of age grades.

Outside the ritual context there is some ambiguity of precedence that may occasionally be expressed in tension between relatives. For example, when a man's father dies, he will be senior to his father's younger brother not only in ritual affairs but, in theory at least, with regard to economic and other matters that may affect both households. Until his father's death the son will have shown considerable deference to the uncle, and his new role of preeminence can sometimes, depending on the personalities involved, lead to tension and conflict. Still, pressures to suppress such conflicts are strong. There is no ambiguity about the values attached to clan cohesion and loyalty, and any kind of open struggle between close kinsmen is scandalous.

If the eldest son of an eldest son is still a child when his father dies, then the uncle or uncles are in a much stronger position in spite of their ritual inferiority. In a situation like this, only a very strong-minded widow would be able to defend her son's interests against a greedy or self-assertive uncle. One man who was said to have defrauded his nephew of some land had a poor reputation and lived in relative isolation. In the other cases where I talked to young widows with children, the family had closed ranks in protective fashion, and the women had nothing but praise for the assistance furnished by the husband's brothers.

Family ritual, or ancestor worship, is an important part of people's lives, and the proper fulfillment of these obligations take a good deal of time and money. The focus is not on some shadowy concept of the supernatural or on cosmic principles, although there is a superstitious element involved in that the

119

ceremony can be seen as guarding against the evil effects of discontented or malevolent ghosts and as helping to ensure the material prosperity and health of the living. A more important purpose in Sŏkp'o at the ideological level, as well as in terms of social function, is to emphasize and reinforce structural kinship relationships. Relatives are brought together in a social context that symbolizes their respective positions in the lineage hierarchy. Family and clan pride and unity are given a periodic boost. The participants themselves took some pains to explain this aspect of the ritual to me, as well as its importance in inculcating proper deferential attitudes towards lineally senior kinsmen.

A this-worldly philosophic orientation is further reflected in the style of ceremonial actions, which might be characterized as demonstrating a simple, intimate, and informal respect. Ancestors are addressed in a conversational tone, and there is no extraordinary solemnity or effort to awe the participants. Professor John Pelzel's remark* that this kind of ritual constitutes a refusal to accept the permanency of death, and that an effort is made to continue the broken relationship in symbolic terms, seems to me apt.

When a parent dies, filial piety requires that the eldest son assisted by his brothers and cousins provide an elaborate funeral (*ch'osang*), followed by ceremonial observances on the first (*sosang*) and second (*taesang*) anniversaries of the parent's death. These are all occasions when large numbers of people gather to eat and drink together. Ideologically the emphasis is on lineage, and in fact patrilineal kin have the most prominent roles at these affairs. In addition, the bereaved son is provided with an opportunity (or obligation) to demonstrate his filial devotion and to acquire status and good will through hospitality in a wider context. For the village as a whole, these are recurring festive occasions when people put on their best clothes and eat and drink together for several hours in an atmosphere of general good will.

After the "three"-year mourning period is over, the *chesa*, a

*In a lecture at Harvard University in 1963.

smaller and more intimate kind of ritual, is performed annually at midnight on the anniversary of death. On these occasions also, large amounts of special food and drink are prepared. In most households only relatives attend the actual ritual at midnight, while neighbors are invited to share a substantial breakfast the following morning.

Because fairly heavy expenditures are made for ceremonial purposes, government propaganda media as well as frequent pronouncements from various sectors of the academic community oppose this "waste of resources." There was no organized church in Sŏkp'o, but throughout the rest of the country numerous Christian missionaries and Korean clergy are constantly on the offensive against traditional ritual practices. The Christians, at least, have a system of morality to offer as a substitute for what they hope to destroy, but the rational modernizers in Seoul offer only "freedom from the burden of superstition."

## MARRIAGE RULES AND AFFINAL RELATIONS

Although formal rules of exogamy require only that marriage be with someone outside the lineage or sib, there is considerable prejudice against village endogamy as well. While at first I was uniformly told that all marriages conformed to such a rule, I discovered later that some of my informants were from households where marriages within the village had taken place.

A fairly detailed study of marriage patterns was made for fifty households. Within this sample 22 percent of all marriages were between village residents, none of which (according to my informants) were between residents of the same neighborhood cluster. Marriages within the village are thought to be somewhat less respectable than those outside for a number of reasons. Marriage choice is still a jealously guarded prerogative of parents, who ordinarily try to arrange a match with someone from another village. Increasingly the acquiescence of the bride and groom is regarded as necessary, but the only effective way for young people to defy their parents is either for the girl to become pregnant or for them to run away together. If pregnancy does occur, marriage usually takes place in a hasty and subdued fashion after a certain amount of angry recrimination and bad feeling between the two families. While much of the bitterness is directed by the older generation against young people, once a household is set up and a child born, the trouble is forgotten. I was not able to obtain accurate figures but I would estimate that about one-third of all village endogamous marriages are the result of such premarital encounters.

Another, related reason given for preferring a bride from outside the village is based on standards of etiquette. In traditional upper-class weddings it was considered improper for the bride and groom to be acquainted before the wedding, and there is still considerable sentiment among older people against any easy public familiarity between young men and women either before or after marriage.

About half (48 percent) of those questioned opposed marriage within the village because they felt it would lead to conflict with affinal relatives. A common Korean proverb, "The toilet and in-laws should be far from the house," is often quoted by villagers. If the wife has a refuge within the village to which she can return and close relatives there to support her grievances, the possibility of domestic discord and strife between the two families is believed to be great.

As part of the study of marriage patterns, I discussed at some length with villagers the relative importance of lineage loyalties on the one hand and obligations to matrilateral and affinal relatives on the other. Although the primacy of the patriline is always enunciated in definite terms, it is accompanied by an equally fundamental although less prestigious principle of solidarity and mutual obligation among all relatives. There is always a possibility of misunderstanding and conflict because of the difference in the responsibilities that well-to-do people are willing to take on towards poor relatives by marriage and the expectations that the latter have of assistance. This troubles many people, who point out the structural advantages of a system that keeps affines at a considerable geographic distance.

I could not discover any special tension, however, among the families in the village that were allied by marriage. In almost every case the result was closer relations and more physical comings-and-goings between neighborhoods than would otherwise have been the case. There were many examples of mutual cooperation and assistance among affinally and matrilaterally related households similar to those normally based on patrilateral ties. Koreans from Seoul often say that relations with their matrilateral relatives are warmer and more intimate than those with the father's side, where formal decorum is stressed. No one in Sŏkp'o would agree with this statement, however, and there was always insistence on the relatively greater closeness and importance of patrilateral ties. Questions about warmth and intimacy among kin evoked little response.

Two cases of village endogamy existed in 1966 in which the household had been established in the bride's neighborhood rather than the groom's. If the girl's family has property and there are no sons, or if a shortage of labor exists in the father's household, this is one possible solution. In both cases the groom was poor but promising, while the daughter's family had some land. The groom retained his own name and lineage membership, and since this arrangement will normally result in the permanent alienation of land from the wife's patrilineage, most families prefer to adopt a son from among their close consanguines.

A number of explanations were put forward to explain these exceptions to the generally observed rule of village exogamy. Parents were enabled thereby to choose a more suitable daughter-in-law, about whose character and industriousness they would have accurate information. The problem of dissatisfaction experienced by many incoming wives with isolation, poverty, and vulgarity (associated with fishing and lack of education) in Sŏkp'o would be avoided. In fact many young men complained about the difficulty of attracting brides, which they attributed to antifishing prejudice among the girl's relatives.

For poor people who belong to one of the small localized lineages (two or three households), marriages within the village are a form of economic and social security and are welcomed. These families need reciprocal good will and a sense of obligation on the part of nearby well-to-do households in order to survive, and in some cases they frankly admitted that this was the reason for preferring such a marriage.

Over the years as a result of marriages among Sŏkp'o families, the moves of sons (both disgruntled and otherwise), and adoptions, an extensive network of kinship relations among the neighborhoods has developed. Prosperous farmers who acquire land at the other end of the village sometimes find it practicable to install a son there in order to lessen the amount of time spent getting to and from the fields. The informal communications system through which messages were transmitted from one neighborhood to another depended in part on links of this sort which functioned to promote village cohesion.

The widely held preference for having in-laws at a distance does not mean that relations with them are avoided. Both husbands and wives look forward to an occasional visit (usually separately) to the wife's family as a pleasant holiday. Other family members find it an agreeable change to stop off at the in-laws' household when on their way to market or the city. The wife's native household is often thought of as a temporarily secure and hospitable haven in the suspicious and dangerous world outside the village. Some people with more education, ambition, and curiosity said they would like to send their daughters as far as Seoul, Taegu, or Pusan in order to establish connections with the distant and glamorous world of city life. Most people preferred nearby villages within the same or a neighboring *myŏn*, however, in order to permit more frequent visits.

## WIVES AND THE STATUS OF WOMEN

The relative status of men and women is complex. All the formal indicators point to complete male domination. Traditional Confucian values enjoin the bride to deference, respect, submission, and obedience to all members of her husband's household. Terms of respect are used by her even towards her husband's younger brothers and sisters. She usually enters the family from outside the village, so there are no influential relatives or even close friends nearby to provide support. A young woman both before and after marriage is surrounded by numerous prohibitions and limitations on her behavior that must be observed if she is to maintain a good personal reputation and not bring discredit on the family.

It is unseemly, bordering on indecent, for a husband to show affection for his wife publicly; to support her in a controversy or quarrel with his mother would be not only a display of bad manners, but an offense against a much more basic principle, filial piety. Male heads of households are supposed to control the family finances, make all important decisions, and represent the family in all official contexts. A double standard with regard to concubinage and adultery was institutionalized until 1945. A man could send back (divorce) his wife for barrenness (failure to produce sons), antagonistic behavior towards his parents, or even laziness. Separation of the sexes in most social contexts outside the inner rooms of the house is an important ethical principle.

Today, all of this discrimination still exists in the village as a part of popular values, custom, and everyday behavior. If guests visit a house, the wife usually retires, appearing only to bring food and drink. In the case of attendance at a social gathering such as a wedding or funeral, a husband and wife would leave their house separately, mingle with different groups, and return at different times. The same principle operates for work groups. Men still occasionally take concubines whether or not their first wives bear sons. Women have no formal role whatsoever in political or administrative matters and do not attend village meetings, even as spectators. In the great majority of families interviewed, informants asserted that the head of the household did actually hold the money and had the final say in economic decision making.

The system does permit a husband to mistreat his wife, or parents to exploit their daughters-in-law without much fear of retaliatory sanctions. A young wife will have some support if her parents live in the village, since they will know the true circumstances of her domestic situation. But there is overwhelming prejudice against the wife in severe family quarrels, even though her situation may evoke personal sympathy. A woman who runs home is regarded as ridiculous and is a source of great embarrassment to her family. She will not be welcomed, and every effort is made to get her back to the only place where she belongs, no matter how great the provocation may have been in personal terms.

Discrimination, then, is real and profound in terms of ideology, institutions, and everyday interaction. An assertion of aloofness and dominance by the male in front of outsiders is more prevalent in households that preserve *yangban* traditions, and differences in this regard are evident in the various Sŏkp'o neighborhoods. It seems to me that the behavioral expression of this ideology of male dominance is even stronger among the traditional elite of provincial towns and in Seoul.

Yet it is necessary to report that in most households the domestic atmosphere is not at all one of bullying intransigence on the part of the husband. This has to be a subjective assessment, but my impression was of generally harmonious informality, within which there is a constant and lively conversational give-and-take between husband and wife. Male superiority is asserted in proportion to the formality of the situation. It is one aspect of proper etiquette. Country women grow up accepting their subservient social role and in most cases determined to display their good manners and morality through conventional, proper behavior. Observance of the forms of etiquette becomes second nature. One striking example that I encountered almost daily involved a poor family in which the wife was notoriously unfaithful to her husband, a man whom the entire village regarded with contempt. Yet whenever they went out to work together in the fields, she walked dutifully behind him, often carrying the heavier load.

There were several couples in the village in which the wife was more competent, more industrious, and more active than her husband in directing family affairs. The man's dependence was evident to everyone. Usually in such households the woman's work, far from being neglected, was performed better than elsewhere, including all the varied services for the husband. Formal rules of respect towards the household head were generally observed, at least when guests were present, although perhaps in a more perfunctory manner.

The quality of family life that I am trying to portray is derived, I think, from the fact that for the most part village women do not have subservient personalities. There is an important contrast betwen the forms of etiquette or social discrimination on the one hand and the actual nature of personal relations on the other. Women are officially and formally denigrated, but in actual fact they are often self-assertive and highly valued.

People in Sŏkp'o point out the important role of women in maintaining a household's financial solvency. In several cases where a family's fortunes had risen or fallen sharply in recent years, the wife was given a large part of the credit or blame. In general, the head of a household should not appear stingy or try to avoid the responsibilities of hospitality and family ritual. Drinking, smoking, and a certain amount of extravagant bravado are not only condoned but expected of men. The ideal woman's role is to keep this kind of flamboyance under control as much as possible and to make compensating economies in other sectors of family life. In addition, her skill and perseverance at gardening and oystering can make an important difference in household revenues. A woman and her teenage daughter will, if they are good at gathering shellfish (and there is considerable difference in individual productivity), not only contribute a major portion of the protein in a family's diet but will also bring in from 10,000 to 15,000 wŏn per year.

In some cases women may have a cooler and more practical head for economic decision making. In an earlier chapter I mentioned the impetuous susceptibility of some men to skilled economic manipulation. "Friends" who know how to inspire confidence on the basis of relatively brief but intimate personal ties are likely to be particularly clever in appealing to a man's self-esteem. Given the impossibility of legal redress when promises are broken, the judgment of a sensible woman can be an extremely useful asset in helping her husband resist this kind of temptation.

There is recognition of the woman's crucial contribution in bringing up healthy, well-behaved children. People comment on the neatness of a courtyard and the quality of food served as additional factors that not only contribute to a man's satisfaction, but raise the reputation of his household in the community.

The bride's relations with her mother-in-law and sister-in-law are often uneasy and sometimes difficult. But the traditional description of a cruel, demanding older woman taking out on her daughter-in-law all the spite and frustration that she was subjected to twenty years previously is a part of Korean folklore that does not fit the average household. Such women do exist, and the system allows them to torture a new bride unmercifully. Still, the value placed on family harmony is great, and both mother-in-law and daughter-in-law normally will make every effort to reach some kind of amicable relationship. Often genuine affection develops, particularly after younger sisters of the groom marry out of the household. It is considered good manners for the young wife to wait for her mother-in-law's suggestion before starting to eat or before going to bed. Possibly customs like these have led foreign observers to exaggerate the degree of domination exercised by older women. Both parents fully realize, of course, that their comfort and peace of mind for the remainder of their lives depend largely on the quality of relationship established with the daughter-in-law, whose relative status in the household will be augmented as theirs declines.

Along with the stereotype of the vindictive mother-in-law there is another of the doting father-in-law, who in contrast to the young husband is able to show his affection for the young woman without restraint. This stereotype does seem to correspond to a considerable extent with reality, and a certain amount of jealousy is probably generated as a result.

In 1966 there were no cases, according to my sources, of severe conflict between wife and mother-in-law. With two male allies in the household the bride is not in such a terribly weak position as is generally assumed, while a mother-in-law is in danger of isolating herself if she asserts her authority in too brusque a fashion.

Three cases of conflict between a young wife and her husband's sisters existed near my house, and at times the noise of quarreling was so great that the entire neighborhood was able to participate vicariously. Village informants said that such hostility was not uncommon. Daughter-father and sister-brother relations are relatively warm and informal, and presumably the advent of a new wife confronts the sisters with a strong rival. I observed one situation in which the father showed favoritism to his daughter-in-law by having her bring his food at ritual celebrations, a function that had been performed previously by the daughter.

Where the sisters-in-law and mother-in-law combine against a young wife, her position can be truly difficult, but the variety of actual situations is so great that generalizations are likely to be misleading. For example, in one of the nearby households a young wife was consistently victorious against her husband's sister, who eventually left to live with a relative in Inchŏn. The wife was able to dominate the situation partly through her own force of character and her hold over the husband, but according to near neighbors the decisive factor was the inability of the mother-in-law, whose hands were paralyzed, to work. With the daughter-in-law in actual charge of the household, the husband's younger sister was unable to challenge her authority.

It is assumed in the village that marriages are permanent unless the wife is found to be inadequate and sent home. An exceptional case involving behavior that contradicts the accepted code illustrates some of the points under discussion. One of the shamanistic practitioners, a subsistence fisherman, also was a confirmed alcoholic. His three sons, all in their twenties, fished on other people's boats and were notable for both their good looks and their excessive drinking. One of them a year or so previously had married an orphan living with her aunt in a town outside Seoul. The marriage was arranged through a friend of the shaman father who had served in the army with him during the Korean War.

The daughter-in-law turned out to be a jewel—thrifty, hard working, cheerful, and attractive. I visited the house a number of times in the course of negotiations to buy an old sailboat, and because I was interested in the old man's shamanistic practice. Often the body of one son or a friend would be stretched out across the floor while the others unconcernedly drank on. The young wife was always busy in the kitchen or courtyard washing, cooking, or sewing in the midst of what could only be called (even by village standards) extreme squalor.

The first hint of trouble came when she refused to show her mother-in-law a letter that had come from her aunt. The mother-in-law, who fully realized the girl's good qualities, had done what she could to make life less difficult, but it was evident that the young wife had written her aunt complaining of the poverty and constant drunkenness. Nearly all the earnings of the four men went into cheap liquor, and there was no money for clothes or repairs to the house.

Eventually at the girl's insistence she was allowed to visit her aunt, accompanied by the husband. The trip by foot, bus, and train took an entire day and cost a considerable amount of money by village reckoning. While there she and the aunt simply disappeared, and the young man after hanging around for two days came home. Two months later, after numerous letters had gone unanswered, he went back to get her. She put him off with promises to return soon, but she never did come back.

Although the entire family was well liked in the village, most women in commenting on the incident sympathized with the girl. They agreed that the aunt must have been glad to get her back, and that she probably could not have gotten out of the marriage so easily if her parents had been alive. Also if there had been a child, she would have had to stick it out or leave the child behind. One man remarked that it was unusual and humiliating for a man to go to such lengths for a woman, and that the husband would have been far better off if he had just stopped drinking.

This incident brings out the fact that marriage derives much of its binding force from the contractual nature of the agreement between two families and from the authority of family heads to enforce the contract. Where exceptional circumstances existed, both with regard to the commitment of the go-between and the nature of the bride's household, it was relatively easy for the wife to evade her responsibilities. The eagerness of the husband's family to get her back, while perhaps natural in the circumstances, appears contrary to the tradition of male superiority and was in fact talked about in such terms by Sŏkp'o residents. What occurred was an open confrontation between formal ideology and the actual importance of a daughter-in-law to the household.

Two unhappily married women confided to my wife that they would have left their husbands if they could. One husband was a notorious philanderer, while the other was mean, often drunk, and an unsuccessful provider. Both women had young children and said there was no place where they could find refuge.

The vast majority of marriages are stable, however, and if wives are not truly content, at least they are cheerful. The status of a woman, which is indeed abysmally low when she first marries, advances markedly with the birth of a child and again with the death or retirement of her parents-in-law. More respect is accorded her as she grows older and acquires authority, a respect that is augmented, of course, if her own personal popularity and reputation are high.

Acquiring too much status too soon can be a disadvantage. One girl in the village had been pushed into marriage at 15 by a father without sons who was eager for a male grandchild. Her first daughter died, and the second was two years old in 1966 when the mother was only 19. Even though her husband was in the army and her mother available to take care of the baby, she could no longer mix with her age mates on informal terms. Unmarried girls, although they had all grown up together, could not use informal, blunt language in talking to a married woman with a child. The young mother complained to my sister-in-law that she had been deprived of her youth and deeply regretted the early marriage, even though she had no specific complaint against her husband.

When wives first marry into the village, there is usually an extended period of homesickness during which they long to visit their own family. Even the routine of domestic activities and the taste of the food is strange. The process of fully identifying with the husband's lineage instead of their own is one that takes time, but I was told that after ten years or so of marriage wives rarely want to visit their parents unless there is an emergency and in most cases no longer bother to keep track of their brothers and sisters.

## Women and Inheritance

Daughters inherit nothing but personal mementos. The right of a widow to hold the deceased husband's property in trust for her sons is recognized. In Sŏkp'o, however, the dead man's brothers farm the land along with their own, and the widow receives whatever share is considered appropriate for the support of herself and the children.

All of the adults under 50 that I talked to stated that they had no objection to the remarriage of widows, particularly if they were still young, often remarking in addition that such old-fashioned traditional prejudices were no longer observed. In actual fact, however, village widows—even young ones—rarely remarry, while widowers almost always do. The deceased man's patrilineage has a tendency to guard a widow somewhat jealously from outside contacts. Two issues are involved: the good name of the family is enhanced since a chaste and modest widow is one embodiment of traditional virtue, and secondly, the widow would have to leave the children (particularly boys) behind to grow up in their own lineage. Her husband's relatives usually are anxious to have her stay in order to help raise them. It was explained that if she took her sons with her they would grow up in another family with other loyalties and personal ties, so that when they received their father's share of the land division it would be alienated from the patrilineage.

In one case an impoverished third son who had an extremely bad reputation in the village had quarreled with all his close relatives. When he was lost at sea, his second wife (whose reputation was equally unsavory) and her three small children constituted an unwanted economic and social burden on the rest of the family. The dead son's share of the patrimony—his father was till alive, and a formal division of land had not yet been made—was hastily calculated and handed over to the widow with the understanding that she would leave the village and make no further claims on her husband's family.

A special geographic factor enters into this unusual case in addition to the low personal status of those involved. The widow had declared her intention of leaving the village and bringing the children up in her own patrilineage. In fact she had shocked the village by "running home to mother" on several previous occasions when her husband was still alive. The dead man's brothers all had sons, so there was no question of family continuity. The amount settled on the widow was minimal, and my informants pointed this out as somewhat unfair to the children while nevertheless sympathizing with the father and older brothers.

A more typical example is that of an Inchŏn woman who was "divorced" (thrown out) by her husband in the city. He kept the son, while she brought the daughter with her when she married into the village.

## Puritanism and Promiscuity

The Confucian tradition in Korea has a puritanical aspect that emphasizes strict rules of physical modesty and reticence regarding sexual matters. Such values are linked to the subordinate role of women and the emphasis on deference and obligation rather than emotion in personal relations. According to the doctrine, boys and girls should be separated at the age of 7 and brought up apart. Women should be secluded within the house or among other women, and the faithfulness of a widow to her deceased husband's memory is an important ideal.

In Sŏkp'o these values are still widely taught and practiced. For example, young children swim in the Yellow Sea or play on the beach without clothes or parental supervision, and they invariably divide themselves into separate groups of boys and girls—even though many may be less than 7 years old. The groups may be only 150 yards apart, but there is never any mixing.

Unmarried girls are supposed to be watched over with considerable care, and when a strange man enters the village they disappear quickly from sight. It is considered improper for a girl to look at a man who is neither a relative nor a neighbor, and some village maidens told my sister-in-law that even after we had been in the village for six months they had never seen my face.

It seemed to me that in addition to the matter of etiquette and reputation there was an element of distrust involved, fear that a girl or woman's natural lust might get out of hand. Whenever I encountered a woman alone and stopped to talk—on a path, when visiting a house, or if she was working in the fields— a man would join us, sometimes a little breathless from running down the beach or across the paddy field dikes. He would usually proceed diplomatically to disengage me from the conversation, and the woman would leave.

The contrast with regard to seclusion between the behavior of women in the *yangban* neighborhood and in the Big Hamlet has already been described, but the uneasiness if a village girl or woman was seen alone with an outsider even for a short time was characteristic of the entire village. The only exceptions were in the case of women past childbearing age and the two or three who kept wine shops in the Big Hamlet.

A profound abhorrence of incest (which is very broadly defined) and the difficulty of hiding any sort of romantic alliance in a small community are additional factors contributing to the repression of sexual drives.

A contrast between this fairly strict ideological atmosphere and the actual expression of sensuality was readily discernible. As in so many other societies, some men may be extremely concerned about the safety of their own women yet eager to poach on those of their neighbors. In Sŏkp'o the mistrust that I have postulated is not entirely unwarranted, as a number of the most attractive younger wives had been involved in cases of adultery. Perhaps the most notable fact, however, is that these incidents were so few in comparison with the total number of families.

Sexual and scatological jokes were frequent in the conversation of approximate age mates. Although the stories were somewhat less raw when women were present, they were by no means omitted entirely. At this level of behavior the contrast between the manners of the fishing and aristocratic neighborhoods was sharp. I never saw men and women telling jokes together in an Yi household.

Children are, of course, aware of sexual matters at an early age, both through the conversation of their elders and because of the crowded sleeping arrangements. The following stages of adolescent development were outlined by informants in their twenties.

Age 12 to 14: There is considerable romantic longing for someone of the opposite sex, but both individuals are ashamed and pretend to dislike each other when they meet, sometimes using insults that provoke real quarrels.

Age 15 to 16: Boys are more friendly with girls and occasionally stop to talk. There is still considerable embarrassment, and clandestine rendezvous are rare. Girls are more aggressive, whistling and calling to boys as they pass.

Age 17 to 19: This is the period of eager, blind passion when premarital intercourse is fairly common. The romances are intense but temporary and do not lead to marriage unless pregnancy occurs.

Age 20 to 23: Young men are thinking more seriously of finding a wife elsewhere and settling down, while girls are concerned about their reputation as the time for marriage negotiations approaches.

The current passionate life of young people provokes a great deal of parental consternation, but there does not seem to be an effective way of coping with the problem. Parents insist that sexual morality was more strictly upheld in their youth and men in their late twenties and early thirties agreed somewhat enviously that behavior has changed greatly in the last ten years. Cousins living in different neighborhoods were often able to serve one another as go-betweens in the pursuit of illicit premarital love affairs. Neighborhood exogamy is still strict but as the wishes of young people are more effectively expressed, the number of marriages within the village is on the rise. Whether this trend will promote or obstruct village-wide cooperation in political and economic matters is a question for further investigation.

The young people find various ways to escape the scrutiny of adults. Girls go off oystering on deserted stretches of the rocky coastline, sometimes by prearrangement but often just on the chance that boys, who know by the tides when the rocks are bare, will find them. Separate groups of boys and girls often sing outdoors at night, and when they eventually break up, a certain amount of merging into smaller groups takes place.

In the last few years an institutionalized form of meeting has developed in which the girls of one neighborhood meet the boys of another by appointment on the beach at night. Again there is only innocent fun and games until the end of the evening when the group gradually dissolves, and pairs wander off.

In Korea there is a fictive older sister-younger brother relation called *uinammae* that young people often enter into. It is supposed to entail only companionship, but in Sŏkp'o it is usually a prelude to sexual relations. Because these often lead to pregnancy and a forced marriage, the custom is bitterly opposed by most parents and must be kept secret.

## BEHAVIOR AMONG KIN

### Family and Household

As in most societies a high value is placed on harmony within the household, in this case a nuclear or extended family. Concepts of family and solidarity are so closely bound together ideologically that it is difficult even to discuss conflict within the domestic group in abstract terms. Sometimes informants refused or were unable to admit that deep-rooted hostility can exist in the family environment.

The Confucian ethical system—or rather the Sŏkp'o variant of it that I observed—is perhaps distinctive in the rigor with which it attempts to regulate kinship behavior in accordance with formal rules. It seemed to me that the ideals of deference, obligation, and cooperation among kin were in fact thoroughly internalized and had a pervasive effect on everyday behavior. This was more true of relations within the family than within the clan, in spite of the strenuous efforts that were made to suppress or disguise contradictions between these ideals and actual performance. Outside the family there was actually in most neighborhoods a pretty clear tapering off of feelings of mutual responsibility, in place of which proper etiquette was substituted. With certain exceptions there was not much difference between related and unrelated households in the same neighborhood with regard to cooperation and mutual assistance.

Inability to maintain harmony within a family is a generally recognized sign of moral failure, and results in loss of status. Obviously villagers make a distinction between noisy, brief family quarrels (particularly those between husband and wife) which provoke only gossip and ridicule and the more serious conflicts that are a source of real concern to kin and neighbors.

Feelings of obligation and deference towards senior agnates are accompanied by formality and restraint. Correct behavior in this context strikes an American observer as awkward, self-conscious stiffness, but men seemed proud of their constraint as a mark of good manners. Informal, friendly relations such as exist among former schoolmates who drink, work, and play together are easier and more relaxed than those with any kin. They are based on personal preference and common experience but lack the foundation of duty and obligation.

Between brothers there can never be this kind of friendliness. An elder brother is always a potential father surrogate and future head of the "big house." Even among cousins who are the same age there is some degree of formality because of a consciousness of age and rank differences. It is extremely difficult to get a village resident to talk about relatives in terms of likes and dislikes or degree of emotional closeness. At the conscious level, structural relations are seen as paramount and it is taken for granted that appropriate feelings and behavior accompany a given degree of kinship.

The family is an institution where most things are shared, where cooperation is constantly required, and where the household head has great authority. Family members are not pre-occupied with individual goals, motivations, and preferences; if they are, there is trouble. Subordination of individual interest to that of the group and the adjustment of personal ideas to fit the consensus, while characteristic of village society as a whole, is most marked within the family.

An extremely difficult problem arises for the outsider who tries to assess the affective component of family life. What is the psychological basis of the family's cohesive strength and durability? Love and affection are not words that villagers use in describing ideal family relations. Terms of endearment do not exist in the everyday vocabulary. Ethically, obligation and deference take precedence over sentiment. I do not mean to imply that strong emotions are not an integral part of most family relations; only that they are cognitively disvalued and repressed. Within the family there exists a permanence and stability that provides great emotional security for the individual.

Except for eldest sons, however, a corollary of this security is psychological dependence. When villagers (and Seoul students studying in the United States) are away from home, it is the immediate family that they miss most. Homesickness in this sense can be acute, even for adults. The need for personal contact with family members, particularly the mother, becomes intense—almost obsessive. For some it has the quality of a physical craving such as thirst. In most cases when direct relations are reestablished with close kin after a long separation, there is no particular continuing pleasure derived from family relationships, which are quickly taken for granted; real enjoyment is found in contacts with friends.

This kind of strong dependence is probably a factor in the importance and durability of ancestor worship, the core of which consists of periodic, ritualized conversations with deceased parents.

As long as a man's father is alive and reasonably active, it is difficult for him to play an independent role of importance in the community. Thirty-five-year-old sons are just not able to speak out with any authority—let alone make controversial statements—if their fathers are also present at a meeting or informal gathering. There were only four younger men in the village (in their thirties) with real influence. All had energy, ability, and intelligence; also they were no longer subject to a father's authority. In two cases the father was dead, while in the third he was senile and nearly blind. The fourth, an elder son, had moved out of his father's house after a series of quarrels. The basic problem was that the lively old man was squandering what was left of the sons' patrimony on wine and a succession of concubines. He was severely criticized by the other villagers, but his son, who was ambitious, economically aggressive, and vigorous in asserting himself in village affairs, was nevertheless not fully accepted as respectable because he had failed in his filial obligations.

When a father dies, younger brothers do in fact seem to transfer their filial deference to the elder brother. The emotional cost in repressed feelings of rivalry showed through occasionally, but public behavior in accordance with the established value was the norm.

A difference between the demeanor of an eldest son and his brother is usually evident. The first-born is likely to be more outspoken and self-confident, while younger brothers tend to be docile, quiet, and without initiative. The extent to which a Sŏkp'o family upbringing conditions personality is problematic. Some young men would brighten up and assert themselves more when the elder brother was absent. Nonetheless they were all used to playing a passive role in decision making, and their smaller inheritance and consequent economic dependence precludes sharp challenges to customary behavior patterns as long as they remain in the village.

## Collaterals

The ideology of deference and respect to fathers and older brothers is extended to collaterals as well. In kinship terminology the word for "father" is included as part of a compound term that stands for paternal uncle. The principle of extension from a nuclear family relationship is explicit, since "big father" (*k'ŭn abŏji*) is used for an uncle older than ego's father and

"little father" (*chagŭn abŏji*) for one that is junior. This terminological distinction has a behavioral correlate; normally a
man will feel considerably more respect and show more deference to his father's elder brother than to an uncle younger than
his father.

Among relatives of the same generation the word for elder
brother (*hyŏng*) is a true classificatory term and it has wide
application. It applies to all patrilateral, matrilateral, and
affinal male kin of the same generation who are senior in age to
ego. In general, attitudes and behavior that are proper towards
an elder brother are appropriate for anyone called *hyŏng* or
*hyŏngnim* (more polite) but to different degrees and with varying emphasis. Ordinarily the degree of constraint diminishes
with genealogical distance. It is much easier, for example, to
drink and joke with a third cousin than with one's own elder
brother or first cousin. Such structural determinants of behavior vary, of course, with the personal feelings of individuals,
but in the village environment formal limitations on casual relations among kin are strong.

Along with the classificatory terminology there exists another frequently used system exactly specifying genealogical
relationships. With regard to collateral relatives then, it is possible (and usual) for related individuals to shift back and forth
between different cognitive frames of reference, one of which
implies a certain general category of formally prescribed behavior, while the other gives a precise indication of position in
the lineage.

## Economic Relations

The extended family is typically a corporate group, and where
it has split into two or more closely related households, the
number of kin who own, operate, and derive income from jointly
held property may be fairly large. Work groups in general are
made up of kinsmen, especially in neighborhoods where relatives live close together. In spite of close economic ties of this
nature, village financial transactions such as buying and selling
property, renting land, loaning money, and hiring wage labor

take place to a considerable extent outside the framework of kinship relations.

Poorer people are eager to obtain advantageous treatment through dealing with relatives, but those who are better off usually prefer to transact business elsewhere. A somewhat different view was occasionally expressed, to the effect that financial transactions with relatives are safer because one can trust them, and because they will feel the obligation to carry out their part of the bargain more keenly so as not to endanger clan solidarity.

The obligation to assist kin diminishes sharply outside the divided extended family or "big house-small house" complex. Some prominent families of the former *yangban* Yi lineage had helped pay off extensive debts incurred by collateral branches as a matter of clan pride, but villagers spoke of such incidents as exceptional. The social status of the debtors was somewhat reduced as a result.

One particularly bright boy from an Yi family was able to continue his studies through college as a result of the combined support of several collateral relatives. Eventually he became the county police chief during the Rhee regime. This is the only such case in recent village history, and it is doubtful whether enough clan feeling still exists to sponsor another candidate through similar collective efforts.

It is no accident that both these examples involve members of the former *yangban* lineage, where ideals of kinship solidarity outside the family group have greater strength than elsewhere in the village.

When asked about the degree of responsibility that existed towards less fortunate kinsmen, most people said they would "try to do something" if relatives approached them for help. However, if repayment or some other form of reciprocity is not forthcoming, it is awkward for someone to ask a second time. One difficulty is that this kind of assistance usually is required to pay off debts or for more immediate needs. Therefore the creditor has little reason to think that his aid will improve the situation enough to enable the poor relation to pay back the obligation. The need for help is usually continuous and often progressively greater, since if a family is going downhill, there is likely to be a time lag before consumption levels are adjusted to coincide with actual resources. Still, an impoverished family is far better off with numerous relatives, even though the aid provided by most will in the long run be minimal.

## SUMMARY

All of the kinship groups in Sŏkp'o are organized according to the same principle, and there is general agreement on the primacy of values that center on the family and regulate relations among kin. But some significant differences exist among the lineages with regard to settlement patterns, the degree of cohesion and solidarity, and the extent to which correct ritual and proper formal relations are observed. Variation is evident, of course, not only among lineages and neighborhoods but among different households within the same lineage.

At one end of the village continuum is the former *yangban* Yi lineage. Except for a single household, all members of this group live together in territorial sections 1 and 2. Ritual observances are scrupulously carried out in most households. Deference to elders is explicit, and old people in their turn act with dignified authority. Poor relatives are assisted financially, and in one notable case joint lineage support was provided to further the education of a particularly bright and ambitious student who eventually graduated from college. There are more middle school and high school graduates in this lineage than in any of the others, although average land holdings (and hence income) are not appreciably different (see Table 8). The other lineages of the village subscribe to the same values, have the same organization, and carry out the same practices. Yet the formal institutional aspects seemed less solid, and the subordination of egocentric behavior to lineage concerns was less evident.

Modes of behavior towards kin are generally characterized by constraint, while relations with nonkin are more relaxed and informal. The easy conviviality of personal contacts among

TABLE 8.  NUMBER OF ACRES OF LAND OWNED IN SŎKP'O BY LINEAGE OF HOUSEHOLD.

|  | | (Kimhae)* | | |
|  | Yi | Kim | Mun | Other |
|---|---|---|---|---|
| Total acreage | 34.3 | 78.5 | 13 | 12.2 |
| Total number of households | 23 | 53 | 14 | 18 |
| Average acreage per household | 1.5 | 1.5 | 0.9 | 0.7 |

*This group actually comprised two local lineages.

men of the same age group contrasts sharply with the stiffness and obligatory nature of close kinship relations. The latter should be characterized ideally by a "deep and weighty" sense of duty and respect. An explicit ranking exists in which emotional attachments outside the lineage are regarded as relatively impermanent and egoistic, while prestige is attached to the proper fulfillment of structurally defined kin obligations. There is a constant interplay, a sorting out of priorities with regard to loyalties and obligations toward lineage mates and neighbors. In every case the bonds of friendship and affection are judged from the point of view of formal ethics as subordinate and inferior to those of kinship.

Formal leadership within the kinship organization is strongly hierarchical and is based primarily on genealogical rank and age, although personal qualities and reputation also affect actual influence. Outside the lineage, a somewhat anarchic egalitarianism exists in which popularity or charisma, wealth, and individual forcefulness determine leadership.

Various forms of ritual play an important role in maintaining the structure of the system, and in promoting kinship solidarity. The most deeply internalized rules of personal morality are closely integrated with kinship ideology.

In the cities and in some rural areas as well, a passion for education, increased geographic mobility, and the declining authority of parents have already destroyed the basis of kinship organization as it has been described for Sŏkp'o, where it is still an important element in the stability of interpersonal and intergroup relations and in the emotional security of individuals.

# 6

---

# BEYOND
# KINSHIP:
# THE ANATOMY
# OF SOLIDARITY

The concept of community solidarity is an intangible abstraction and difficult to define, but this chapter will attempt to document and analyze the sense of social reciprocity and collective responsibility that characterizes a good deal of interpersonal behavior in Sŏkp'o. Instead of finding endemic hostility and group conflict in the village as I had expected, I was compelled to recognize a well-integrated set of attitudes and values for heading off disputes and for calming things down when serious conflicts did develop. At the ideational level specific statements by residents regarding solidarity were rare, but the concern with maintaining not only peaceful but cordial relations throughout the village was expressed in numerous ways.

People from neighboring villages and towns somewhat patronizingly commented that Sŏkp'o residents had good *insim,* literally, human heartedness—the implication being that they possess this quality at least despite their poverty and lack of cultivation. Good *insim* might best be translated as not only maintaining proper relations with others, but infusing them with a certain amount of warmth and good will as well. Villagers are proud of this reputation and often compliment themselves on their own goodheartedness.

Cooperation, both in traditional tasks and in connection with village development projects—most notably the construction of a road—was also cited with pride as characteristic of the village. Physical aggression is strongly condemned, and if there is trouble, the fact that everyone feels an urgent need to patch things up quickly is evident. It is only in the case of drunkenness that quarrels get out of hand, and even then most of the severe fights were with outsiders.

Structural divisions, deep-rooted conflicts, personal rivalries, hostility, and malintegration in various forms all exist and will be discussed in a separate chapter. But their expression and effects are usually controlled so that in the short run, at least, a degree of peaceful equilibrium is maintained. Villagers showed enormous tolerance for the failings of others. Although critical gossip about specific acts was normal, it was rare to hear someone being judged or categorized in absolute moralistic terms. While there were plenty of brief, explosive, emotional outbursts, such antisocial acts were regarded as temporary lapses rather than as an indication of evil nature. Everyone is eager to make allowances, find excuses, and encourage the person responsible to resume normal behavior. There is a concerted effort, in which even the participants eventually join, to smooth over the break and restore harmony—or the appearance of harmony. Also, from the point of view of the individual participant in a quarrel, holding a grudge is really a kind of self-punishment, since one of the main recreations of villagers is the pleasure they take in one another's company.

Although ridicule in the form of friendly (and sometimes not so friendly) banter is frequent, there is reluctance to put others in a situation that will shame them publicly. It is far more important to maintain good personal relations than to insist on performance in accordance with abstract standards. Thoughts such as "But it's a matter of principle," or "They should get to the bottom of the trouble and hold the offender responsible," frequently occurred to me as an American observer, but they did not seem to figure importantly in the thinking of village residents.

## INTERPERSONAL RELATIONS

In describing informal relations such as exist among approximate age mates who frequently play, work, drink, and chat together, villagers use the terms *ujŏng* or *ch'ingu*. The Chinese characters stand for closeness or intimacy, and friend. These ties are easier and more relaxed than those with any kin and are not based on duty or obligation except where reinforced by the bonds of fictive kinship. Friendly relations of this sort across clan boundaries constitute an important part of all village social interaction. From an ideological point of view friendships based on personal preference are not invested with great significance, and rules of etiquette are not prescribed.

People in Sŏkp'o congregate naturally in informal groups. This is particularly true of young unmarried men and older men who are semiretired. During the intervening years a man, particularly if he is a farmer, will be somewhat more involved with family affairs and agricultural work so that he has less

*At this informal drinking and singing party, the man on the left is beating out a rhythm on the wine pail for the singer on the extreme right. Except for two third cousins, members of the group are unrelated.*

time for conviviality. Fishermen, on the other hand, have a good deal more leisure and are faithful patrons of the wine shops and open-air meeting places.

Certain standard gambits are used to create an atmosphere of equality and informality. Status differences often are deliberately ignored or even reversed, sometimes with outrageous language and sometimes with clowning or horseplay. Liquor is, of course, a great leveler. But for the most part members of such groups are approximately the same age, and close kin are not present.

Being alone, even for an hour or so, is an unusual and unwanted state in Sŏkp'o. People hurry to catch up or wait for others so as not to walk by themselves. Those who work alone in the fields will call out to passers-by to stop and share a cup of coarse rice wine called *makkŏlli*. Certain spots that are sunny and sheltered in winter or cool and shady in hot weather become habitual meeting places for small groups. Often there are others around who may not quite fit in because of age differences, but they still participate as spectators on the fringe. Members of a group will make an effort to include anyone else in view who is eligible, so that as far as I could tell there are no outsiders except by choice.

A concomitant of all this sociability is one obvious feature of village existence that practically every ethnographer has to confront: lack of privacy. Participation in the social collectivity means that one loses the right to lead a private life. There is no way, as I discovered with considerable exasperation, to disassociate oneself from neighbors and friends. Everyone seems to be at anyone else's disposal for unlimited periods of time. In my case it was often difficult to follow a work schedule, either because I would be hailed and invited to join others as I walked about the village, or because my own veranda became a preferred meeting place in the summer.

The variation among neighborhoods with regard to occupation and etiquette has already been emphasized. While nearly every adult acknowledges the priority of Confucian ethical values and canons of behavior, there is a great deal of difference among individuals within the same hamlet in the actual degree

147

of internalization or commitment to these values as a guide to everyday activity. Certain persons in every neighborhood cluster stood out in sharp contrast to the predominant orientation of the surrounding households, although such nonconformity did not seem to constitute an obstacle to cordial relations. For example, the village carpenter from the Mun lineage of section 4 was quiet, respectfully correct in his relations with others, conscientious, and able. He had a middle school education, never drank, and was sometimes spoken of as a potential village head. He rarely joined the informal men's gatherings that were so conspicuous in this part of the village, and everyone knew that he strongly disapproved of alcohol and idleness. Nonetheless—and this is the intangible quality of interpersonal relations that is so striking—whenever he did appear, there was never any awkwardness. He was welcome in any group and although less noisy than most he would be immediately at ease, laughing and joking with the others.

Some people, of course, were more popular or more respected and formed a kind of nucleus that attracted others, but no one was excluded. A man with a bad reputation, who is neither liked nor respected, easily joins groups without apparent discrimination and participates in the general cordiality. On the rare occasions when a decision is made to turn against someone and have nothing to do with him ("Let us all refuse to cooperate"; *Ilch'e hyŏpcho haji mara*) it is done jointly, and enforced, by an entire clan or by the village as a whole. An individual who tried to do this on his own would merely be depriving himself of participation in a major form of relaxation and recreation.

Group life continues after dark with the same intensity. Young people gather almost every night, either outdoors or at someone's house; when the weather is good, they will surround a guitar player on the hillside and sing for hours. Often there will also be a girls' singing group nearby, and a certain amount of rough banter goes on between them. On a typical evening, from my vantage point on the hill several drinking groups could be distinguished by the noise alone, and a walk at night among the houses revealed that men were also gathered here and there just for conversation. Even during the busiest agricultural seasons the two hours between about 8:00 and 10:00 p.m. were devoted to sociability as usual. In the other neighborhoods things were somewhat quieter, but there was a good deal of visiting back and forth in the evening by men and young people. Wives, however, were far more restricted to their houses than were those in the Big Hamlet.

Only two individual exceptions to the general predilection for sociability came to my attention. The head of one large and well-to-do farming household situated between neighborhoods 5 and 6 rarely associated with the other villagers. Two other related and to some extent economically dependent families lived close by forming a tiny neighborhood cluster, and members of these households (including the younger brother of the landowner in question) mingled readily with the rest of the village. Informants were unable or unwilling to explain his peculiar behavior and were careful in conversations with me not to criticize the man for remaining aloof. Comments that he was "different" or "strange" were as far as they would go. This individual had a slight hereditary physical disability, and like several others in that sector of the village his family had been subject to harsh retaliation for collaboration with the Communists when South Korean forces reoccupied the village.

One other morose person who remained aloof was a member of one of the poorer branches of the Yi lineage. As a youth he had left the village and worked for many years for the Japanese railroad system in Korea. After the war, bothered by bad health and discouraged by the meager existence that his rail road job provided in Seoul, he returned to the village. Without land or influential close relatives, his life was difficult. In addition, whenever cash from odd jobs was available, he drank. He had partially adopted the city dweller's contempt for peasants and fishermen and was anxious to display his relative sophistication to me. His conversation was unique in that he never had a good word to say about anyone and constantly complained about the way that life had dealt with him.

There were no children in the schoolyard who stood off by themselves and had difficulty adjusting to play groups. The primary school teachers were puzzled by my inquiry and could think of only one kind of example, whereby a child who was crippled or had some other health problem was unable to keep up with the others. The establishment of primary schools, first at a neighboring village under the Japanese occupation and then at Sŏkp'o ten years ago, has promoted contacts and friendships across neighborhood lines, at the same time undercutting clan solidarity somewhat among the younger generation. Previously a child grew up in one neighborhood playing with his siblings and cousins in an atmosphere dominated by kinship. Now childhood friendships are on the basis of personal preference and seem more often than not to be with age mates from other neighborhoods. The teachers insist that no cliques existed at school on the basis of lineage.

The children of an impoverished fishing family that had recently moved into the village from South Chŏlla Province had some trouble making friends, according to their parents. But in this case the children did not attend school. Older members of the same family had no complaints about their treatment in the village.

## Hospitality and Sharing

Hospitality and generosity rank high among informal values. Providing food and drink for others is a recognized way to acquire prestige. One traditional image of success, in Seoul as well as in Sŏkp'o, includes the maintenance of a large house where friends, neighbors, and kinsmen frequently gather to talk and be entertained.

Eating and drinking are an important accompaniment to almost every occasion when men congregate. At any kind of ritual, cooperative work group, or economic transaction—and often at informal meetings or even a chance encounter—something will be served if it is at all possible. People in the village constantly are being treated by others and reciprocating to the best of their ability. On those occasions when large amounts of special food are prepared (for example, when a pig is killed) neighbors, friends, and others to whom the household is obligated are all invited to come and share. If a work group in the fields or on the beach has stopped to eat and drink, passers-by will be asked to join in. A casual two-hour stroll about the village can produce six glasses of wine and ten kinds of seafood without infringing at all on mealtime. Soldiers and other parasites from out of town sometimes made deliberate use of the

*Women from neighboring houses join in the preparations for a wedding feast. Here they are cooking noodles.*

custom in order to obtain entertainment at the peasants' expense.

Residents denied that there was any ritual significance to eating and drinking together. Still, it would not be an exaggeration to say that the sharing of food and wine does have symbolic meaning as part of a continuing secular ritual of solidarity.

## Ritual and Ceremony

Several kinds of ritual or ceremonial observances functioned directly to promote integration within the village. In addition to the major festivals at the lunar New Year and at harvest time, large feasts associated with the first and second death anniversaries of parents (*sosang* and *taesang*) take place several times a year and are attended by a substantial portion of the village's adult population.

Although the principal bereaved persons (that is, the children of the deceased) maintain a somber demeanor throughout the day, their near relatives (*chiban*) who do most of the work also act as hosts and join in the general festival atmosphere. Women from neighboring houses, whether kin or not, are likely to be helping in the kitchen and courtyard where vast quantities of food are dished up in noisy, happy confusion.

Usually relatives and friends come from nearby villages, and some inhabitants of Sŏkp'o, particularly the elderly, frequently walk considerable distances to attend similar ceremonies elsewhere. A wealthy family with a substantial reputation to uphold must be prepared to entertain lavishly five or six hundred guests from all over the *myŏn*.

The *chesa*, or annual ceremony in honor of a deceased parent or grandparent, obviously takes place much more frequently since every "big" house has at least one such anniversary each year. Even though these ritual occasions reflect the most intimate and exclusive aspects of family solidarity, they are frequently celebrated in such a way as to maximize friendly informal relations among all members of a neighborhood, serving as another link in the endless chain of reciprocity (see Chapter 5).

As in most societies, weddings are occasions where the entire community plus affinal relatives from the bride's village join in prolonged feasting.

In addition to these formal events there are relatively unstructured and smaller gatherings, usually among approximate age equals to commemorate a special event, repay past favors, or provide a suitable send-off for a young man going into the army. While not particularly "ceremonial," such occasions are less casual than the informal men's groups described below, and there are likely to be some ribald toasts as well as dancing and singing.

The traditional festivals of New Year's (*sollal*) and harvest or thanksgiving (*ch'usŏk*) are lavishly celebrated over a period of several days. In each case nearly every household (except the poorest) prepares a variety of special food and drink and then keeps open house while groups in every stage of inebriation wander about taking advantage of the hospitality. These are periods of general euphoria, when consumption attains gargantuan proportions. To quote from my field notes at *ch'usŏk* (October 1st, 1966):

The main emphasis of the festival seems to be on the preparation of large amounts of food and drink. There is also a display of new and brilliantly colored clothes for children. Houses are repaired, and new white paper is pasted on doors and windows.

Everyone who has a boat performs *kosa* (the propitiation of animistic spirits) the night before *ch'usŏk*, and it is a lengthy business with preparations going on in the darkness for hours, although the actual ritual—presentation of food and the pouring of wine all around the boat accompanied by prayers—takes just a few minutes.

Hospitality is offered to all who stop by, but the groups of men who wander around don't go to just anyone's house. An informal and subtle kind of inviting goes on, partly by forethought and partly through chance encounters. No plans are firm and a group on its way to one house is easily detoured to another—and then another. The women stay home and must be prepared to get elaborate meals for several people on short notice. The normal requirement that one abandon oneself to the social collectivity is particularly pressing at any festival

153

period. I am allowed no private business or work or time that is not subject to interruption at any moment. People come by to drag me off with no warning, and I'm expected to drop everything and go. Others come by and sit down, and one is expected to entertain—interminably.

Life during the festival period is a sort of timeless passage through endlessly similar gatherings where almost identically heaped trays of food and drink appear and are soon disposed of. Mealtime loses all meaning as the revelers just keep on going, always managing to have room for more. There is no schedule, no apparent pattern, not even a clear definition of groups. I am pleased because everyone insists on including me, but after several hours of being dragged here and there without any control over my own actions, I am wild to escape.

At New Year's, in addition to prolonged revelry similar to that described above, there is annual worship on behalf of the entire village when an offering is made to a mountain or, according to others, an ocean spirit addressed as grandmother. This kind of animistic ritual is widespread in Korea and each locality has (or had) its own resident guardian spirit. Prayers for the prosperity and health of everyone are offered at a small thatched-roof shrine (*tang*) located on high ground near the geographic center of the village. The building is empty and unused during the rest of the year.

## Neighborhood Groups and Cooperation

Except for the former *yangban* neighborhoods (sections 1 and 2) and some of the house clusters in sections 5 and 6, relatives and nonrelatives are pretty well mixed together. For any given household there will always be relatives nearby (with the exception of a few of the very small lineages), but there will also be unrelated neighbors with whom interaction is close and constant. Neighborhood cooperation is an important value expressed in the proverb, "A neighbor is better than a far-off cousin" (*Mŏn sach'on poda kakkaun iusi natta*). In fact many Korean proverbs make fun of cousins on the grounds that relatives who are supposed to assist in time of need actually try to evade their responsibility.

Whenever a ceremonial event of importance such as a wed-

*Neighbors from three households help a poor family thrash its meager grain harvest. The work, which would have taken members of the family two or three days, was quickly disposed of in a few hours of intense, jovial activity.*

ding, a funeral, a man's sixtieth birthday, or a death anniversary celebration takes place, neighborhood men and women help with the preparations along with relatives. In the case of a household without nearby kin, neighbors do most of the work.

In one funeral that I observed, the deceased was a younger son who was on exceptionally bad terms with most of his numerous relatives as well as his neighbors in the fishermen's district. He was lost at sea in a fishing venture with two other men, but of the three only his body was recovered. Sŏkp'o inhabitants have a horror of such violent deaths because of the particular malevolence of the resulting ghosts, but the fact that in this case a proper burial could be performed was regarded as an important mitigating circumstance. No one pretended, however, that the death was a loss to the community. An absolute minimum was spent on the funeral, and not many rela-

155

tives attended. Most of them were young and delegated by their families to serve on this unpleasant and inauspicious occasion. As it turned out, the cortege was composed mainly of the man's close neighbors who also contributed a considerable part of the labor in carrying the bier and digging the grave. At such a time the obligation of neighbors is inescapable, particularly in an exceptional case like this where the deceased's kin neglected him. Neighbors are conspicuous at any funeral, regardless of kinship ties or the degree of pomp with which the ceremony is carried out.

On another occasion the "big house" of a lineage that contained only two households put on an extravagant ceremony (*sosang*) to observe the first death anniversary of the father. This family had been prosperous many years before, but they were quite poor in 1966. The son and household head was not a particularly hard or able worker and had no other economic competence that might have compensated for his easy-going attitude towards agriculture. He was agreeable to everyone, however, and his reputation in the village was good. In particular he was concerned with upholding family prestige by unstintingly carrying out his ceremonial obligations.

What really happened in this case was that the village as a whole—especially his neighbors—carried them out for him. Neighborhood women took over almost the entire job of food preparation and service, while the men attended to the numerous other tasks. It turned out to be a memorable party, and there was a good deal of joking afterwards when the "official" in charge of donations revealed that the collection had fully reimbursed the bereaved for his ambitious display of filial piety.

It would be misleading, I think to look at these examples of neighborhood cooperation and solidarity as an extension of kinship behavior patterns to nonrelatives. It is true that ties of fictive kinship are not infrequent, in which case appropriate kin terms are commonly used. But there is never any confusion as to who is a blood relative and who is not. Some people expressed the opinion that what counts most is being on good terms with one's neighbors, and that the obligations of kinship can occasionally become a burden. The basis of close permanent ties among nonrelatives is different from those among kin, even though participation in joint activities may be identical. There is a voluntary, nonhierarchical element to such relationships. Mutual confidence and respect are based on long association and detailed knowledge rather than the moral doctrine of kinship ideology. Restraint in egoistic and aggressive behavior as well as the quick settlement of disputes reflect a sense of community—the acceptance of certain imperatives without which harmonious life in the neighborhood would be impossible.

If the neighborhood and lineage are coterminous, kinship bonds are reinforced in countless ways. Where nonrelatives live close together, the sense of community acts in most cases as the functional equivalent of kinship. The highest incidence of quarrels was in the Big Hamlet where the mixing of clans spatially was greatest, but since most of the trouble was within families or between related households, it can hardly be attributed to the residence pattern. This kind of overt conflict reflects instead a far less strict adherence to formal norms of kinship behavior.

Any given individual will maintain that he is free to emphasize either his social ties with relatives or those with friends and neighbors. There are exceptional cases in all four major lineages, however, where members have moved to other neighborhoods in order to avoid constant intimate association with their kin. Such cases are truly exceptional, in terms of both their rarity and the amount of critical comment they provoke. In other families where personality conflicts or differences over property exist, they have been subordinated to the concern for respectability, to habits of dependency and cooperation, or to economic pressure. Acquiring land and building a new house are such a major expense that the vast majority of villagers have little choice but to adapt to the social demands of lineage values or the ethic of communal solidarity. For most households, naturally, there is a mixture of both that varies depending on their lineage and neighborhood affiliation.

Two of the major activities that bring women together are gathering oysters and washing clothes. For both of these, women are grouped on a neighborhood basis. Oystering and washing at the well, although time consuming and uncomfortable in cold weather, are favorite occupations because they enable women to spend long hours together exchanging gossip outside the family environment. Frequently groups from more than one neighborhood will gather shellfish in the same general location, so there is plenty of opportunity for contacts on a village-wide basis as well. This is one of the few occasions when young married women (or girls in households where there is a lot of work) can get away and relax by themselves. There are days when young women go out on the rocks for hours but bring home few oysters.

Another kind of neighborhood grouping that is not based on kinship has already been mentioned in the chapter on status and authority—that of men, usually heads of households, who more or less regularly meet in the guest room (*sarang pang*) of an influential person. Here in addition to ordinary conversation and gossip there is discussion of issues at every level from neighborhood irrigation problems to national politics. The system is quite informal and ties in with the general obligation of well-to-do persons to provide hospitality. Some men visit *sarang pang* in other neighborhoods as well as their own in accordance with ties of friendship, kinship, or economic interest. Often curiosity or simply a search for recreational variety is the motive. The somewhat solemn and dignified atmosphere of most *sarang pang* groups results largely from the presence of older men.

Village diversity is reflected also in this kind of association. In the former *yangban* sections, wealth is perhaps less important than lineage, rank, and reputation as a determinant of which house will attract a following. There is some division according to age, since the formalities of etiquette prevent younger men from enjoying any of the recreational aspects of a meeting dominated by elders. But when substantive matters are under discussion, the village head (43), the school principal (36), and the wealthiest man in the village (34), all of whom are members of the Yi clan, frequently join the older men and state their views. In the sixth section, the most remote and in some ways the most conservative neighborhood, one house clearly dominates the rest on the basis of all three criteria: wealth, rank, and personal character of its head. Because his ideas are so influential, it is usually assumed in village affairs that the entire neighborhood will think and act in accordance with the decisions of this man.

The situation in sections 3 and 4, the Big Hamlet where fishermen predominate, is quite different. The wineshops are located here, and although the groups that meet in them are somewhat analogous to the *sarang pang* as a kind of men's club, the atmosphere is distinctive. Group membership is much more flexible and often will include men from other neighborhoods as well as occasional traders, soldiers, or fishermen from out of town.

When men meet repeatedly at some other house in this section, it frequently is a reflection of some enterprise or project in which the owner is playing a leading role. Patterns of influence seem to be more variable and temporary in accordance with the economic success, energy, and popularity of forceful individuals. Whenever money is being spent, and men gather to work on boats, engines, or other gear, the house of the entrepreneur becomes a focal point of activity where large amounts of food and drink are available without reckoning to everyone connected with the project. Ambitious men in this part of the village can acquire almost instant prestige within the neighborhood by such activity and considerations of lineage, rank, and ethical reputation carry less weight.

An informal kind of grouping in the Big Hamlet consists of fishermen who gather to work on their hooks, lines, and nets high up on the beach just in front of a line of houses that faces the harbor. Another favorite spot for such work is the enclosed courtyard of a house that is sandwiched between two wine shops facing the boats. Here gear can be safely stored, and there is plenty of sunshine—while refreshment is never far away. The house belongs to a fisherman who, although well enough liked, has no particular outstanding qualities and little

*Fishermen mend nets on the beach. No fisherman in the village had enough money or influence to buy a boat as large as the one shown. In this case it was chartered for one season.*

influence in the community. But in addition to the convenience of the place his young wife, with good looks, charm, and skill in joking with men, provides a considerable attraction.

The importance of cooperative labor as a way of expeditiously accomplishing certain traditional tasks while at the same time reinforcing social bonds in an atmosphere of mild euphoria has already been mentioned. The personnel of these groups derive from three sources: kin, neighbors, and friends. House building, moving, rice transplanting, thrashing, and the hauling of boats are the chief occasions for such festive work groups.

An emergency such as a fire or a bad storm also stimulates excitement and intense cooperative effort. On one occasion part of the thatched roof of a house near mine caught fire while the evening meal was being cooked. Neighbors rushed to the house from all sides, and three men climbed onto the roof, hacking at the thatch in a frenzy of activity. A bucket brigade from the well was established simultaneously, and the fire was out before any real damage occurred to the house. It was an extremely efficient operation, although the atmosphere was one of wild excitement. The large numbers of helpers and spectators ruined a nearby vegetable garden, however, and when things had calmed down somewhat, the lady of the house took out her feelings on those who were still trampling the young plants. (Kitchen gardens near the house almost always are tended by women, and no assistance from other households is needed.)

In many rural areas it has been traditional that men of substance who have passed their sixtieth birthday should retire and spend much of their time traveling about the countryside visiting friends or entertaining at home. In Sŏkp'o it is a long and grueling walk to the next village, and the expeditions of the elderly generally are confined to death anniversary ceremonies, weddings, funerals, and visits to kin. Except for these occasions most of the old men continue to work at home, and many of them take particular pride in their ability to do so. The standard answer if I asked why they did not spend more time visiting was that poverty made it impossible.

## Two-Person Relations

In spite of the strong group orientation of village life, most interaction takes place between two people, and it is through these dyadic relations that much of the process of accommodation of differences is worked out. As far as I could determine, only the village head and a few others think and talk in terms of such abstractions as village cohesion and solidarity, although similar concepts are used consciously more often in the context of lineage ideology. The importance attached to behaving correctly or at least circumspectly towards individuals in actual situations works out in practice to promote good relations in a wider context. In other words, immediate sociability in face-to-face situations with another individual often takes precedence over group solidarity in the abstract sense of a psychic or emotional bond uniting all inhabitants of the village. Some examples may be useful to illustrate the point.

(1) All over rural Korea, and Sŏkp'o is no exception, efforts

at innovation have been opposed by conservative sentiment. The veto of one or two influential older men often has been enough to block a proposal that had the backing of the rest of the community. As eager as people are to promote development, and in spite of the fact that innovations are clearly in the public interest, villagers can be discouraged quickly by the effects of strong opposition and the prospect of a permanent rift in good relations. The ingrained deference to elders reinforces the ability of the latter to defend the status quo, but the point is that to be successful, joint effort must be whole-hearted and unanimous, while the prospect of trouble makes most people shy away.

(2) A foreign foundation provided some money to the village for the purchase of engine-powered fishing boats, and it was decided that each of five owners should put up an amount equal to the loan received. A village fund was established to which the loans were to be repaid, so that additional credit could be made available subsequently for other projects. At the meetings held to discuss this project, there was great stress on proper fulfillment by the borrowers of their obligations in the interest of making the project a success and promoting general village welfare. One man, however, through fraud and manipulation of personal relations, was able to establish himself as a prospective boat owner and received a loan. He was neither liked as a person nor respected as a fisherman, and when it became evident that he had obtained the money on false pretenses, I expected there would be a general outcry against the unfairness to others who had dropped out because they could not meet the conditions. An informal meeting was held to discuss the possibility of canceling his loan so as not to endanger the viability of the project, but no one was willing to become the apparent cause of the man's public disgrace by replacing him. The idea of fairness to others, operation in accordance with the rules, and village welfare all turned out to be less important than the safeguarding of personal relations within the face-to-face community environment.

(3) A narrow sandspit, connecting the main part of the village to the rest of the peninsula, faces the Yellow Sea on one

side and a bay (or mudflats when the tide is out) on the other. As a part of the effort to reclaim tidal land for rice agriculture, grass and small trees were planted on the sand dunes, both in order to strengthen them as a barrier against the ocean and to keep sand from blowing onto the proposed rice fields. As soon as the grass really took hold, a nearby farmer staked his ox on the dunes every day in order to take advantage of the free fodder. He persisted in spite of a few protests, including that of the village head. Finally the village's only college graduate, who lived at the county seat and enjoyed enormous prestige in his native place, publicly rebuked the man and threatened him with official retribution if he persisted. This worked, but no one in the village had been willing to maintain the "public" point of view at the risk of acquiring an enemy.

There were other occasions too when the will of the majority or the general interest was blocked by one man's stubborn opposition, and concern with avoiding direct conflict always resulted in negotiations designed to reach unanimity rather than consideration of a resort to some form of coercion. Restraint in pursuing one's own interests and sensitivity to the feelings of others are highly prized qualities, however, so that the kind of individualistic insistence described in these examples is not common.

Another instance of personal ties taking precedence over community solidarity involved the resident anthropologist. Initially something of a conspiracy existed to deny me access to information that was considered unfavorable. On one occasion the village head even exhorted everyone at a large meeting to act and speak in such a way as to give only good impressions of the village. By and large his advice was followed, and people were reluctant to talk about adultery, drunkenness, gambling, anti-administration opinion, or crime of any sort. But with the development of personal friendships and obligations, certain people not only began to answer my questions more frankly but also volunteered information. One informant told me that the conflict between village pride and the obligations of hospitality and friendship towards me was occasionally the subject of heated debate in informal men's groups.

*Chapter 6 / Beyond Kinship*

## Local Administration

The village head man (*ijang*) is appointed by the county administration (*gunch'ŏng*) usually on the basis of the *myŏn* chief's recommendation. Formerly it was an elective office, but everyone I talked to in the village said that the present system worked better. Elections at the local level had had a divisive effect, since the more diffuse criteria for leadership such as education, ability, and reputation tended to be subordinated to lineage ties and personal obligations in the heat of partisan campaigning. The *ijang* is an important man in Sŏkp'o, and his prestige is great. The job is a fairly onerous and time-consuming one, largely because he must make the round trip on foot (four hours) so frequently to the *myŏn* office. The material rewards are meager; each villager contributes a small amount of rice that is determined in proportion to his wealth. In 1966 the *ijang's* income from this source amounted to about 30,000 *wŏn*, which was of course in addition to the food obtained from his own fields.

*Panjang* are hamlet or section leaders chosen by the village head after informal discussions with the residents concerned. The *panjang* were all in their thirties and forties, representing generally the middle and upper middle economic categories. Appointment as *panjang* amounts to recognition of a man's solid respectability. The material incentives are minute, however, and the duties mostly unpopular, since he must collect taxes in his neighborhood and mobilize people for work on county roads.

Village meetings are held quite often, usually at the school in section 3. Some meetings were attended by most of the adult males; as a rule smaller numbers, those directly concerned with a given issue, were present. Women and young unmarried men do not attend.

Word is passed around by mouth beforehand, and the school bell is rung before the meeting, which eventually seems to get under way an hour or two later than the originally announced time. The role of the village head at such times is that of moderator. He announces the problem and then sounds out opinion, attempting to reach a consensus that all can support. He may

164

offer his own recommendations, but unless they are a reflection of pressure from the *myŏn* chief, he will not try to insist on any single point of view in the face of strong opposition. Usually the outlines of a decision will have been reached ahead of time at smaller informal meetings of village leaders, so that the larger meetings are often just chances for residents to sound off themselves and hear what more influential persons think. A good deal of impassioned oratory takes place, and when a particular grievance or opinion on some issue obtains wide support, the *ijang* will always make some effort to show that he is responsive to popular feeling.

Decisions concerning village contributions of labor and resources, either in response to demands from the county administration or as part of local development projects, are carefully balanced so that no neighborhood or clan has reason to feel unfairly treated. Similarly when anything is being handed out, scrupulous care is taken to maintain the existing equilibrium. For example, when loans for the purchase of fishing boats became available, they were portioned out among clans and neighborhoods in a way that almost exactly paralleled the system of informal leadership by influential men. Only one of these leaders actually obtained a loan, however, the others going to kin and neighbors. Conversations with the village head indicated that the system did not operate on the basis of a positive abstract principle requiring some sort of proportional distribution of effort and rewards. Rather the negative point of view— that anything leading to conflict among either kinship groups or neighborhoods should be avoided—was uppermost in his mind. So, just as in interpersonal relations, political decision making is marked by restraint and a reluctance to push hard on an issue if the opposition is at all determined.

## Transactions and Economic Interdependence

Within the village the use of money is ordinarily avoided. But when major exchanges of property take place such as the sale of land or a boat, substantial amounts do change hands in an atmosphere of considerable formality. Also, money is borrowed and repaid fairly frequently. Minor purchases are made at the single store (run by an outsider), and small amounts of cash are ostentatiously flung around in hospitality contests at the wine shops. Money donations are made by all who attend major ceremonies in order to help offset the substantial cost of food and liquor. At such times the money is formally received by a friend of the household head (usually not a close relative), and the amount as well as the donor's name is ceremoniously written down.

In most other situations the use of money between friends and neighbors seems to create disagreeable restraint and embarrassment. The act of treating others provides considerable satisfaction and increased status, but the role of the recipient can be humiliating unless the obligation is promptly discharged. Most villagers are not only poor but extremely conscious of their poverty, and money often is desperately needed. Yet all seem concerned with protecting personal ties from the dangers presumed to be inherent in cash transactions, as if in recognition of the incompatibility of a money economy and the collective basis of village ideology.

There are plenty of indirect ways to maximize personal profit and, of course, the greed of some individuals is insatiable. A good deal of the reluctance to accept money presumably is feigned; still, the demands of collective responsibility and generosity can result in a contempt for hard cash that is surprising.

There were two occasions when I tried to pay for labor. After living in Sŏkp'o for about three months, I asked for help in hauling and stacking firewood. When I tried to find out how much money should be paid, I was told that the only problem was finding men with enough spare time, and that there was no need for money. Convinced that this was merely a conventional expression of etiquette, I calculated an approximate amount according to the wages currently paid for work on the dike and handed it around. The result was a wild party that lasted until everything had been spent on liquor.

Some months later, when summer rains had washed away much of the packed earth terrace in front of my house, two neighbors with whom I had been discussing the problem turned up one morning carrying heavy loads of dirt. They spent the entire day rebuilding the terrace. By this time I had learned that it was appropriate in such cases to provide copious food and drink. Along with the hospitality goes the understanding that the labor will be returned if needed. Not having an adequate catering service and realizing that my labor was relatively useless, I again gave them money. This time I was summoned to the wine shop after the party was well under way. My neighbors were treating everyone they could find, and I was forced to join in the general intoxication. The whole sequence of events may well have been planned in advance in order to manufacture an occasion for drinking, but the point is that as neighbors performing an act of assistance, they did not feel they could accept and keep payment in money. In this case the money was used as a means of obtaining the proper medium of exchange.

The distribution of most other goods within the village is accomplished by various kinds of nonmonetary transactions. A complicated maze of obligations based on kinship, friendship, neighborhood ties, and past acts connects nearly everyone, facilitating the exchange of goods and services. A migrant fishing family from South Chŏlla Province who had been in the village about a year operated to some extent outside this exchange network. They had set up a large fixed net along the shore, using techniques learned from the Japanese that were unknown in Sŏkp'o, and as a result they obtained different varieties of fish during the seasons when local fishermen caught little or were away fishing among the offshore islands. These fish were often sold or bartered within the village and the negotiations resembled those with commercial buyers, but I never saw local fishermen sell their catch to village residents in this fashion. When I wanted fish, they were either given to me or I was told there were none; no one would sell.

When in need of minor articles such as salt, buttons, vegetable seeds or a few fish hooks, villagers often go next door to a kinsman or neighbor and ask for them. It seemed to me that their manner on such occasions was somewhat brusque rather than supplicating, as if refusal were out of the question. If the request is considered exorbitant and rejected, there will probably be a harsh exchange of words.

167

A good deal of borrowing of tools and implements take place. Where a major item such as an insecticide sprayer or a foot threshing machine is loaned, a predetermined rent is paid in grain; for most things such as shovels, a bucket, or even the use of a boat, there is no compensation. All such acts go onto the informal balance sheet, and the necessity of reciprocating at some future time is universally recognized. Some people said they hesitated to ask for things because of the obligations entailed, and others confessed that they dreaded requests from those who were slow or forgetful in returning the favor.

The system operates continuously and effectively to tie people together across the boundaries of kinship and territorial groups. When my house was being built, people from all over the village came to help, which was useful later on in making informal contacts. People who had worked on the house felt free to stop by and drink coffee or whiskey or ask for a cigarette, and they urged me to continue the exchange by going to them if I needed anything. In other words the obligation to reciprocate in a constant exchange of goods and services is explicitly recognized and utilized as a means of establishing and reinforcing personal ties.

Exchanges of labor (see Chapter 3), often across neighborhood boundaries, are important in the economic and social life of the village. Men, particularly the idle poor, are content to work all day just for food and drink plus the companionship and certainty that they can call for similar services in the future.

The dependence of a large portion of the village on neighbors and kin for extra labor, tools, loans, and other assistance can be seen as one more factor promoting the preservation of good personal relations. Most people are very poor and can hardly afford to antagonize neighbors who might provide crucial help in time of need. I had no success in trying to follow up this kind of deterministic interpretation of solidarity, however, since villagers invariably described their acts of mutual assistance in more positive and idealistic terms.

Barter, as a direct commercial transaction or disguised as an exchange of gifts, takes place on a considerable scale. Villagers occasionally used the technique of coercive giving or favor-doing preparatory to asking for something, particularly in dealing with the resident anthropologist, but among themselves most exchanges seemed to follow established patterns of rights and obligations. In particular, a substantial portion of the fish catch was regularly distributed within the village despite efforts by the wholesalers from town to buy as much of it as possible. Through a wide variety of transactions fish are exchanged for agricultural commodities, a process that not only ties the third and fourth "fishing" neighborhoods economically to the rest of the village but also reinforces many social bonds across kinship and neighborhood boundaries.

## Relations with the Outside World

The nature of those shared sentiments that give people in a society a feeling of belonging together can also be examined from the point of view of relations with the outside world. A more complicated situation exists in Sŏkp'o than the simple in-group, out-group distinction, but something like it can be said generally to occur at the boundary separating village society from the rest of the country. Most inhabitants of Sŏkp'o have an ambivalent outlook towards strangers, particularly those from towns and cities. There is on the one hand distrust, apprehension, and a feeling of inferiority, while on the other envy, admiration, and the longing for closer ties are also present.

Different groups within the village express the ambivalence in different ways. Substantial farmers and influential members of the Yi clan are inclined to be formal and on their best behavior with outsiders, adopting an air of respectful restraint that seems to fluctuate between aloofness and humility. The didactic homily, "One is respected only if one shows deference to others," is a guide to conduct.

Residents of the third and fourth sections, however, often seem to exaggerate certain aspects of their normal behavior in relations with outsiders, as if they are acting out special roles for the occasion. Here the emphasis is on directness, crudity, and a kind of simple, noisy honesty in contrast to what is felt to be the wily sophistication of townsfolk. Extremely sensitive to criticism of their "backward cultural development," fishermen are deliberately boisterous, often using particularly crude language in order, it seemed to me, to show that they are not ashamed. Of the two alternative ways of dealing with the strangers, I suspect that the aggressive, noisy one is a reflection of greater anxiety or a deeper sense of inferiority.

At the same time it is the fishermen who seemed most susceptible to the blandishments of outsiders in speculative business transactions or in forming disastrous partnerships. Anyone who can project an air of confidence, refinement, and experience gained in the city, makes a great impression in spite of the natural suspicion towards strangers. To some extent lack of confidence in dealing with outsiders, which is based on the stigma attached to fishing, educational disability, and geographic remoteness, is shared by everyone, including those who are predominantly farmers, while the generalizations set forth above are subject to numerous exceptions because of variations in individual personality.

County and subcounty officials concerned with administration, health, production, and education visited the village infrequently, usually in connection with some ceremonial observance. Beyond these minor chores their interest in the village is largely exploitative. In Korea when considerable amounts of money, grain, or other goods change hands at local levels—in both the public and private economic sectors—functionaries and whatever other brokers are involved usually manage to retain a certain portion. So if the dike project at Sŏkp'o is approved for financing under the Food for Peace Program, or if the National Fishery Cooperative decides to lend money to Sŏkp'o fishermen, opportunities for profit arise. The practice of helping oneself in such situations is so ubiquitous and traditional that there is little sense of popular indignation except in cases of exaggerated abuse. Military officials responsible for the coastal defense units guarding against infiltrators from the north also made occasional tours of inspection.

Whenever such dignitaries did arrive, riding in a jeep and wearing western suits or uniforms, there took place a rather dramatic downgrading of the status of older men. The county (*gun*) or subcounty (*myŏn*) officials were not actually rude; they simply ignored the old men, or if forced into a confrontation, greeted them in a perfunctory and somewhat patronizing manner. Then they at once turned to younger men such as the village head or one of the townsmen living temporarily in Sŏkp'o in order to conduct their business. It was strange and somewhat pathetic to see men whom I had come to regard as influential pillars of the community standing around the edges of a small crowd gawking at the visitors just like some of the schoolboys.

Sŏkp'o does have one representative who can deal with the mighty on relatively even terms. He has already been introduced as the only college graduate ever produced in the village. Formerly county policy chief during the Rhee regime, his prestige in the village is infinite. In 1966, aged about 45, he still lived in Sŏsan (the county seat) struggling to maintain his former status and standard of living. He has since moved to Seoul, where thanks to his education, social competence, and administrative experience, he has many important connections.

In recent years this man, a member of the Yi lineage, has made something of a career out of promoting the development of his native village, motivated partly by gratitude for the efforts made in sending him to college. The people of Sŏkp'o are proud of their representative and fortunate in having one so able, energetic, and dedicated to promoting village development. Without him Sŏkp'o would be completely ignored as far as official benefits are concerned. The parallel with traditional China, where local literati intervened informally with the bureaucracy on behalf of their "constituency," is striking.

## VALUES AND SANCTIONS

### The Learning of Values

An intensive study of child-rearing practices should be the subject of a specialized program of research conducted by someone with extensive training in psychology. John Whiting and his associates have emphasized the importance of rigorous methodology, including statistical control of the observations, if scientific results are to be obtained (Whiting *et al.*, 1953, 1961).

171

While none of these conditions was met by the Sŏkp'o project, it seemed useful as part of the study of values to take a hard look at the way children were instructed and disciplined. This was feasible only because my sister-in-law, a Korean, was accepted into the world of women and small children—a milieu closed to me. She spent long hours with them, sharing household tasks or out on the rocks gathering oysters. In the evening she was frequently invited to supper, particularly in our neighborhood, and sat around talking with girls and young women until long after dark. All this provided ample opportunity to watch the way young children were handled. The generalizations that emerged from these observations are naturally focused most sharply on behavior that contrasts with practices in the United States or in Seoul.

The apparent neglect of all children after infancy was particularly striking to both of us. A mother's attention is concentrated on the newest baby, who remains in almost constant contact with her day and night. Older children, including those who are only 2½ or 3 years old, are left very much to their own devices or in the care of an older sibling. During the process of socialization parents make little effort to explain or instruct, and learning is almost entirely by imitation and negative prohibitions. For example, in one house when an elderly man sat down on the porch, a child of 7 or 8 was lying nearby. The mother said, "Don't lie there," but the child did not move. The mother then raised her voice and lifted her hand threateningly, but there was still no compliance so she half-heartedly tried to strike the child, who gauged the exact moment to slip out of reach. Or again, if a child is playing near a boat that is being readied for sea, it will merely be chased off with an angry shout. In general, no attempt is made to explain the reason for a prohibition or to enunciate a rule of conduct. The child learns only that some acts are wrong in a certain social context. Discipline is usually exercised in terms of situations and specific individuals rather than abstract principles.

There is a paradoxically integrative aspect to the "neglect," however. Parents do not take the trouble to create a special world for children in which there are separate rules and indulgences. There is no catering to a child's ego so as to give him a strong sense of separate identity. As soon as children are old enough, they naturally help (or try to help) with whatever work is in progress. They are nearly always under foot when anything of interest is going on. As constant spectators of the life of the village, they press in as close as they dare and while sometimes thrust aside, usually they are ignored.

It is as if the child, while having the potential for becoming a full-fledged member of the community, is not yet regarded as being fully human. At the same time, however, there is far less separation from the adult world than we are used to. For example, at night there is no bedtime; children listen to the conversation of their elders until they fall asleep draped across the lap of an older relative. Thus, as spectators and partial participants, they are constantly receiving an "initiation to adult life" and a "realistic introduction to the ways of the world" (Hsu 1963:201).

Parents, especially mothers, frequently scold and threaten their children in what seem to be violent terms. As a rule the children pay little attention. When they are beaten or slapped, it is usually for disobedience rather than wrongdoing. In fact, most people are extraordinarily tolerant when a child causes trouble by breaking something, by making his younger brother cry, or through any other mischief. "He is only a child and doesn't know any better," is a phrase that is constantly heard. But once a command is given, strict compliance is required. Parents strike children for failing to obey such orders as, "Bring the dish," "Light the fire," "Carry the baby on your back," "Stop teasing the baby," "Don't eat that," and so on.

If it can be said that children over 2 or 3 are left pretty much on their own, it must also be added that few demands are made on them. Children are encouraged to be dependent, obedient, and cooperative. There is no strong parental expectation that they should compete and achieve.* The inferiority of his own status, the importance of deference to elders, and the subordi-

*This is in striking contrast to many Seoul families in which children are often subjected to extreme pressures in order to fulfill their parent's ambitions.

nation of his individual ideas to those of the group are heavily emphasized in a child's upbringing. After infancy he rarely asserts himself, and he learns to accept hardships such as cold, hunger, and sickness without complaint. Productive skills are learned very gradually through imitation, not organized instruction, in an atmosphere of cooperative effort.

## Values and Sanctions in the Small Community

Many writers on Far Eastern society have pointed out the particularistic or situational aspect of values as they are applied to everyday behavior. At the village level people can be regarded as belonging to a series of hierarchically organized, concentric or overlapping groups such as the family, lineage, neighborhood, age grade, work or recreation group, and formal meeting. In all such groups norms of behavior are applied differentially according to individual status, role, and immediate situation. Such factors as wealth, degree of inebriation, reputation, and even knowledge of individual personality quirks are considered in determining what kind of behavior is appropriate.

Social censure in a milieu where everyone is always watching constitutes the most important sanction for the enforcement of conformity to acceptable standards of behavior. When villagers leave the small face-to-face community, this "shame" sanction loses a good deal of its force. For example, a small detachment of six soldiers was in Sŏkp'o for a few months on antispy duty. Although they were farm boys from similar villages, they were often arrogant, frequently drunk and disorderly, and made crude advances to several women. One explained sheepishly that he had always been an upright person in his native place, but that in Sŏkp'o criticism did not bother him. Eventually a soldier was so badly beaten in a drunken brawl that he had to be hospitalized, and the detachment leader was replaced with one who maintained better discipline.

When Sŏkp'o residents go to Inchŏn, Seoul, or Pusan, they no longer are subject to the same constant scrutiny of relatives and neighbors and they feel more free to act in accordance with individual feelings and goals. At the same time they are leaving a relatively stable and secure environment in which other people's behavior usually can be predicted. The city is seen as a kind of dangerous and exciting battleground where a man survives through cunning, toughness, and the ability to remain inconspicuous.

Initially at least, visits to city relatives or migration results in an intensification of kinship values. The boundaries of cooperation, mutual obligation, and responsibility that formerly included the whole village are narrowed down to a few persons or families within a much larger society that is hostile or indifferent. Four, and possibly more, families have returned to the village after extended periods in a large city. They were lured away by the possibility (remote, as it turned out) of upward mobility and came back to Sŏkp'o not only because it offers subsistence, but because of the permanent network of relatively secure personal relationships.

If social censure is important in enforcing a degree of conformity with many rules, internalization still is profound with regard to two basic focal areas or clusters of values: (1) filial piety, which although most intense within the household, has diffuse aspects throughout the kinship organization; and (2) cooperation and reciprocity.

## Cooperation and Reciprocity

Cooperative work groups have already been described in some detail. People are proud of this tradition, and the willingness to contribute one's labor on behalf of others is, according to my informal opinion survey, one of the most important factors in establishing a good reputation, ranking above honesty, sobriety, and pleasing personality. The second most important ideal characteristic is proper behavior (*parŭn haengdong*), a concept that combines formal etiquette and good heartedness.

Also included in the idea of cooperation is a sense of mutual assistance (*sŏro towa chunŭn kŏt*). Out of fifty heads of household who discussed the issue with me, thirty-eight (76 percent) preferred a man who was concerned with the affairs of his neighbors even to the extent of intervening in disputes or offering unsolicited advice. In talking to people, I framed the questions in a slightly pejorative way so as to give the connotation of a busybody meddling in his neighbors' affairs, and yet three-fourths of the informants preferred such a person to one who minded his own business without concern for what went on next door. This may appear to stretch the meaning of cooperation pretty far, but from the point of view of Sŏkp'o residents the concepts are closely related. Many respondents were surprised by the question, considering the answer to be completely self-evident. The 24 percent who preferred that a man mind his own business was composed largely of persons who had lived elsewhere and a number of younger men in their late twenties and early thirties.

Another related and fundamental value is that of reciprocity. It is a basic principle of ethical behavior but curiously unformulated linguistically. Obligations are keenly felt, both individually and collectively. Help, favors, and presents must in theory be returned in order to establish some kind of reciprocal balance.

Some people take these obligations more seriously than others. Unlike cooperation, which requires only personal participation, material goods or money as well as labor are often involved in questions of reciprocity. It is a value that can be manipulated by someone who is skillful and unscrupulous, particularly in the larger more anonymous society of the cities. In Sŏkp'o occasional noisy disputes arise when two people or families calculate the current balance differently. Such conflicts are frequently settled in a sort of public arena through the informal expression of social censure (see Chapter 7).

The theme of tolerance comes up again and again in my field notes. Although children and adolescents are constantly scolded and badgered, young men and adults are rarely corrected or criticized in public. For example, when tools are being made, many people gather at the forge to watch and some always help with the bellows or the hammering. If a man blunders, there may be a nervous giggle on the part of a child, but no one will say anything and immediate efforts are made to cover up and forget the incident.

The same thing is true when fishing or tinkering with an

engine or building a roof. Excellence of productive performance is not usually the focus of primary concern. It is a quality
that is appreciated, of course, and other things being equal, the
most skillful fishermen are preferred when making up boat
crews. But other things rarely are equal, and cooperative spirit,
proper etiquette, conscientiousness, honesty, and considerations of kinship usually take priority. Allowances are made for
failure in all aspects of behavior, and most villagers are not
accustomed to judging others in terms of some abstract standard of perfection. When people are criticized, it is generally because of ethical shortcomings rather than incompetence.

Conversely, individuals are rarely singled out for praise in
technical matters, and extra skill usually gets no special reward
beyond the esteem of fellow workers. Nor is intelligence a quality that receives much attention. Moderation is far more admired than incisive brilliance. Intelligence is useful not in
itself but because it qualifies a boy for education. All of this
seems to be less true among women, and critical gossip around
the well or when out oystering often deals with the practical
shortcomings or special skills of wives and daughters.

Familiarity engendered by a lifetime of living closely together creates a special kind of subtlety in interpersonal relations. Censure is more often sensed than expressed. People
know how their neighbors think and feel, so that a combination of gossip and imagination is usually enough to enforce
conformity.

## Territorial Loyalty

Despite considerable effort I uncovered very little evidence
of allegiance to Sŏkp'o as a geographic entity. Land is highly
valued, but there was laughing denial when I would ask
about something deeper—an emotional attachment, either to
family rice fields, to a specific house, or to the area in general.
Geographic isolation has undoubtedly contributed to the
maintenance of village cohesiveness and a sense of mutual
interdependence, but loyalty to the place is a less important
integrating factor than identity with a group of people. In other
words, common participation in a network of human relations,

a society, takes precedence from a conceptual point of view over joint occupation of a piece of territory.

Most villagers take the attitude that residence in Sŏkp'o is the result of an unkind twist of fate. They make constant references to their poverty, lack of education, and backward way of life, all of which are blamed primarily on the village site. (In spite of all this self deprecation, social morale—or community spirit—is high, a fact that is perhaps best expressed by the pride in "human heartedness" referred to previously.) Ambition on behalf of one's children usually includes the hope that they can eventually move or be married out, either to an inland agricultural village or to town.

The strong prejudice in Korea against those who fish has already been mentioned. What surprised me was the extent to which it was shared by villagers in thinking about themselves. On the other hand, many fishermen, while dedicated to the goal of insulating their families from the stigma, preferred fishing as an occupation to farming and were eager to expand their operations. Within the village this prejudice was carefully concealed in everyday interaction between farmers and fishermen. I never heard any disparaging remarks, except by outsiders, on the subject, which was nonetheless expressed locally through marriage choices and the desire of most fishermen to acquire more land.

There are significant exceptions to the general dissatisfaction with Sŏkp'o and the desire to move away. Some respondents in the age categories over 45 said that they wanted their eldest sons to stay in order to carry out family ritual properly and look after the ancestral tombs. In such cases kinship continuity and the welfare of spirits was at stake rather than attachment to a piece of ground, and except for the eldest son it was still regarded as preferable that the children try to find their opportunities elsewhere.

Some "rich" farmers were content to see their children stay in Sŏkp'o and were reasonably optimistic about future development. In particular two prominent household heads in the former *yangban* lineage indicated a somewhat paternalistic sense of responsibility for taking the initiative and guiding the process of village economic development. A prominent member of one of the Kim lineages, an aggressive and successful fishing entrepreneur, also thinks of himself as a potential leader in promoting economic activity.

In all these cases ambition is expressed in terms of a role where the emphasis is not on personal aggrandizement but rather on the promotion of community welfare and goals. The orientation or frame of reference is collective, and such men see themselves as organizers of group activity, human catalysts promoting cooperative self-help. Success and prestige for them exist in being at the center of energy and movement and thereby gaining the esteem of their follow villagers. They do not disassociate their own personal fortunes from those of the village as a whole; or at least they are unwilling to express their goals in wholly egoistic terms. Once economic security is achieved and additional resources are available beyond those necessary for bare subsistence, it is still far more prestigious in Sŏkp'o to align oneself with administrative functions such as leadership of the village, school teaching, or economic development rather than with amassing wealth and living luxuriously.

Another more intangible factor connected with territoriality as a basis for village cohesion is the attitude towards nature. Thoughts and beliefs concerning land are strongly influenced by geomantic concepts* rather than emotion. Residents of Sŏkp'o never comment on aesthetic aspects of the scenery, although they are deeply concerned with the shape of hills, the flow of water, and the orientation of topographic features in relation to the compass. Natural beauty, however, is not re-

---

*Geomancy, an import from China, was enthusiastically adopted in Korea, where it underwent additional refinement and development. It is based on the belief that if tomb and house sites are properly chosen with respect to wind, water, compass direction, and topographic land features, good fortune and prosperity will result. In Sŏkp'o a number of old men refer to it as the true science (kwahak) in contrast to recent notions brought in from the West. All village residents make a sharp distinction between geomancy (p'ung su) and superstition (misin). The former is quite respectable, whereas the latter, which refers to a variety of shamanistic practices, is contemptuously rejected by the more progressive villagers.

ferred to except as a potential economic asset that might bring tourists to Sŏkp'o from the city as it has to some nearby and more accessible sections of the coast. It has no discernible and consciously expressed affective meaning for the inhabitants that I could discover.

## Economic Egalitarianism

There is still a fairly strong prejudice in Sŏkp'o against ostentatious consumption that might put too much social distance between rich and poor households. This straining towards equality has several elements. On the one hand, it is composed simply of local tradition in a poor and backward area. Villagers have modest ideas regarding standards of living, and the taste for many luxuries has not yet been acquired. It is really a question of priorities in the use of what meager additional resources exist beyond those required for subsistence. Out of forty-seven heads of household who were asked how they would use 1,000,000 *wŏn* ($2,700) if it were suddenly available with no strings attached, not one replied that he would spend the money for immediate consumption needs. The table below summarizes the replies, which when broken down by neighborhoods provide an interesting clue as to value preferences:

PREFERRED INVESTMENT OF 1,000,000 *WŎN*

| Sections | No. of households in sample | Percentage preferring— | | | |
|---|---|---|---|---|---|
| | | education | fishing | commerce | land |
| 1 and 2 (*yangban*) | 14 | 43.0 | 0.7 | 0.7 | 21.6 |
| 3 and 4 (Big Hamlet) | 25 | 12.0 | 24.0 | 32.0 | 32.0 |
| 5 and 6 ("Over There") | 8 | 12.5 | 25.0 | 12.5 | 50.0 |

The persistence of *yangban* prejudice against fishing in sections 1 and 2 is particularly striking, while the emphasis on fisheries and commerce in the central neighborhood is also marked. All three neighborhoods are hungry for land.

Most people expect that the well-to-do will redistribute much of their surplus in ceremonial festivities and hospitality, and there is always gossip about substantial new expenditures for personal or family consumption. As one fisherman who migrated to Sŏkp'o in 1961 from a nearby town put it, "No one here wants to see anyone else live better than he does." Or, stated more positively, one can say that even though a surplus exists, a sense of collective responsibility inhibits spending when so many people live so precariously.

Another factor is the traditional fear that any evidence of wealth will result in a rapacious onslaught by officials. As recently as the Rhee administration, exactions by local police who visited the village in search of "voluntary contributions" gave a certain substance to these lingering fears of administrative exploitation.

Two younger men in the well-off farmer category were considering putting tile roofs on their houses when I left the village. A tile roof is a definite status symbol in the Korean countryside, and Sŏkp'o was the only village in the area without a single such house. As new opportunities for production, investment, and commercial activity open up, some individuals are bound to become successful entrepreneurs on the basis of their personal capacity and energy. This process, which directly challenges traditional egalitarian values, has proceeded much further in some neighboring villages than in Sŏkp'o where it is just starting. An unfortunate concomitant is that the sense of collective responsibility, which in effect guarantees a certain minimum level of subsistence to incompetent or unlucky members of village society, fades away in proportion to the rise of individuality, and the gap between rich and poor widens.

## TOPOGRAPHY AND INTERACTION

Certain environmental factors are important in promoting village cohesion. The minor topographic barriers between neighborhoods are far less formidable than those between the village as a whole and other communities. Individual plots of land are scattered widely so that a farmer often must trudge back and forth throughout the village and even beyond to reach all his fields. Prosperous farmers who acquire land at the other end of the village sometimes find it practicable to install a son there in order to lessen the amount of time spent in getting to and from their fields. The result is an expansion of the scope of kinship relations beyond concentrated neighborhood clusters.

Aside from patterns of residence, the fact that most well-to-do farmers own land in different localities compels them to move constantly about the village and interact with residents of other neighborhoods. Such contacts may be brief and perfunctory, but often enough they consist of prolonged conversations, mutual assistance, and shared food and drink. Fishermen, of course, are still more mobile, their activities being limited by the tides, winds, and location of fishing grounds rather than by neighborhood residence patterns.

It is difficult to obtain any historical perspective on the question of village unity. In the late Yi dynasty period (circa 1900) Sŏkp'o neighborhoods were just as widely dispersed as they are today, while political and economic factors promoting cohesion were probably less strong. Administrative policy under the Japanese and Republic of Korea governments has contributed to a sense of territorial unity in many ways. On the other hand, because of the village's isolation there may have been formerly an even stronger in-group feeling vis-à-vis the outside world.

## SUMMARY

This chapter has described the kinds of groupings that cut across kinship divisions and the values and attitudes that mitigate a pervasive lineage ideology. Informal convivial men's groups, the importance attached to maintaining correct dyadic relations, and the way many lineage rituals are expanded to include everyone are all integral aspects of village social organization that promote solidarity. Cooperation, reciprocity, and hospitality rank high on the scale of informal values, while tolerance and restraint are a nearly constant ingredient of interpersonal relations. Neighborhood loyalties and obligations are strong and in some situations challenge the cohesiveness of the lineage.

These disparate elements are not linked together in any systematic way either by the villagers or in any Korean intellectual tradition. They do have in common a focus on the entire community, and they contribute to its unity.

A conscious effort is made by village leaders to maintain an approximate balance among the territorial, kinship, occupational, and class divisions with regard to all matters affecting the whole community, so that no one element will feel unduly slighted. The balance is not symmetrical since the *yangban* and "Over There" neighborhoods with less population have a disproportionate share of wealth and influence. Their greater moral authority has several components: an emphasis on agriculture, education, and lineage, all of which are associated with a slightly different style of life. While the fishing neighborhood shows occasional resentment, residents there share the values that give greater prestige to the more sober and conscientious men who own rice land.

The list of influential persons consulted in advance when an important decision is pending represents a judicious mixture of neighborhood and lineage representation. When economic benefits are available for distribution, the same principle is maintained. This does not mean that there is a conscious effort to promote economic equality. Some neighborhoods and some lineages are considerably better off than others. Nevertheless, there seems to be a common recognition of permissible limits to inequality in wealth and influence, and there is resistance if the current balance is threatened.

# 7

## CONFLICT
## AND
## MALINTEGRATION

Many studies of contemporary peasant societies have emphasized the prevalence of suspicion and conflict among individuals
and groups, and as a result a lively theoretical discussion of
such behavioral phenomena has ensued (Foster 1960, 1965,
1967; Balikci 1965; Turner 1957; Lewis 1963; Norbeck 1963;
Gluckman 1955, 1965; van Velzen, Thoden, and van Watering
1960; van Velsen 1964).

The efforts of Gluckman, Balikci, Turner, and others to relate
quarrels to structural and environmental factors as well as to
processes of individual decision making, and to analyze them
in terms of specific causes and classes of persons involved,
would seem to offer a more sound and productive line of approach than Foster's attempt at a total explanation of peasant
society in terms of hostility, suspicion, and conflict.

In any case there are no objective standards for judging
whether a village is characterized by strife or by harmony. The
ethnographer's state of mind—possibly his visceral reaction to
life in a strange environment (or defense against such reaction)
—is all too likely to influence the choice of what to emphasize.
A similar problem exists in any discussion of the relation between ideology and behavior. The observer can either emphasize the conformity of acts to a system of values or the

contradictions, but there is no absolute scale against which a given society can be measured.

In contrast to the relative anonymity of western social life and the sharp separation of the environments where interaction takes place, most village interpersonal relations occur in an open public arena where they are of intense dramatic interest to every member of the community. The sound and fury of conflict is there for all to see, and it invariably makes a strong impression on the ethnographer, particularly if he is from a relatively repressed society. The point may be obvious, but it is perhaps worth stressing in any attempt to estimate the extent of an anthropologist's personal bias in interpreting his material.

Another possible source of distortion is derived from the perspective of applied anthropology. An outside observer tries to show "his peasants" the path to a better life and is frustrated by their obtuse and irrational conservatism. He is then perhaps led to generalize about their mutual distrust and hostility in order to explain why they refuse to cooperate in transforming their society and economy in accordance with his plan.

Is it not just as likely that much of the conflict and suspicion arises from the pressures and strains to which traditional peasant societies have been subjected during the past fifty or one hundred years? It is easy for the westerner from a city to conclude that peasant villages have "changed little from the time of Christ" because they still use the same kind of plow. Yet it is the large population increases during the last hundred years or so that have increased human pressures on limited agricultural resources to the point where economic competition does threaten traditional ways of reconciling interests within a society. Is peasant hostility preventing change, or is change introducing new tensions?

Distrust, envy, and conflict are plentiful in Sŏkp'o, although (and this is where my own bias must be made apparent) they seemed a less deeply rooted part of individual personality than in the other societies where I have lived. The immediate reaction of most villagers in difficult interpersonal situations is to attempt to brush aside the trouble, to make allowances for the behavior of others, and to seize on almost any concession or show of good will as an adequate basis for the restoration of harmonious relations.

These subjective estimates are paralleled by an interesting statistical comparison made by McGinn, Harburg, and Ginsberg of "Responses to Interpersonal Conflict by Middle Class Males in Guadalajara and Michigan" (1965). The Americans in this study felt themselves to be far more threatened by implied criticism on the part of friends and reacted with more hostility than did the Mexicans.

There is no doubt that the limited size of the economic "pie" contributes to tension and disputes. But to abandon the inquiry into the nature of conflict at this point as Foster seems to (1967), and rest the case on such a sufficient cause would not only be a gross oversimplification in the case of Sŏkp'o but would also give an entirely misleading account of social relations.

Potential and actual conflicts between groups or individuals are headed off or resolved with a minimum of subsequent recrimination and bitterness by a complex, subtle combination of self-control, social censure, and on-the-spot arbitration. The frequent use of intense oral aggression as an immediate expression of tension and hostility is a significant factor in village life. Strong feelings do not remain bottled up for long. There is little verbal restraint once a real quarrel is launched, the principals often continuing to shout at each other until every conceivable grievance and bit of resentment has been dredged up and spewed out. Where serious conflict exists, the process may go on for days; in other cases it will last an hour or two, while work continues uninterrupted. Despite their frequency, such individual outbursts do not permanently disrupt the overall atmosphere of tolerance and good will.

Some deep-rooted animosity does exist, in particular as a result of political events that occurred during the Communist occupation and subsequent liberation of the village in 1950. There is widespread agreement, however, that the bitter memories of this period, which in any case are fading, should not be reflected in everyday relationships. Occasionally an incorrigible thief or bully has been permanently ostracized from the village, but such cases are rare and occur only after repeated and extreme provocation.

In this chapter I will discuss the kinds of disputes that are most frequent and the way in which they are resolved. An effort will be made to relate interpersonal conflict both to ecological and structural areas of contradiction or malintegration, and to considerations of personality and ideology. A number of illustrative examples are included to show how things actually work out.

## SOURCES OF CONFLICT

It is difficult to classify many disputes in the village by specific cause. Even the separation into economic and noneconomic quarrels often is unreal. Although some quarrels arise for obvious reasons, others are of long duration with complex causes. This situation is no less complicated than that faced by a marriage counselor in America or the judges of a dispute in Barotseland when they are confronted by a whole series of grievances, "a record of quarrels and breaches of obligation on both sides" (Gluckman 1965:10).

Probably the most frequent economic cause of disputes is the failure to pay back money or return property. Such acts as overworking a borrowed ox or damaging property in some other way were also frequently cited as leading to bad feeling. Failure to keep promises or to reciprocate in labor exchanges can cause trouble. If a man is sharp in his dealings with fellow villagers, they will eventually call him miserly, an insult that almost invariably provokes a quarrel.

Land division among brothers is a recognized point of strain in the village. The considerable difference in status and standard of living between elder and younger brother has already been described. If the elder brother does not balance this dominant position with generosity and a benevolent sense of responsibility, the younger will resent his position.

Two forms of poaching by boys and young men of poor families occur now and then. The areas of sand and rock enclosed in stone fish traps are considered private property, and netting fish or digging for octopus there when the tide is out is regarded as a serious offense. On the other hand, the owner understands the family circumstances of the offender and knows he would not be there if there was enough food in his family. A monumental bawling out is the usual punishment, but repeated offenses damage a boy's reputation—and that of his family. Some families have no forest land, and there is a certain amount of surreptitious cutting of branches for fuel and other uses in the more remote hilly areas.

Children are strongly disciplined for taking ripened crops of any kind, and there is little stealing of this sort in Sŏkp'o. During my stay in the village some minor pilferage of cabbage and drying rice sheaves occured that was attributed to children. Also, a kind of institutionalized pilferage called *sŏri* does exist as an adventurous prank for young girls between about the age of 15 and the time when they leave the village to get married. At night they sneak out and take persimmons, corn, or sweet potatoes which are then eaten raw in secret. A sharp distinction is made linguistically between this and stealing. In nearby villages across the bay where some farmers are quite prosperous and there are more landless poor, theft of crops is a major problem.

The only form of sorcery practiced in the village is used to punish theft. According to women informants, most of whom had married into the village from outside, people are afraid of it and therefore there is little stealing. Men were reluctant to discuss the practice and usually claimed that there was no stealing in Sŏkp'o because of the "human heartedness" of the villagers. Small thefts are ignored or attributed to children. If larger amounts are involved and people get to know about it, the injured person catches a small aquatic salamander (loach; *misqurnis fossilis*) in the paddy field and pokes out its eye on the birthday of the thief while uttering a suitable incantation. Thereafter the thief goes blind. Two cases of blindness caused by this practice were mentioned.

# MALINTEGRATION

Certain built-in factors that might be labeled structural contradictions or elements of malintegration contribute in various ways to interpersonal conflict. Most fundamental is the tension between kinship loyalties and cooperation or solidarity on a village-wide basis. One dominant theme of this paper deals with the effective way in which this opposition has been reconciled. Nevertheless, there were enough disparaging remarks made in the context of lineage distinctions to provide evidence of some degree of competition, envy, and distrust.

During the Korean War a serious split along kinship lines was provoked by the conflict in political doctrines. One of the Kim lineages became identified with the Communist occupation. With a membership composed mainly of uneducated farmers possessing an unimpeachable commoner background, they were utilized by the North Koreans as agents of class warfare. The most prominent man of the Yi lineage was executed as a rich landowner by North Korean political officers, and the Kims collaborated with the Communists in requisitioning oxen and grain from well-to-do farmers of the other kinship groups. When the village was reoccupied by the South Koreans, retribution was extreme. They killed between ten and fifteen villagers (stories differed) and redistributed a certain amount of property. The Kims on the north side of the ridge are still occasionally referred to as "the red ones" (*ppalgaengi*); villagers, when asked whether bitter feelings remain, answered to the effect that such events could never be forgotten—at least in people's hearts. It is noteworthy that everyone agrees the past should be forgotten, however, and members of all the lineages interact today in both productive and social activities without restraint.

Similarly the traditional class division between *yangban* and commoner is still part of the cognitive outlook of middle-aged and older men. Yet only one old man ever spoke out openly with what might be called class prejudice, and those who heard him considered it a shameful and embarrassing act. A good parallel exists, I believe, with certain subcultures of Americans who although intellectually committed to racial equality, can not shed a whole cluster of beliefs and feelings all at once. Prominent members of the Yi lineage consider it natural that they should take the initiative in village affairs and that their influence should be a little weightier than that of the other neighborhoods. From their point of view, residents of the Big Hamlet are cantankerous at times, failing to cooperate just to show their independence. The fact that this slightly patronizing attitude was resented became abundantly clear at the time of the great incest scandal (see page 209), when residents from the Big Hamlet and "Over There" provoked several quarrels by pointing out the discrepancy between the *yangban* assumption of moral superiority and the glaring actuality of a specific incident.

## Tradition and Change

A working compromise has existed between hierarchical principles as expressed in the authoritarian organization of the family or lineage on the one hand and egalitarianism as expressed in the rivalry of peers on the other. Egalitarianism can also be associated with the importance of consensus and a preoccupation with solidarity across kinship boundaries. This reconciliation of opposing structures and clusters of values is threatened by the modernizing process. Along with technological innovation and the expanding influence of national markets, a whole new way of thinking about individuals in relation to other men and to the natural environment is starting to permeate the village.

In many cases youth welcomes the challenge to traditional patterns of authority and behavioral codes, and consequently strain between the generations is increasing. Currently the expanding expectations of youth are focused on the desire to obtain more education and—some years later—on the right to choose one's own spouse. Strict deference to elders is regarded less as a moral principle than as a form of etiquette. Nevertheless etiquette of this sort is still a determining factor in establishing a man's reputation, and young men fear social censure. Older men sometimes accuse the young of failing to behave morally, contrasting the present with their own youth. If pressed to be explicit, they usually emphasize lack of deference as the major shortcoming.

Under the Japanese occupation there were periods when considerable economic change and new ideas were introduced, accompanied by unrest. During the thirties many young men left to work in the cities or in Japan. Today a period of two or three years after a boy finishes primary school is recognized as something of a crisis, and quite a few boys do run away then. Most, but not all, come back. At this time a boy fully realizes that his education is over and with it the chance for advancement. He is expected to do almost a man's work from the age of 15 or so, and the contrast with his lackadaisical years of schooling is abrupt.

The discontent of young men and their desire to leave the village reflects the increased pace of ideological change today. The idea of success and achievement, measured in material terms and resulting from individual effort, has been indirectly promoted in many ways, most notably in recent years through radio broadcasts from Seoul. Today these ambitions are accepted without question. Many young men complained to me of the oppressive, stifling quality of their environment and the lack of opportunity to seek individual goals. Competitive striving, originality, and forceful initiative are qualities that still get a child or youth in trouble. The collective orientation of the village requires conformity to cooperative norms and acquiescence in the consensus once it is established. Ruthless pursuit of individual goals brings a quick rebuke to young people, or malicious gossip and even subtle sabotage in the case of adults.

In addition to conscious opposition by youth to the confining nature of village society, there exists a more fundamental and usually unrecognized contradiction between traditional ways of thinking and new expectations. Some of the problems involved have already been discussed in Chapter 2. Certain attitudes regarding intelligence, initiative, excellence, competition, achievement, and saving, that are an integral part of the new modernizing ideology, are still relatively undeveloped in Sŏkp'o,

191

and young men are not particularly well equipped intellectually by village upbringing to fulfill their new expectations in an economic environment dominated by competition.

One implication of ideological and economic change for the future is that an emphasis on individual achievement may be incompatible with a system of weak leadership in the context of cooperation and interdependence. Considerable strain can be expected as part of the process of reconciliation between a tradition of community solidarity and the growing demand for progress and economic viability.

## Morale and Joint Effort

An indication of the limits of cooperative effort was provided by the failure (as of mid-1967) of a major project, a proposed dike about 500 yards long to reclaim tidal mudflats for use as irrigated rice land. This negative instance also contributes to an understanding of some psychological elements involved in successful group action. In preceding chapters the term "euphoria" has been used in connection with joint work projects of a traditional nature, and the importance of cooperation has been stressed as an informal value. On the other hand, there has been some indication of tension between this aspect of village life and the individual described as volatile, self-assertive, and resentful of secular authority.

During a four-year period from 1960 to 1964 the village undertook almost entirely with its own resources the construction of a vehicle road linking it with the outside world. This was the first step in the overall scheme of the village "developer." There was lengthy discussion in the village before the project got under way, and it took all of the developer's great prestige to overcome the objections of elderly conservatives. But the proposed road offered at least some prospect of eventual economic improvement to the remote impoverished village, and men, women, and children used most of their free time during those years to hack it out of the mountains, almost with their bare hands. Building on the tradition of cooperative work, the entire village devoted itself to a monumental joint effort without any clear idea of immediate concrete rewards. Eventually county officials, impressed by the undertaking, provided some necessary materials and the road was finished. During my stay in the village it was used by one or two trucks a week, not counting an occasional American soldier or wealthy Korean who came by jeep to shoot pheasants.

On the basis of the village's new reputation for self-help, the developer was able to obtain official assistance for the dike project in the form of American flour under the United States "Food for Peace" Program. Several hundred tons of flour were allocated and a construction company was established under the direction of the developer's brother-in-law, a townsman from some distance away. It was evident that the addition of more than one hundred acres of reclaimed rice land would revolutionize village resources, eliminating poverty and turning every family head into a substantial landowner.

All went well at first as nearly every able-bodied male—including teenagers—participated enthusiastically in the brutally hard labor. Men and boys from other villages in the region also came to work at the standard wage of 3½ kilograms of flour per day. Crops had been poor the year before and no other work was available, so the project was welcome during the slack seasons of winter and early spring. Progress was rapid, and the flour flowed steadily from official channels through the construction company into the village.

Then rumors began to circulate that an excessive amount of flour had been siphoned off by the brother-in-law and the large group of technicians and foremen that he had imported with him; the village learned that most of the flour allocated had been used up, with more than half the dike still to be constructed. Shortly after this, flour deliveries stopped altogether because of an unrelated interruption in shipments from the United States, and workers stopped appearing on the job. Eventually when the remaining flour did reach the county, it was held up by officials with the stipulation that because of the poor performance so far, it would not be released unless the village guaranteed to finish the entire project without requesting any more aid. It soon became common knowledge that it was being held on orders from Seoul until just before the presidential election of 1967 so as to have an imagined favorable impact on the voters.

Furthermore, the operation seemed to be overdirected by a sizable leadership group of managers and foremen who were mostly from outside the village. Some of these were either intoxicated by their lofty positions or determined to emphasize status differences, and they continually harassed the workers. It may be that forceful direction was necessary to complete the job, but what actually occurred was a loss of enthusiasm for the whole project, with more and more villagers failing to show up for work.

Removal of the direct economic incentive in the form of flour coincided with a bumper barley harvest, so that anxiety over food supplies was temporarily removed. With the arrival of summer, agriculture and fishing occupied many villagers full time and other opportunities for work became available. The few men who continued somewhat lackadaisically to work on the dike had no other employment and still had some hopes of getting paid eventually. But when the rains came in July and August all work halted.

In the meantime the portion of the dike that had already been built was steadily being eroded through tidal action. In this situation every effort by the village head and the dike committee to mobilize residents for work was unsuccessful. The initial enthusiasm had been replaced as a result of the series of setbacks by the disgusted conviction that the dike could not be completed, and that working on it was a waste of time.

The job proved to be more onerous and time consuming than anyone had expected, but the fact that villagers were working not for a diffuse common objective but for individual daily wages was probably a more important causative factor. When the wages ceased or were no longer desperately needed, so many people left the job that the rest lost confidence in the final goal. The dike changed from a symbol of hope to one of failure, and local informants showed a sort of uneasy distaste for the whole business. Influential villagers complained as they watched the dike crumble that if the spirit of the road-building period had been still alive, the whole thing could have been easily finished in two or three months.

So the problem seems to have been basically one of morale. Once the sense of participation in a common endeavor for the collective welfare had been shattered by the charges of profiteering, it proved impossible to put it back together. And once men became used to working for wages, they were no longer willing to go without for the sake of some intangible promise of future plenty. Of course many families were so near the margin of subsistence that they could not postpone current consumption in the expectation of future rewards. Others had work to do in their own fields or on their boats. But even in the summer there were fifty or sixty people who could have been mobilized every day.

In this case even though the immediate economic incentive (wages) was much greater and more specific than the vague benefits villagers had expected to receive from the road, it was not enough to sustain joint effort. Some irrational but crucial quality of total participation—of collective engagement—was necessary in order to mobilize effective cooperation. It is within an atmosphere of confidence, mutual trust, and familiar egalitarian uproar that work is usually accomplished without any precise calculation of individual reward. In terms of incentives it seems evident that the psychological rewards of collective social action are in some circumstances even more important than rational economic considerations.

## Contradictory Aspects of Personality

One might protest that in describing villagers as group oriented and lacking in individual initiative, I am contradicting the image presented in an earlier chapter of self-assertive farmers and fishermen clamoring for leadership roles. There is a sense in which such a contradiction does exist, a contradiction that is closely associated with the ideological distinction between a lineage-oriented and an egalitarian ethic. When a Sŏkp'o resident lists the ideal attributes of a moral man or describes those values that he regards most highly, he nearly always talks in terms of moderation, gentleness, and proper etiquette. This is official, upper-class ideology having the flavor of formal textbook maxims. Most people pay more than lip service to these ideals, which (as pointed out earlier) influence actual behavior in the various neighborhoods to a very different degree.

On the other hand, there is a contrasting set of behavioral norms that can be associated with informal interaction among people who are not closely related. In place of moderation there is likely to be excess; instead of dignified restraint, noisy self-assertion—a kind of male swagger or bravado. The careful concern for proper etiquette is often replaced by an intense, if temporary, intimacy based on sentiment. In such a mood one can ask anything of a friend, and one is likely to offer him anything in return. If there is dislike or a difference of opinion, it can be equally intense with heated exchanges of fierce language. This kind of behavior is reinforced by alcohol on the frequent occasions when men gather to drink together. It is not legitimized by any formal ideology, but it is an important part (statistically) of social life. Men in all walks of life shift behavioral frames of reference along with their social roles from one pattern to the other. Koreans are not aware of any contradiction, however, probably because the cooperative, nonkin pattern is not explicitly conceptualized and is without prestige, so that it is not cognitively set alongside accepted doctrine for purposes of comparison.

Foreign observers since the earliest missionaries visited the country in the 1860's have been struck by the contrast between a refined sense of propriety on one hand and extreme volatility on the other (Kennan 1905; Griffis 1882; Moose 1911; Rockhill 1891; Osgood 1951; Hamel [1653] 1918).

In another sense, the contradiction may be more apparent than real. When a farmer or fisherman in Sŏkp'o shouts out his suggestions in the form of blunt commands (commands that are often disregarded), he is probably not competing seriously for authority, but is merely participating in group activities and expressing himself in a normal, acceptable manner. It seems to me that it is often more a matter of style than of ambition to prevail over his fellow villagers. Nevertheless, it is true that some men become overbearing if unchecked by opposition. When through economic strength or coercive political force someone does achieve a preeminence that effectively silences those under him, he often will act the role to the hilt. Opposition then becomes passive taking the form of noncooperation until the moment when the tyrant can be cut back down to size.

In the personality of most villagers there seems to exist another kind of contradiction between simultaneously existing attitudes of dependence and fierce pride. Emotional and economic dependence is strongly developed in the family environment. Frequently, where material aid and direction has been available from outside sources, Koreans have shown themselves eager to adopt a subordinate, even a humiliating, position in order to take advantage of it. But this "mendicant mentality," as it has been called by foreign critics, is eventually interrupted by the explosive reassertion of claims to individual autonomy. Leadership that is not based on true consensus—implying the right to oppose and withdraw—is likely to come up against this somewhat "ornery" individualism or "cussedness" sooner or later. Any assertion of dominant status that is not legitimate (that is, based on seniority, education, or formal rank) is resented, and eventual opposition can be expected.

## SOCIAL CONTROL

In the *yangban* neighborhood men of the Yi lineage, when discussing how disputes were settled, emphasized the important function of elders in supervising the moral behavior of clan members. This was made possible, they thought, by a clear geographic separation of kinship groups, and they pointed out that the same situation existed "Over There" in sections 5 and 6. The predominance in village affairs, both numerically and in terms of wealth and prestige, of the four "respectable" sections (1, 2, 5, and 6) offset in their opinion the more disreputable elements in the Big Hamlet (sections 3 and 4), where different clans were jumbled together and more quarreling took place. Whether this purely structural interpretation is correct or not, it is significant that the former *yangban* tend to think in terms of lineage and hierarchy in describing the proper way of ordering a harmonious society.

If a youth or young man commits a number of serious offenses, the problem is discussed informally at night in the *sarang pang*, and a decision may be reached to call him before one or more of the most respected older men. At this formal meeting the offender sits in a position of extreme humility with his head bowed, while the elders as a rule try to encourage him to mend his ways through kindly advice. When asked what would happen if a youth ignored this kind of gentle admonition, there was a puzzled silence, and someone said, "He would have to be crazy or planning to leave the village." In some cases a sterner approach is used, but there was general agreement that the system worked to keep deviance within acceptable limits.

The same procedure is used among the Muns, Kims, and Kangs of the Big Hamlet, but less effectively. If the advice of older kinsmen is ineffective, there is little more that can be done and the "case" is left to a diffuse form of social censure for correction. Residents of this neighborhood maintained that when disputes occurred, they were quickly and easily settled. Resignation, tolerance, and understanding are apparently the main factors depended on to limit the seriousness of quarrels. My informants asked rhetorically, "If a person meant no harm, how can you blame him?" "If a man is poor with a wife and children, how can you take away his property?" "If the injury was done by a child, how can you hold his parents responsible?" To them an impersonal formal system of justice with universal rules seemed highly immoral.

What actually happens throughout the village in the vast majority of cases is that the bystanders, friends, and kin play an important role in patching things up. Once someone with a grievance starts to let himself go, other people usually do not interfere. Afterwards, when a consensus regarding the merits of the case had been established, someone will convince the "guilty" person that he is wrong and should apologize. The usual form is to shake hands and say, "Let's live together!" As soon as one person admits his fault and promises to "live together," it is extremely difficult for the other to maintain the grudge or seek further redress. Overwhelmingly, public opinion expects that he will soften his attitude and accept a reconciliation. In the thinking of everyone but the injured person, compensation is far less important than restoring good relations. Sometimes two or three days may be necessary to restore peace, but most quarrels are settled more quickly—often over a glass of wine.

When controversy over the division of land or other property causes bad feeling among brothers, an older collateral relative will often try to settle the affair in order to protect his family from scandal.

When a difficult situation appears to be developing, or something has been done that might cause anger, the proper way to handle it is to assist the person involved in ignoring the trouble rather than in dealing with it directly. It can be surprisingly effective. Diverting questions are asked, jokes are told, and on one occasion, a game of arm wrestling was initiated—all to change the mood and avoid trouble. Primary concern is not with fixing the blame or assigning responsibility. Compensation or punishment are not usually required in order to settle cases of damage or injury. Priority is still given to reestablishing harmony, not to revenge or material redress.

Police intervention is extremely unwelcome, and all residents are agreed on the desirability of settling conflicts within the village. If someone is badly enough injured to require hospitalization or if a major theft occurs, the police investigate and take action, but even then formal legal proceedings are unusual. The normal procedure is one of mediation in which the police officer at the *myŏn* or county level tries to reconcile differences and restore harmony rather than singling out a culprit for punishment. In recent years some of the more sophisticated farmers in the region have begun to talk of taking legal action, but I could discover no actual case in which this occurred. In 1962 or 1963 a poor fisherman, the younger brother of a well-to-do and influential man, had killed someone from another village in an argument at sea over damaged fishing gear. After spending a year in jail, he returned to the village where he lived without any visible signs of discrimination or prejudice.

The leader of the local coast defense detachment, a sergeant, tried in 1966 to intervene twice to maintain law and order and uphold public morality. In one instance a drunken fisherman struck his father, and two soldiers were ordered to reprimand him. In the process the fisherman was beaten up and one of the soldiers injured. In the long run the effect was salutary, as the fisherman stopped drinking altogether. On another occasion when a hysterical woman got drunk, burning her daughter's arm and driving a son to attempted suicide, the sergeant tried to calm her down and restore order. She promptly attacked him with blows and curses, and his hasty retreat from the Big Hamlet provided the spectators with considerable comic relief in an otherwise grave situation.

A widespread and intense fear of malevolent spirits, in the context of lineage ideology as well as in that of shamanistic beliefs, can be regarded as another element of social control. Two illustrative examples follow.

A neighbor of mine, a younger son with very little property, was married and had small children. His mother had died the previous year under mysterious (to villagers) circumstances; she collapsed while weeding in the rice paddies and although brought back to her house never regained consciousness. It was rumored that she had been much troubled shortly before her death, because this son had received almost nothing when the property was divided.

Some months after her death, while crossing a small dike that provided a shortcut to his house, the young man suddenly saw his mother rise up out of the sand at the water's edge. He immediately lost consciousness, and when he came to, his eyes bothered him. Along with his neighbors and kin he was convinced that his eye trouble was caused by the ghost, and thereafter he refused to return to his house by this route after dark. Villagers say that no matter how close or beloved someone was in actual life, if the ghost appears, it is an evil and fearful thing.

This man's elder brother paid for a series of expensive shamanistic curing ceremonies, and since I was also treating him at the time with sulfa eyedrops, I was invited to attend. Both the afflicted man and other village informants (in this case young women at the well) expressed satisfaction at the willingness of the elder brother to accept some of the responsibility, and family relations became more cordial. Also, there was some improvement in his eye condition by the time I left the village two months later.

A more tragic incident occurred two years before the period of my field study. A small coastal freighter traveling between the port of Kunsan and Paengnyŏng Island went aground in a storm off the entrance to the village harbor. The crew got off safely, but an officer went back in an attempt to salvage money and was drowned. One young man from Sŏkp'o who was a noted swimmer went out to the ship even before the gale had subsided and was the first on board. He found money in the pockets of the dead man and brought it to his father, who was subsequently able to buy additional rice land. Shortly afterwards the boy went mad, declaring that he had seen the dead man's ghost. After wandering around the village in a pitiful state for a few weeks, he swam out to sea and was drowned. This suicide was mentioned a number of times when the idea of retribution by a ghost for misdeeds was brought up.

## EXAMPLES OF DISPUTES AND THEIR SETTLEMENT

Quarreling within the family, particularly between husband and wife, can be severe and the tranquility of an entire neighborhood may be disrupted for several days at a time. It is always difficult for outsiders to intervene in domestic fights, and if the couple is over 40 mediation by neighbors becomes practically impossible. The intensity of such outbreaks is probably related to the everyday repression of emotion in the interest of preserving domestic harmony. It would be misleading, however, to draw the facile conclusion that because of such repression family relations must be characterized by an underlying tension and anxiety. I had the impression rather that within the family there exists a permanence and stability providing great emotional security for the individual. From an ideological standpoint it is believed that relations with close kin should be immune from the vagaries of egoistic feeling, and my own subjective assessment is that in most households harmony and strong mutual attachment do in fact prevail.

Obvious conflict between sons and parents or between brothers was infrequent but not rare. Out of 108 households there were possibly ten that could be called aberrant in this sense. None of these was in section 1 or 2. In other cases a son's migration from the village had removed the cause of trouble. In a few families the parents live with the second or third son instead of the first because of mutual dislike and a history of incessant conflict. Invariably in such a situation the first son had either moved to a different neighborhood or left the village. The economic dependence of most younger brothers on the "big house" makes their situation particularly difficult if there is conflict, which is usually attributed by villagers to unfair land distribution.

The fishing industry serves as an outlet, both for younger sons who are too ambitious or independent to accept a subordinate role, and for some elder sons who are unable to submit to a father's domination. They live and eventually marry in a major port such as Inchŏn, Kunsan, or Pusan, and their occasional visits to the village are important events.

When an eldest son moves away or builds a separate house, it is not always the result of bad relations with the parents, however. If the family is large and his younger siblings still unmarried, it may be necessary for an older married son with children to move in order to obtain adequate living space.

Those households within the village where antagonism between a son and his parents or between brothers had caused an open break were notorious, and critical comments by neighbors made it plain that they had lost a considerable degree of respectability. On the other hand, when discussing specific quarrels and individuals, informants are likely to be tolerant and fair minded, sympathizing with the problems involved. Ordinarily they are reluctant to brand any one person as at fault, although in a couple of instances responsibility for the trouble was clearly assigned.

The contrast between repression and explosion is likely to be dramatic. Anger or disapproval is often expressed at a level of sound and with an apparent intensity of emotion that impresses western observers as the prelude to violence, although violence is rare. If one maintains that it is merely a matter of verbal style, it must be admitted that the style does permit an immediate release of tension. Hostile emotions towards a father or an elder brother must be repressed indefinitely, but their expression in other contexts and to other individuals is provided for. Of course, some individuals are more restrained; and in theory at least, moral education should develop composure and dignity in difficult situations. In Sŏkp'o the village head and the schoolteacher were, in fact, far more moderate in the expression of their ideas than most other residents.

Often hierarchical status relationships are utilized for this kind of working off of emotion. Sŏkp'o residents ordinarily are permissive and understanding about such outbursts, although young men occasionally complained that they resented the tirades of their elders. A great deal of this kind of ego-expressive behavior is ignored or shrugged off with some such comment as, "He feels strongly." If it goes too far, however, retaliation in kind can be triggered and trouble will develop, particularly if the protagonists arc of similar age.

Once a certain pitch of emotional involvement occurs, particularly in the case of women, the quarrel may go on for two or three days with suitable pauses in the oral fireworks for sleeping and eating.

It is the women who must repress their frustration and irritation most often, and except for their own children there are few outlets for displaced aggression. Their explosions of rage can be more violent and uncontrolled than those of the men, amounting to a kind of hysteria. Many of the disputes among kin are precipitated by women, and a household that is unlucky enough to have a quarrelsome wife or grandmother is frequently in an uproar or at odds with both neighbors and kin.

Fights with outsiders such as soldiers, passing fishermen, or casual laborers on the dike are more frequent, more violent, and more likely to result in injury than intravillage troubles. The former are usually the end product of sustained drinking, and the police are summoned if someone is badly hurt. Where disputes occur between village residents, it is easier for bystanders, neighbors, and relatives to intervene, and their mediation usually is successful not only in restoring order, but in producing an apology and a resumption of good relations.

## Mother-in-law and Daughter-in-law

In a prominent Yi household the daughter-in-law, an efficient, hard-working mother of six, was about 35. She came from a good family at the county seat. Her husband's mother, from a commoner family in the village, was still very active, and the two women ordinarily worked together harmoniously in accomplishing household tasks for an extended family of twelve persons. One morning a discussion about misplaced kitchen utensils led into a critique of food preparation and eventually management of the family finances. For about three hours while they went on working in the kitchen and small courtyard, the two women shouted at each other, bringing up all sorts of minute causes of irritation during the previous months. Their tone of voice would fluctuate, but often it would rise to a level that I labeled "uncontrollable fury." The young wife was as voluble and intense as her mother-in-law, although her language was somewhat more respectful. After the grandfather returned to the house, his wife's scolding continued in a somewhat milder tone, while the daughter-in-law no longer answered back. As a result of the uproar a 2-year-old daughter went into a hysterical tantrum, and it was finally the grandfather's annoyed insistence that something be done to quiet the child that brought an end to his wife's nagging.

In this case the women remained inside the completely enclosed courtyard of their house, and it is doubtful that they would have let themselves go so completely anywhere else.

They made no effort to keep their voices down, and the neighbors must have heard everything nearly as clearly as I did. Perhaps they did not know I was in the guest room.

The incident represents a fairly typical example of how interpersonal hostility is discharged through the airing of an accumulated store of minor grievances without restraint. The phrase "verbal aggression" perfectly describes the mood of the occasion. Subsequently there was nothing to indicate (to me, at least) that any conflict had existed.

In the fishing hamlet there was a still larger, well-to-do, extended family household where two married sons and one unmarried son lived with the parents. The young wife of the second son, a particularly attractive girl from a village across the bay who still had no children, was visiting her parents before the harvest festival. Thinking her husband and his family might worry, she came home to let them know she would stay in her native village for another week. Her mother-in-law, who had a reputation for being strict, said she would have to stay home and proposed that the son visit his in-laws instead.

The resulting quarrel took place in front of the house (not in the courtyard) where all the neighbors could watch, and the girl raged at both her parents-in-law in extremely disrespectful fashion. This shocked and in some cases delighted the spectators. She did not return home, and opinion in the neighborhood was divided pretty much on generational lines; young people sympathized with the girl, while their parents upheld the right of the mother-in-law to control her activities.

## Breaches of Filial Piety

A branch of the Mun lineage in the Big Hamlet was commonly known as the "fight factory" (*ssaum kongjang*) because of frequent family quarrels. The eldest son did not live with his parents. Six years previously he had left the village as a result of friction, mostly with his mother, who was a notoriously difficult person. After his return to Sŏkp'o he was even more independent than before and showed open disrespect for his mother, father, and uncles. A limit of sorts was reached when he ignored his father's sixtieth birthday, not even bothering to send a present. This is one of the most important ritual occasions in a man's life, and the entire village was indignant. An older collateral relative with a knowledge of Chinese characters and considerable personal standing delivered a formal reproach, and the son's age mates also urged him to apologize. Eventually he did take a present to his father and paid respect according to customary form. Relations between son and parents continued to be strained, however.

In the same neighborhood a more tragic conflict with wider ramifications grew out of difficulties between a man and his adopted son. A farmer with some property adopted a nephew in order to have someone to look after him in his old age and carry out the proper rituals after his death. The adopted son became a heavy drinker who showed little respect for his new father. He married a woman who also drank and who after a few years was having more or less flagrant affairs with other men in the village. The couple managed to run through the old man's property and turned their house into a wine shop. By then the father was in his eighties, and his expectations of a tranquil old age had been shattered. As a traditionalist and stickler for etiquette, he constantly complained at home of the degradation, criticizing everything that his son or daughter-in-law did.

They in turn found his carping intolerable, and when the woman drank, she went berserk, striking the old man and raging for hours. On one occasion after repeatedly hitting her father-in-law, she threw hot bean paste at her daughter, seriously burning her arm. A 22-year-old son, who reportedly was dominated by his mother and had no other way to protest against the situation, ran out of the house, jumped into the water and started swimming out to sea. The screams of his sister finally alerted rescuers who went after him with a boat while the mother yelled, "What is a human life? Something to be crushed like a fly!" We watched all this from our vantage point on the hill as if it were some violent tragedy performed on a far-off stage.

The boy was brought back unharmed, and the mother went on cursing and screaming for several hours. She roamed about the neighborhood pounding on the doors of houses and commenting on the sexual peculiarities of the men who lived inside; anyone in her path was likely to be sworn at and pummeled.

A day or so later when she had calmed down, a group of neighbors visited her to ask that more consideration be given to the children. It was also pointed out that a repetition of such acts would probably bring a police investigation.

Despite the exceptional and scandalous nature of these cases as well as the intensity of the animosity that was generated, none of the persons involved considered leaving the village or even renouncing his family ties. In both cases neighbors and kinsmen intervened in an attempt to promote some sort of acceptable settlement. Villagers spoke disparagingly of everyone concerned, however, and their low personal status was further emphasized.

## Friendship, Kinship, and Sex

A refugee woman who married into the village after the Korean War had a close younger friend from the same town in the north. Their relation was one of fictive kinship, and they addressed each other as elder and younger sister. The younger woman, who was in her thirties, had lived with a man in Inchŏn for a few years, but after being thrown out with her daughter (he kept the son), she became a peddler in Ch'ungch'ŏng Province. She always made a point of spending a few days with her "elder sister" in Sŏkp'o when passing through the region.

On one of her visits a cripple in the village whose wife had temporarily deserted him gave her presents and offered marriage. The "elder sister" was married to the cripple's uncle. The peddler woman refused the cripple, but a few weeks later she accepted the offer of a fisherman who had moved to Sŏkp'o from a nearby town, and they settled down right next door to the house of the rejected suitor. One day in a quarrel with the new husband over the price of fish, the jealous cripple said that he had slept with the woman on the night that he had originally offered marriage and that the baby she was carrying was his. The newly pregnant wife summoned her "sister," who was the cripple's affinal aunt, to prove that she had had no sexual relations with him, and the resulting fight lasted all day. After the aunt had denounced her nephew as a liar in terms that were extreme even for the fishing neighborhood, he was beaten up so badly by the pregnant woman that eventually he had to be rescued by neighbors—none of whom sympathized with him, however.

Subsequently, at the urging of neighbors, the cripple apologized to the wife next door, admitting that he was wrong. When he tried to apologize to his North Korean affinal aunt, however, she shut the door in his face and refused to listen. There was some talk of prosecution by the new couple, both of whom had lived in the city, but the cripple was so poor that it made little sense except as an expression of their outraged feelings.

## Economic Bargaining

An elderly member of the Yi lineage with a forceful personality, considerable property, and a reputation for stinginess was negotiating on the beach for fresh fish. Possessor of the only forge in the village, he had made a couple of gaff hooks at the request of a fisherman and was intent on trading them for as much as he could get. The fisherman had recently migrated to Sŏkp'o from South Chŏlla Province because, according to his account, a storm had wrecked his boat and washed away all his gear. People in Sŏkp'o assumed that he had left home in order to avoid paying debts.

The landowner having apparently agreed on a price, transferred several fish to his basket. Then taking advantage of his age and the relatively insecure position of the fisherman in the community, he began to renegotiate the transaction, offering a much smaller price. The fisherman was in a difficult position. He had lost possession of the fish and was obliged to maintain a fairly respectful demeanor, while the old man was bullying him unmercifully. At this point a local resident and boat owner from the Kim lineage who was standing nearby announced in a loud voice to no one in particular that in his opinion the fish were cheap at the original price. The old man was eventually shamed into paying what he had first agreed to, but not until he had extracted another small fish.

## Incest

A monumental scandal with explosive repercussions occurred in the village when it was discovered that two third cousins of the Yi lineage, who could of course never marry because of strict exogamy rules, had been regularly having sexual relations. The incident triggered a whole series of separate, though related disputes, most of which were between members of the Yi clan and individuals from other kinship groups. People who had economic grievances or old resentments against the former *yangban* brought up the matter as an example of moral degeneracy, and bitter quarrels resulted. There was even conflict among the Yi clan members regarding who was at fault and what measures should have been taken. Women in particular were enraged over the accusations, and several hair-pulling contests took place.

Both the boy and the girl were sent away in disgrace, but the entire Yi clan was forced by the rest of the village to accept a collective burden of shame.

As a result of this incident a certain amount of latent animosity on the part of the rest of the village towards the former aristocratic lineage was crystallized and openly expressed. The lineage as a whole and some of its most influential men in particular suffered a substantial loss of prestige. The bitterness and resentment that were generated constitute a far more serious challenge to village solidarity than any of the other incidents that I have described. It remains to be seen whether the immediate disruptive effects will have permanent significance.

## Theft

In addition to the incestuous cousins, only one other case of expulsion from the village in recent years came to my attention. The younger son of a "small house" in a minor lineage composed of only three households boarded a visiting fishing boat one night and stole the cash box. It was full of money, and the police were called. They promptly arrested someone who had been seen on the boat—it later turned out that he had been adjusting the mooring lines of his own boat lying alongside— and beat him so badly that he "confessed."

In the meantime the real culprit was spending money so lavishly on his fiancée in a nearby village that her parents became suspicious and reported it to the police. The thief was arrested and sent to jail for six months, after which he returned to the village. Although both this young man and his mother had had a reputation previously for small thefts, this was his first serious crime and the village was prepared to accept him back. The man who had been beaten by the police was not, however, and announced publicly that he would kill the thief at the first opportunity. It was this threat that forced the informal village council to take action, and the boy was told to leave.

There were rumors of other cases of expulsion in the past, but no one was willing to discuss them in detail. The principle of family responsibility for acts committed by any member is still strong, and an unsavory incident reflects on the reputation of an entire household, extended family, and lineage. Once the matter is settled and some sort of equilibrium restored, most people are very reluctant to bring it up again.

I learned about the theft of the cash box, an incident that had taken place three years previously, only because someone in the family of the man who had been unjustly accused felt that I was becoming too intimate with the thief's older brother.

## Dispute over a Concubine

This man (the elder brother in the previous account) had led an eventful life. In 1964 and 1965 he had been living in Seoul, where he dealt illegally and profitably in cosmetics. During that time he acquired both a wife and a concubine and maintained two houses.

This style of living combined with a disastrous police raid forced his return to Sŏkp'o with the two women as a penniless dependent of his parents. His relatives and wife were anxious to get rid of the concubine, who was pregnant, but the son was adamant and they all continued to live together. The wife's account of this story was somewhat ambivalent; at one point she boasted of her husband's prowess in attracting and satisfying two young women, and then complained that the situation was unbearable.

At any rate, things deteriorated to a point where she attempted suicide in protest, and the concubine was eventually moved out of the house with her baby to a room in a different neighborhood. Then while the son was away on an extended fishing trip, his mother and wife simply refused to give the girl any food and she was forced to go back to Seoul. When the husband returned, there was a big family quarrel with lots of noise and he beat his wife, but the situation had finally been resolved to the relief of kin and neighbors.

The weakness of the concubine's position, which depended entirely on the personal support of her lover, is readily apparent. Since the wife had provided a son, there was no justification at all for the woman's presence in the village. Still, if the husband had been able to provide more generous material support, he probably could have maintained his polygynous household, at least for a time. While the impulsive and tyrannical behavior of this eldest son was tolerated temporarily, without wealth he was unable to have his way in the face of the united opposition of parents, wife, and village opinion.


## DISCUSSION

A fight involving deep hostility or violence is regarded as a serious matter by neighbors, kin, and bystanders. If relatives are involved, it is a much more grave offense against morality. But intensity of feeling regarding quarrels among kin as well as their actual incidence differed strikingly in the various neighborhoods. Men of the former *yangban* lineage spoke with feeling of the deeply sinful nature of such quarrels. Efforts to preserve proper family relations were more fundamental than mere attempts to keep up appearances. Rather, lack of filial or proper fraternal feeling was rejected intellectually as out of the question in one's own family, and in fact behavior largely conformed to this pattern of conflict repression.

In the Big Hamlet there were more quarrels of all sorts, but except for the violence of casual drunken brawls with outsiders, the most severe were among kin. Principles of kinship solidarity were just as firmly enunciated in this neighborhood by everyone I talked to about matters of right and wrong, but tensions within the household were more frequently translated into overt conflict. When I confronted informants with the fact of numerous family quarrels, the reply often consisted of some variant of the following statement: "Quarrels between brothers or cousins can never be a real threat to family or clan solidarity, because nothing more serious than a momentary display of temper is involved." The examples show that this was not always the case. On the other hand, people in this area seemed to be more concerned with preserving harmonious relations among unrelated neighbors, and cooperative norms were scrupulously observed.

Residents of Sŏkp'o believed themselves to be peaceable and they claimed there was less trouble in their village than in others of the region—a claim that was somewhat grudgingly supported by a number of people from nearby areas that I talked to. My impression as a resident was of conviviality and harmony punctuated by occasional violent outbursts, most of which were quickly and permanently settled. I made a special effort to uncover evidence of hostility and quarreling, and the cumulative effect of the detailed examples may give an impression contrary to my intent, which is to show that conflict is effectively resolved.

The ubiquitous concern with maintaining good relations and restoring equilibrium if a quarrel does break out, might be explained as a kind of defense against repressed hostility and therefore as an indication of anxiety and tension. My own interpretation is more straightforward. Conscious values derived from Chinese social ethics still have tremendous force. The virtuous man avoids involvement in disputes, since they are regarded as both immoral and shameful—an admission of human failure. A man's reputation and prestige depend in large part on his success in getting along well with his fellow villagers. Pride and manly courage in defending personal honor are not held in particularly high esteem and therefore do not challenge the preeminence of social harmony as an objective of human effort.

Korea's political history of continuing internal discord provides a striking contrast to the situation that I have described for Sŏkp'o. Even among expatriate Koreans in the United States today there are likely to be "instant factions" whenever organizations are formed. But the village situation in which there is no anonymity and no escape from the pressure of collective censure requires much greater individual responsibility for avoiding disputes.

In the historical context as well as in some of the accounts of "clan" villages, conflict seems to occur most frequently along predictable lines corresponding to the pattern of group loyalties (Lee 1960:56; Kim 1964:63). In Sŏkp'o, however, a sense of community and the mechanisms through which it is expressed helped to prevent the hardening of lines of permanent cleavage.

There is perhaps another, less conscious element involved in the concern with preserving solidarity in a small community; according to functional theory, the "existence and continuity" of society is at stake (Radcliffe-Brown 1959:200). Since everyone's security is threatened when discord erupts, there is general participation in the efforts to restore tranquility.

# 8

---

# THE
# INDIVIDUAL
# AND THE
# COMMUNITY

In order to understand better the kind of cohesion, as well as the threats to it, that exist among individuals and lineages or neighborhoods, it will be helpful to examine some actual cases. There has already been considerable general discussion of social integration in terms of what might be called the *yangban* and egalitarian stereotypes. The fact that these categories are neither rigidly fixed nor exclusive has also been emphasized. For example, it was pointed out in Chapter 2 that any individual might be obliged to shift both his ethical frame of reference and his behavior according to specific social situations or role relations.

## SMALL LINEAGES

Members of minor kinship groups in Sŏkp'o provide especially good examples of the interplay between lineage and territorial loyalties and responsibilities. Unless particularly wealthy or talented, such persons are regarded to some extent as second-class members of the community and only rarely can they achieve influential status. Relations among the two or three households that comprise such a small local lineage may be especially close and each family is more than usually dependent on the good will and cooperation of its neighbors (see Chapter 6).

In the Big Hamlet there was one lineage of just three households; although spatially separated, they formed a cohesive, cooperating unit that participated in each other's rituals. At the same time, members of each family were closely tied to their own immediate neighborhoods in ways that were in some respects similar and in others distinctive. All three households shared a predilection for fishing, strong drink, and conviviality, while none had pretensions to traditional high status in terms of education, restrained dignified behavior, or elaborate ceremonials.

The "big house," although not "rich," had considerable property, and its head, a gregarious and energetic man in his middle thirties, was the *ban* or subsection chief and an ebullient, noisy participant in most informal men's groups of the fishing neighborhood. He owned a sailboat as well as rice fields and acted in an official capacity connected with building the dike. Because of his informality, heavy drinking, and lack of a strong kinship base he was never mentioned as a potential candidate for village head or as a future member of the power elite, but he had considerable popularity and influence in his own immediate neighborhood. He showed little deference to the village elders, including his own relations, for which he was occasionally criticized.

Naturally, insistent demands on his generosity were made by the two other households of the lineage, both of which were much poorer. His success in providing some assistance while fending off most of their requests and at the same time maintaining good relations was commented on favorably by other villagers, who said he was in an awkward position.

The second household of this lineage was headed by an uncle of his, who lived together with his own three sons. Without land or capital, the family subsisted on its fishing skills and the shamanistic practice of the old man. Poverty, constant drukenness (both father and sons), the association with shamanism, and an almost total dependence on fishing put this family near the bottom of the social scale according to conventional criteria, and the sons had some trouble in obtaining and holding brides. Nevertheless as individuals everyone in the family was well liked and even respected for their generosity, trustworthiness, and hard work on other people's boats. The father was the most sought after of the local practitioners, and at New Year's time he received large amounts of food and drink for his services.*

The third household of this minor lineage was the least respected of the three, with a reputation for numerous serious violations of "proper behavior." Its head, a man in his thirties, had spent some years in Seoul, returning to the village only when destitute and unable to support his family in the city. A younger brother had been ostracized from the village for theft (see Chapter 7), and the marital arrangements of the eldest son provoked constant criticism. His position in the village was precarious and his status low. Economically, in terms of kinship base, and with regard to personal reputation, he was a marginal member of the community. He himself dreamed constantly of returning to the city to engage in trade and regarded residence in his native village as a temporary misfortune.

Yet this man, like his kinsman, possessed great personal charm and was popular among his age mates in the Big Hamlet. He could sing well and practiced a crude form of acupuncture without charge. He was physically strong and a jovial drinker, while his sexual exploits were much admired. These personal qualities enabled him to live a reasonably cheerful life and interact on good personal terms with most of his neighbors in the fishing hamlet.

The strength of the egalitarian outlook and the importance of neighborhood ties with nonrelatives in the case of this lineage is obvious. Yet the lineage itself was tightly knit, and the responsibility to assist kinsmen was deeply felt and frequently acted upon. Family rituals, while somewhat confused and sloppy by *yangban* standards, were regularly carried out. In this case

---

*The mixture of fear, suspicion, awe, and contempt that attaches to genuine shamans in many societies, including the typical female *mudang* in Korea, was not characteristic of popular attitudes in Sŏkp'o. Perhaps this is because the village practitioners, although they used some hypnotic techniques, were not ecstatic performers who could enter real trances.

there is an association of strong kinship ties with more communalistic patterns of behavior. The social situation of these households highlights the contrast between a kind of basic cluster of kinship values and the elaborate formal lineage ideology that is still so influential among former *yangban*. Norms of mutual assistance and affective integration are strong but in a much more casual and egalitarian context.

## MIGRANTS TO SŎKP'O

The integration of outsiders with kin groups and neighborhoods in the village normally occurs either through taking advantage of consanguinal (usually matrilateral) ties or through marriage. While it is almost a truism of anthropological literature that one has to be born in a peasant village to be accepted as a full-fledged member of the community, in Sŏkp'o this sort of statement needs considerable qualification, particularly with regard to close interaction among immediate unrelated neighbors.

On the one hand, it is probably true that prolonged residence —even for two or three generations—will not give the "newcomer" a status exactly equivalent to that of residents whose family tombs go back six generations or more. On the other hand, it is part of the essence of the community ethic in Sŏkp'o that, even though unrelated, if people live next door and behave "properly," they can in a relatively short time build close neighborly relations on the basis of hundreds of little exchanges of objects, services, and general good feeling. A man who is open and direct, willing to assist his neighbors, not stingy, and able to hold his own in the give-and-take of informal conversation or drinking groups will be accepted quickly. He may even have a special vogue initially because of his novel experiences and general entertainment value. If his wife refrains from malicious gossip and any suggestion of provocative behavior towards other men, she too will probably acquire a good reputation— provided, of course, that domestic family conflicts are kept under control.

A good deal of tolerance—a kind of communal expression of

compassion—was displayed towards one of the poorest house-holds in the village, a couple without children who had drifted to Sŏkp'o for lack of any other refuge. The man, who was then in his early fifties, was the disowned son of a well-to-do family in a town some 50 miles away. He had become infatuated with a wine shop waitress (a low-class entertainer and prostitute), and after his father had refused to support the affair any longer, he had left home with her in tow. According to the villagers' accounts, she had left him more than once to go off with other men, but he had always taken her back. In Sŏkp'o he dug for octopus in the tidal mudflats and worked as an agricultural laborer. Their house was the nearest thing to a hovel that existed in the village, and the wife was frequently drunk or tipsy.

Middle-aged members of the Yi lineage across the bay found all this so distressing that they refused even to acknowledge such people as villagers, going so far as to tell me lies, such as that it was a transient fishing family residing only temporarily in Sŏkp'o. (The couple had been there for five years and had no intention of going elsewhere.)

What is more interesting is the fact that their immediate neighbors invariably spoke well of them. The man was gentle, kindly, and always well mannered, while his wife was usually cheerful and ready to lend a hand whenever it was needed nearby. He accepted his low economic and social status without making demands on anyone, and he seemed content to struggle along on the thin edge of subsistence, bolstered by amicable relations with the other poor fishing families of the neighborhood. Their way of life was perhaps bearable only because of the special local opportunities for gathering octopus and shellfish.

Two less dramatic examples of neighborhood and village integration deserve mention as being somewhat more representative of the statistical norm, at least insofar as in-migrants to the village are concerned. Both households were located in the *yangban* neighborhood, so that the overwhelming majority of their neighbors belonged to one of the tightly-knit branches of the Yi lineage. Both were members of the same sib as the

218

largest village kin group, but they made no effort to assert any sort of lineage connection with the other Kims.

The grandmother of one of these household heads had originally come from a Sŏkp'o Yi family, and her daughter had returned with a grown son after being widowed in a nearby village. The son therefore had entered the village thirteen years previously with a small amount of land, a house, and a host of matrilateral relatives. He worked hard at both farming and fishing, married fairly well, and at the time of the investigation (when he was 38 years old) was rising economically to a position near the top of the "middle farmer" category. His house was neat and as far as I could tell his behavior was exemplary. No one made disparaging remarks about him, so that my initial impression was of a family differing from the *yangban* norm only in surname.

The single peculiar fact about him that made me follow up the case was that he almost never appeared at informal gatherings or joint work parties, either in the Big Hamlet or in his own neighborhood. The trouble seems to have been that he lacked the essential qualities of openness and conviviality on which village communalism thrives. Further questioning revealed that some of his neighbors thought him too aggressive and grasping in economic matters, and he seemed jealous of his time, lending a hand to others only when absolutely necessary. It was evident that his family's relatively isolated position even after thirteen years in the village was due more to his own special personality characteristics than to any village discrimination, on the part of either his relatives or members of other kin groups. He himself stated that he was content with life and seemed unconcerned by the fact that he participated only marginally in the intense social interaction that was going on around him.

This kind of social self-sufficiency was extremely rare in Sŏkp'o. By way of explanation it can be pointed out that there were neither patrilineal ties nor close associations from childhood to bind this man to the community. The crucial importance of individual personality as a factor in social relations is emphasized by the contrast between this case and the one that follows.

The other household, possessing considerable property, had been in Sŏkp'o for more than forty years. Although the family head had no pretensions to *yangban* descent, members of the household had adapted their style of life and manners to that of the well-to-do Yi families around them and neighborhood relations were excellent. The old man had stuck to farming and was a welcome if slightly sententious member of the local *sarang pang* group. His reputation for honesty and generosity was good and his opinions were listened to respectfully, even if his influence was not particularly great. He invariably assisted others in cooperative work sessions, and when his only son was in the army, neighbors—unwilling to let the old man try to carry the entire agricultural work load alone—stepped in and helped out at the crucial seasons. The son, although competent and a hard worker, was more interested in fishing than farming and mixed freely with fishermen from every part of the village. He was cheerful and straightforward, a moderate drinker, and was rumored to have remained faithful to his wife even though subjected to considerable temptation.

This family, then, although comparative newcomers to the village and without local relatives, had been thoroughly assimilated in every other conceivable way, exchanging labor and services with a large number of people on the basis of mutual respect and good will.

## LARGE LINEAGES

It was suggested earlier that seriously improper behavior on the part of a native member of an established lineage is likely to be accepted with greater tolerance than in the case of a relative outsider. People know all about each other's lives and reputations since childhood, and while deviant acts by an individual are regarded as a great misfortune to his family or lineage, the community has grown used to the fact that certain persons drink too much periodically and get into fights, that they beat their wives, or that they fail to fulfill important obligations.

One such individual in the Big Hamlet was particularly notorious. He was the eldest son of a prominent branch of the largest lineage in the village. Further, he was related matrilaterally to one of the most highly respected of the *yangban* households and his grandfather had been an important village leader. The man himself, a household head in his forties with eight children, drank constantly, mostly by means of elaborate—if transparent—strategems devised to take advantage of the ethic of hospitality that governed so many everyday occasions in the village. A kinsman's ancestor ritual, a wedding, helping to haul a boat for repairs or launch a new one, the celebration of a good fish catch, or the arrival of *Old Crow* in a rucksack from Seoul to be consumed on the anthropologist's veranda were all occasions when he could be found at the center of things, making sure that the liquor continued to flow freely. He ruthlessly exploited his numerous ties throughout the village in every way possible to obtain loans, favors, or other assistance. He frequently lied or seriously misled friends, relatives, and even the village head. He was brutally negligent to his family. His father, who had retired as household head, was a man of absolute honesty who never drank but continued to work conscientiously both at farming and fishing as if to make up for his son's devious laziness.

Even more striking to most villagers than the son's personal faults was the truly monumental bad luck suffered by this family. In fact the man's character, although no one liked him personally, was usually described fatalistically and without real malice as just one more item in the series of family misfortunes. Consequently he was able to continue to insert himself as a central actor in village events, despite behavior that was frequently outrageous and that might have provoked organized reprisals against an outsider.

In each of the larger lineages there are one or more household heads who have quarreled extensively with their parents or close relatives and live apart, keeping this particular sector of their kinship ties to a minimum. The severity of the events that lead to such clashes and the stubbornness of the individuals involved must be extreme to overcome the value indoctrination and constant social pressures that promote kinship loyalty and cohesion.

Fifty years ago the authority of parents and elders was so great that this kind of overt opposition was virtually impossible, and the only escape from domination for the individual was to leave the village. Filial piety was the central principle of the formal lineage ideology, in which status differences and deferential behavior were an essential manifestation of morality. Although this whole cluster of values is losing its intensity, the desire to associate with kinsmen and the tendency to turn to them in time of need remains strong in most families no matter what the class background. Most middle-aged parents today are far less intransigent than the older generation, however; while there are struggles and arguments over marriage, occupation, migration, and finances, young people increasingly are able to get their own way without pushing things to the point of breaking off relations.

The ambitious elder son of a "big house" in section 5 ("Over There"), who had broken off all normal kin ties with his father because of disputes over the old man's profligacy (see Chapter 5), still was an insistent proponent of the importance of close cooperation and mutual trust among relatives. A fishing entrepreneur, he entrusted his boats only to his younger brothers and a first cousin, while the crews were made up almost entirely of kinsmen. He pointed out that a certain amount of stiffness and respect characterizing such relations (he had the advantage of superior lineage rank as well as age) were helpful in maintaining effective control of fishing operations.

This combination of trustworthiness and control as characteristic of dealings with relatives constitutes a strongly pragmatic incentive for the enthusiastic participation of wealthy and powerful men in a kinship system that otherwise makes extensive demands on their generosity. It has probably been more important in the relatively anarchic social situation that exists in Korean towns and cities, where communal sanctions for enforcing proper behavior are much weaker, and the universalistic controls inherent in contractual relations are only beginning to be decisive.

## Migration to the City

The greatest challenge to village solidarity today comes from the city. With rapid industrial and commercial development taking place in the Seoul area since about 1964, low-paying jobs in factories and small shops have been increasingly available. Although unemployment remains high in the city itself, country boys and girls usually are able to find some kind of work through the network of friends and relatives who have already migrated. As a rule they are willing to work longer, more conscientiously, and for less pay than most urban youth, so that entrepreneurs often prefer to recruit in villages despite the low levels of education and lack of skills.

In the summer of 1969 I heard frequent complaints about a severe labor shortage in the village caused by the migration of young men and women. The lure of the city, while strongest among the young and unmarried of both sexes, affects others as well. It is probably greatest for the sons of poor families who see no possibility of improving their situation in the village, but many sons and daughters of middle-level farmers as well as those of some substantial landowners are also eager to leave.

It is much more difficult for the head of a family with small children to make such a radical move. His skills are no greater than those of a 20-year-old and he risks much more, since it is usually necessary to sell land in order to pay the expenses of getting a household established in the city. If he does sell everything and leave for the metropolis, the chances of losing his money in some abortive retail trade venture or of getting fleeced by clever city parasites are considerable.

Nevertheless, restlessness is growing as more and more people feel that they are living depressed lives in the village, and that some new and wonderful experience can be found in modern society. The main impetus for migration no longer comes from worsening rural economic conditions as in the past. Today some slight improvement is taking place, although it is very slow. The farmer's traditional resignation is being replaced by rising expectations among the young.

I had a series of long conversations with two young men in their late twenties who were anxious to leave Sŏkp'o. Both were from large, well-established, well-to-do branches of major lineages. Both were recently married, had young children, and owned (or would inherit) considerable property. At first it seemed strange to me that they were so eager to exchange economic security and a substantial, respected position—including the prospect of becoming influential local leaders—for the squalor and precarious, competitive existence that was all they could expect in Seoul.

One, who was from the village's largest kinship group, had attended middle school plus a year or so of high school in the city and felt that farming was a demeaning occupation for one with such educational attainments. As a result of his city experience he had the greatest contempt for all traditional aspects of village culture, even to the extent of feeling acute embarrassment when I, a foreigner, attended ancestor worship ceremonies or listened to the old men chant ancient poetry (*sijo*). His ambition was to pass the police examination and enter public service in Seoul. In contrast to the village norm, he admired strong leadership and believed one should speak out forcefully and without hesitation in order to destroy old ways and promote innovation. He did not get along very well with his relatives. Perhaps most important of all, he spent little time with his age mates and did not particularly value this kind of personal relationship, at least in the village. In other words, there were a number of resemblances to the typically isolated, emotionally self-sufficient, restless, upwardly mobile American nuclear family.

This farmer had little attachment to Sŏkp'o, as either a territorial or social entity. While he prided himself on his advanced ideas and sophistication, he was forced to suppress their overt expression (except in conversations with me) in order to live in some sort of reasonable adjustment with the community. His most prized possession was a wristwatch,* which he said he

*Wristwatches are totally unnecessary in Sŏkp'o where everyone is able to tell time with remarkable accuracy by the state of the tide. In any case, they are a mark of high status and as such are properly worn only by mature men. My sister-in-law, a graduate of a women's college in Seoul, stopped wearing hers after word reached us indirectly that it had been considered offensive.

could not even wear in the village without being censured by elder kinsmen. His only concern about leaving was whether he could secure a position in the city that would provide adequate status and some degree of security. Having already received his share of the family property, he lived separately from his parents and younger siblings with an attractive wife of his own choosing.*

The other young man, a member of a *yangban* family with high genealogical rank in the lineage, did not have the same modern attitudes. His upbringing had been strictly traditional, so that he was deeply enmeshed in the kinship-oriented atmosphere of his neighborhood. Even though he had been raised as a farmer, he was intensely interested in boats and fishing. After a drink or two in the company of former schoolmates from the fishing neighborhoods, his somewhat stiff and pompous manner changed to relaxed conviviality. With only a primary school education and no intellectual pretensions, his formal qualifications for respect on a village-wide basis were not high. On the other hand, he was still famous for his athletic exploits as a schoolboy and he continued to demolish all challengers in the village at wrestling and other feats of strength. One of his sisters was married to a prominent family in another neighborhood of the village, so that he had many affinal relatives with whom he could relax in casual intimacy. By contrast with the previous example, then, he seemed to be well integrated with the community in terms of personality and behavior, as well as through more formal ties.

In this case there were other factors that promoted a deep restlessness. As the only son (and youngest child) he would eventually inherit all his father's property without division, thereby becoming one of the wealthiest farmers in the village. But the old man, who was still vigorous, remained very much in control. A hard-headed, tight-fisted, conservative peasant, he had chosen a quiet, plain, and hardworking daughter-in-law, and he would not permit his son to invest any money in fishing

*In this case the separate establishments of father and eldest son were necessary, because three unmarried brothers and a sister were still living at home with their parents.

ventures. In conversations with me, the young man confessed his desperate longing to live a different kind of existence that would bring him excitement and adventure. "There's a better way to live, and I have to see what it's like," was the way he put it. "Perhaps afterwards I'll come back here and farm."

### Kinsmen and Neighbors

In the *yangban* and solidly agricultural neighborhoods of Sŏkp'o, wherever kinship grouping and residence patterns coincide, the element of choice in associating with either kinsmen or neighbors practically disappears. Such people are predisposed by ideology, custom, and habit to live and work together with relatives.

The following example of a nine-man work group rethatching the roof of a large house is taken from a detailed account in my field notes. In addition to two grandfathers in their sixties, all the men involved are brothers, first and second cousins, or nephews and uncles. The men on the roof placing rice straw and binding it in place are household heads in their thirties and forties. Younger men are throwing up the straw, while the

*Relatives are thrashing barley in an agricultural neighborhood.*

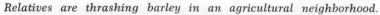

*A highly respected and influential elder is at work on a roof covering.*

two bearded patriarchs sit on the ground finishing off a complicated roof tree covering. Small children tumble around underfoot. The women work in the inner courtyard except when they go out to get water, borrow something, or join others in the neighborhood to collect oysters.

In contrast with the boisterous house building scene de-

227

scribed in Chapter 2, it is a picture of tranquil and comfortable cooperation. There is relaxed talk among the mature men, occasionally interrupted by a rough order to an adolescent for more cordage or straw. The old men sit a little way off by themselves engaged in desultory conversation as they skillfully tie knots in the homemade twine. One makes a sarcastic, half-joking comment about a bulge on the roof that provokes laughter but no rejoinder.

When work stops around noon, everyone gathers on the polished wooden veranda for a few minutes of talk, but as soon as a tray with wine, pickles, and some dried eel appears, the younger men move inside leaving their fathers in undisputed possession. They know that similar trays have been prepared in the guest room where they can drink and smoke without restraint. The actual meal is also segregated, with adolescents and unmarried men relegated to the opposite end of the veranda.

It has become fashionable in recent years for some unsentimental, hard-headed anthropologists to deride any account of the traditional pleasures, or comforts, or benign qualities that are supposed to have been inherent in peasant society. They have emphasized instead the poverty, disease, backbreaking work, lack of opportunity, economic exploitation, and mutual distrust that has impressed them so unfavorably in village life.

But nostalgia for a bucolic way of life has been a persistent theme in the literature and political thought of many cultures, and the quality of secure personal relations and individual integrity that dominates a scene such as the one just described is not a fantasy dreamed up in retrospect by some discontented migrant to the city. Hard as it is to pin down, a special mood does exist among most of the house clusters in the village. It exists as one particular expression of the social system—a way of life that is probably desperately fragile and subject to being easily undermined through aggressive personal ambition, exaggerated family pride, greed, a money economy, and modern technology. Dignity, etiquette, naïveté, and an unselfconscious poise seem to be essential behaviorial ingredients. There is also the kind of certainty and directness that comes from knowing what constitutes moral uprightness, combined with the conviction that life is being conducted pretty much accordingly. Just because such traditional patterns are clearly doomed in Korea and are disparaged by most of the village youth, it by no means follows that this form of social organization is somehow inferior, or that it has been less successful than more modern modes in effectively solving some of the major problems of human association.

# 9

## IDEOLOGY AND SOLIDARITY: A STRUCTURAL INTERPRETATION

It is hoped that by now the bare structural skeleton set forth at the beginning of this book has acquired some ethnographic flesh and blood. The general dualistic scheme that has been imposed on village social organization distinguishes two separate systems of ethical principles, beliefs, behavior patterns, and institutions, each of which demonstrates a considerable degree of internal consistency and integration. In ideological terms the first of these systems has been described as lineage oriented, formal, hierarchical and Confucian, while the other has been labeled the egalitarian, community ethic.

### LINEAGE ORIENTATION—THE IDEAL

Despite the fact that everyone in the village acts and thinks in terms of both systems, there are numerous respectable farmers, particularly those in the former *yangban* (Yi lineage) neighborhood, who somewhat self-consciously exemplify the formal tradition. They spend nearly all their time farming (although relatives may fish), and they live surrounded by households of the same lineage. Much of their agricultural work is carried on cooperatively among relatives, and most of their social relations are also with kin. Not only their wives and children but all other genealogically junior persons in the neighborhood show them deference, both in speech forms and other kinds of behavior, and they in turn are elaborately courteous to their elders. Actual kinship distance in terms of generation and degree of collaterality is an important determinant of behavior throughout the lineage.

In the evening these men gather in small groups for ponderous discussions in the *sarang pang*. There is great concern over the moral behavior of youth, particularly with regard to filial piety, and the older men take it upon themselves to guide and reprimand where violations have been particularly obvious. The heads of such households are faithful in their observance of the rituals of ancestor worship, they are likely to invest whatever meager extra resources they have in education for their children, and they consider themselves somewhat superior to the rest of the village because of their traditions, their manners, and the cohesion of their lineage. Their women, who marry into the village from outside, are shy and retiring (in manner, at least) and are not chosen for good looks or charm. Wives and daughters rarely wander to other neighborhoods except on their way to work in the fields, to gather oysters, or visit the houses of relatives. The atmosphere of calm and restraint in the neighborhood is only rarely shattered by quarrels.

The description above amounts to a thumbnail sketch of the standard, consciously held village ideal. Everyone recognizes the moral values and social prestige inherent in such a way of life, and to some extent every household tries to live up to this tradition.

## THE OTHER IDEOLOGY

For residents in other neighborhoods of the village there are as many unrelated as related households next door, and while questions of kinship still have pervasive importance in every aspect of daily existence, they do not dominate social relations as they do among the Yi in the former *yangban* neighborhood. Both at work and in recreational groups there is a combination of kin and nonkin, and relatively intimate, informal, and unrestrained contacts between friends and distant relatives are most characteristic of the numerous casual men's groups. There is less concern with the forms of etiquette, and interpersonal relations seem correspondingly blunt and rough. Noisy quarrels are much less evident than laughter and singing but they are not infrequent. Older men, who do not receive as much deference as they do in the Yi lineage, exert little influence outside the extended family.

Men acquire prestige and authority not so much through lineage rank and dignified bearing as through energy and personal charm, and as a result the exercise of leadership is relatively impermanent.

Social relations, then, in these neighborhoods are more open, both psychologically and in terms of physical comings and goings. There is a less intense in-group mentality at the lineage level, while strong neighborhood bonds are matched by close kinship ties with households in other parts of the village. Women and girls are more evident on the paths and in front of the houses, and they join in the conversations and quarrels far more than among the former *yangban*. Fishermen are more numerous in such neighborhoods; their way of life entails more leisure, more physical mobility, less attachment to tradition, and speculative rather than stable prudent attitudes towards productive activity. Finally, there is greater utilization of shamanistic practitioners and animistic ritual than among the Yi.

The description above may perhaps not appear to be an ideological one, yet the strong sense of community and egalitarianism that confronts the *yangban* ethic emerges out of, or is embedded in, all these elements. Community ideals of reciprocity, tolerance, and collective responsibility across kinship boundaries have no codified expression, either oral or written, to give them a legitimacy and prestige rivaling the lineage ideology.* Yet these ethical concepts, along with an almost automatic resistance to the exercise of direct personal authority

---

*The Confucian ethical principle of *Pao,* which is frequently translated as reciprocity, also involves elements of exchange and repayment. In his fascinating discussion of this concept as "a basis for social relations in China," Lien-sheng Yang makes two state-

outside the family, are an important part of every villager's cognitive makeup, and flagrant violations are condemned.

## EFFECTS OF THE ENVIRONMENT

The egalitarian tradition is powerfully reinforced by environmental and institutional factors, the most significant of which is the number, composition, and settlement pattern of the lineages. Of these, four are prominent in Sŏkp'o, but none can be regarded as dominant. The former *yangban* Yi lineage holds a slight edge in educational attainments and prestige, but since they do not represent a preponderance of either numbers or wealth, important members of this kinship group are unable to exert a controlling influence in village affairs. Although a strong lineage base seems to be a necessary condition for prestige, real authority on a village-wide basis is exercised also in terms of wealth, education, reputation, and personal popularity. The process of decision making is a slow and indirect search for consensus among influential leaders in contrast with the much more authoritarian organization of power within the family and lineage.

Another important factor reinforcing the egalitarian point of view is the relative economic equality within the village. While there are considerable differences between "rich" and "poor" with regard to property and income in all the lineages, actual living standards vary much less widely. The well-to-do feel an obligation to redistribute much of their income in ceremonial and casual hospitality or through assistance to poor relatives. If there is an additional surplus, most of it goes into education. The rewards for such prestigious activity are almost entirely social and not as a rule financial. Today there is

---

ments that fit neatly into the scheme presented here. With regard to upper-class, official Confucianism (the hierarchical aspect) he writes: "Duties to the emperor and to one's parents therefore tended to receive increasing attention. Particularism along these two lines became still more predominant, and the principle of reciprocity was further modified." The egalitarian, vulgar aspect is stated as follows: "For the not-so-well-educated small men, whose ethical code is preserved in proverbs and other forms of folklore, reciprocity was always the normal standard" (Yang 1957:308,309).

no really large landowner in Sŏkp'o and this has been true historically as well. Until very recently there has been a marked reluctance on the part of wealthy individuals to adopt a strikingly ostentatious style of living, or to permit that of relatives and neighbors to sink below a certain minimum level.

Geographic remoteness has played its role in promoting community values. The traditional division of labor between farming and fishing along class lines imposed a mutual economic interdependence just at the point of greatest potential structural cleavage. Also, the difficulty of the *yangban* in maintaining close social and official ties with more powerful branches of their lineage elsewhere probably has been a factor in the past that prevented the more effective exercise of aristocratic authority.

## IDEOLOGY, BEHAVIOR, AND SOLIDARITY IN SOKP'O

There is infinite variation in the way each individual in the village combines elements of both ideological systems in his normative thinking as well as in actual daily behavior. Both sets of norms are such an integral part of Korean cultural tradition that exclusive participation in one or the other is impossible, and an individual is constantly shifting his frame of reference back and forth somewhere between the two extremes in accordance with changes of role and situation.

At a different level of analysis the two systems of ideas and behavior can be regarded as separate interacting forces that promote or reduce community cohesion. Kinship loyalties are strong, particularly where relatives occupy the same neighborhood. Solidarity of the kinship group is constantly reaffirmed through a whole series of Confucian rituals ranging from those that include only members of a single household to others that encompass the entire clan or lineage. The ideology embodied in these rituals not only emphasizes allegiance to kinsmen and group solidarity, but it stresses a stable, hierarchical ordering of personal relations, according to principles of genealogical rank and age. Actual behavior among relatives reflects these rules of conduct to a remarkable degree.

234

It would be logical to assume that four kinship groups, organized according to such principles and of approximately equal size and strength, would confront one another in a small community with considerable mutual hostility. Although some animosity and envy is generated along kinship lines, investigation revealed rather that social life in the village is predominantly harmonious, and that a widespread concern with cooperation and integration throughout the entire community is prevalent. The divisive effects for the village as a whole of the ideological emphasis on lineage loyalties are mitigated by institutions and patterns of normative behavior that cut across kin boundaries.

One striking example of the preoccupation with preventing a rigidly exclusive definition of group loyalty is the way most of the lineage rituals themselves have been adapted to include nonrelatives at some stage of the festivities. In everyday associations the formal values that require cooperation and a sense of mutual responsibility among kin are matched by the more diffuse commitment to neighbors and fellow villagers regardless of lineage membership. On recurrent traditional occasions for both work and recreation, community solidarity and morale across kinship boundaries is reaffirmed in a euphoric atmosphere. The conviviality of ordinary, informal relations usually depends in part on the fact that close kin do not participate together in the small groups where joking and drinking constitute the main recreation of most adult men. Finally, in terms of status and authority, the formal hierarchical principles on which lineages are organized and controlled give way for the village as a whole to egalitarian institutions, and the attempted exercise of strong leadership outside the lineage is likely to generate an immediate and correspondingly strong opposition.

## INADEQUACIES OF THE MODEL

This book has attempted to show the way in which different and in some ways conflicting ideological and institutional factors are expressed in one village in interacting patterns, and how they contribute to the maintenance of a considerable measure of social harmony. While most behavior, as well as the verbal expression of norms, can readily be allocated to one ideological system or the other, there remains an in-between area or overlap of considerable importance that resists clear categorization.

Confucian doctrine, as it is expressed in Sŏkp'o, goes beyond the boundaries of kinship in inculcating values of restraint and moderation as a general guide to all interpersonal conduct. In this respect it reinforces the more egalitarian ideals of cooperation, reciprocity, hospitality, and tolerant accommodation of personal differences. Similarly, the willingness to compromise and a tendency to avoid rigid moralistic interpretations that might lead to a break in good relations can also be discerned in the organization of lineage affairs.

In cases such as these where there is an inextricable tangle of lineage and community-oriented values, the attempt to define behavior as belonging to one category or the other becomes somewhat artificial, and a clear dualistic distinction may not always be tenable. One of the hypothetical propositions of this thesis, however, is that the success of Sŏkp'o villagers in preserving harmonious relations and in accommodating differences arises out of the close interrelation and simultaneous operation of both the hierarchical and egalitarian systems of organization.

Another area of behavior that is not fully accounted for by the model is in the expression of egoistic drives. Both ethical systems require subordination of the individual to group interests. The community ideology, as defined above, does emphasize conviviality and relaxed informality among peers so that self-expression in joking behavior, singing, and informal oratory is provided for. Furthermore, personal energy, ability, and popularity are necessary in order to acquire status and exercise leadership outside the system of lineage ranking. Such qualities as these can be assigned, therefore, to the informal egalitarian tradition.

But the acquisitive and competitive achievement drives that are a necessary condition for success in modern industrial society have had no real legitimation in either the lineal or egalitarian ethical scheme. Energetic men of ambition have had to work slowly and indirectly to achieve their goals; in many cases the obstacles to achievement are so great that they have left the village.

The new ideology of modernization offers freedom from most traditional restraints and promotes the expression of individual energy in many ways. In this sense it is a truly revolutionary influence for a place like Sŏkp'o and is reflected in the increasing dissatisfaction of young men with village life. The enormous lure of the city for rural youth can be partly explained in terms of the new opportunities offered there for self-expression. For the first time an alternative to the stifling environment of the village is available to young people, as they become conscious of another world where their aspirations need not always be subordinated to family and community interests.

## VILLAGE ORGANIZATION, COOPERATION, AND CONFLICT

While the existence of marked differences among Korean villages with regard to various elements of social organization has already been mentioned, the point deserves further emphasis. The most important variable factors from the point of view of this discussion are the numbers of households in each lineage, their cohesiveness as kinship organizations, and their spatial distribution. In one kind of arrangement several loosely organized kinship groups with a commoner tradition may make up most of a village population. In some areas there is a territorial division into clan neighborhoods within the village, while another settlement pattern will show an indiscriminate juxtaposition of related and unrelated households. If former *yangban* households are present, they may or may not have wealth and influence. A somewhat different kind of pattern is represented by a village like Sŏkp'o where a cohesive, well-organized *yangban* lineage coexists with other kinship groups of approximately equal size and wealth.

Although the number of community studies made so far in Korea is still too small to provide decisive evidence, the results of several investigations indicate that there is a tendency for village social organization as a whole to reflect the combination of lineage structure and ideology that predominates in the community. For example, if a single lineage is dominant, particularly if it is one with a strong *yangban* tradition, the village is likely to be run in somewhat authoritarian fashion by the elders of high genealogical rank. The lineal organization of the kinship group with its emphasis on form and etiquette then becomes characteristic of the entire community. Social stratification is more marked, reflecting the importance of traditional ascripive status differences, and there is likely to be a fairly high concentration of land ownership among a few lineal corporate groups. Any threat to the dominant position of the village elite provokes strong conservative reaction.

In Korea there seems to have been a tendency for hierarchical lineage organizations in rural areas to become extremely rigid. Arbitrary leadership usually has been exercised by men who are senior in age and lineage rank, with opposition not tolerated. There has been little or no prospect of mobility upward into elite positions for men of energy and ability who were not part of the dominant hierarchy, and such structures seem almost automatically to have engendered equally rigid opposition.

Although there are plenty of examples of conflict and division on the basis of other issues, hostility between rival kinship groups (in some cases the factions may be segmentary branches of a single major lineage) has often been intense; cooperation on a village-wide basis then becomes difficult or impossible. In villages this kind of group conflict seems to be associated with the authoritarian hierarchical tradition that I have described as *yangban* or lineage oriented. While egalitarian norms of mutual assistance and neighborhood cooperation undoubtedly exist in such communities as well, they will have priority only among the poorer households and cannot compete with the kinship loyalties that support the dominant groups.

The modernization process presents a direct challenge to this kind of village structure, which is gradually giving way before the forces of accelerated economic and social change.

The contrast is clear between a true "clan" village and a place like Sŏkp'o where community sentiment and a built-in resistance to authority checks the efforts of any one group to pursue its own interests without consideration for other segments of the population. In many other communities the mixture of hierarchical and egalitarian forces is more even, and there is likely to be a combination of intense rivalry on the one hand and frequent cooperation across lineage boundaries on the other.

A fundamental question remains: Can the concept of two opposed and interacting traditional ideologies at the village level together with the hypothesis outlined above (which suggests that hostility between groups is likely to be associated with a dominant kinship organization) cast any light on the more general problem of the prevalence of factionalism in Korean society? Conflict, rivalry, and competition among individuals and groups exist, of course, everywhere. Max Gluckman has postulated that certain kinds of institutionalized conflict have an integrative effect for society as a whole (1955), and Americans take for granted the proposition that competition is a constructive force resulting in increased production and progress. It seems clear that the expression of hostility and conflict is culturally determined, at least in part, and that each society imposes certain limits on behavior aimed at maximizing the wealth and power of one individual or group at the expense of others.

Nevertheless, in Korea, endemic pervasive factionalism often has been blamed for most of the country's ills, past and present (Hong 1967:134), while almost no systematic study has been made of its basic sociological elements and how they operate. Until very recently leaders of large political units or organizations seem to have been unable to find appropriate symbols or methods that would stimulate a sense of identity and common purpose capable of unifying the loyalties of diverse groups of people. The limits of solidary association have remained the small face-to-face community, the kinship organization (or segment thereof), and the unstable political faction, whereas the common interests of members of a community, an association, a class, a region, or the country as a whole often have been obscured or forgotten in the intensity of the struggle between competing groups. Frequently a contest for political and economic spoils has been waged in terms of moral issues that introduced an aura of religious fanaticism, providing additional emotional bonds among members of the warring factions (Wagner 1959).

This study of solidarity in Sŏkp'o has shown that social cohesion there is intimately associated with an egalitarian community ethic ranking far below the formal lineage ideology in terms of social prestige. Elements of this lower-class and possibly more ancient tradition have persisted throughout all levels of Korean society. But during the course of a long historical development, Confucian ideology and aristocratic structural principles so dominated institutions and higher culture above the village level (and in many villages as well) that egalitarianism and the accompanying spirit of accommodation and tolerance were eliminated or submerged as a basic unifying factor of social organization.

# BIBLIOGRAPHY

Balikci, A. "Quarrels in a Balkan Village," *American Anthropologist* 67:1456–1469 (1965).

Bodde, D. "Harmony and Conflict in Chinese Philosophy," in *Studies in Chinese Thought*, A. F. Wright, ed. Chicago, Ill.: University of Chicago Press, 1953.

Choi Jai Seuk. *A Study of Korean Family.* Seoul: Minjusokwan, 1966. (In Korean with English summary.)

Epstein, T. *Economic Development and Social Change in South India.* Manchester, England: Manchester University Press, 1962.

Feng, Han Yi. "The Chinese Kinship System," *Harvard Journal of Asiatic Studies* 2:141–275 (1937).

Foster, G. M. "Interpersonal Relations in Peasant Society," *Human Organization* 19:174–179 (1960).

————"Peasant Society and the Image of Limited Good," *American Anthropologist* 67:293–309 (1965).

————*Tzintzuntzan.* Boston, Mass.: Little, Brown and Co., 1967.

Frankenberg, R. *Communities in Britain.* Middlesex, England: Penguin Books, 1966.

Fried, M. *Readings in Anthropology*, vol. 2, *Cultural Anthropology.* New York: Crowell, 1968.

Gluckman, M. *Custom and Conflict in Africa.* Glencoe, N.Y.: Free Press, 1955.

241

# Bibliography

———— "Ethnographic Data in British Social Anthropology," *Sociological Review* 9:5–17 (1961).

———— *The Ideas in Barotse Jurisprudence*. New Haven, Conn.: Yale University Press, 1965.

Goodenough, W. "Introduction," in *Explorations in Cultural Anthropology*, Ward Goodenough, ed. New York: McGraw-Hill Book Co., 1964.

Griffis, W. E. *Corea: The Hermit Nation*. New York: Charles Scribner's Sons, 1882.

Halpern, J. M. *The Changing Village Community*. Englewood Cliffs, N.J.: Prentice Hall, 1967.

Hamel, H. "The Description of the Kingdom of Corea," *Transactions of the Korea Branch of the Royal Asiatic Society* 9:129–148. New York: George Stechert, 1918 (written in 1653).

Hong Sung Chick. *The Intellectual and Modernization: a Study of Korean Attitudes*. Seoul: Seoul University Press, 1967.

Hsu, F. L. K. *Clan, Caste and Club*. Princeton, N.J.: Van Nostrand and Co., 1963.

Kennan, G. "The Korean People: the Product of a Decayed Civilization," *The Outlook* 31:409–416. New York: Outlook Co., 1905.

Kim Taek Kyoo. *The Cultural Structure of a Consanguinous Village*. Ch'ong Ku University, 1964. (In Korean with English summary.)

Leach, E. R. *Political Systems of Highland Burma*. London, England: G. Bell & Sons Ltd., 1954.

Lee Chong Young. "The Canal across T'aean Promontory." *Tong Bang Hak Chi* 7:99–133, 1963. (In Korean with English summary.)

Lee Hae Young. "Tradition and Change in Rural Korea." Unpublished manuscript, 1969.

Lee Man Gap. *The Social Structure of Korean Villages*. Seoul: Korean Research Center, 1960. (In Korean with English summary.)

Levi-Strauss, C. "Social Structure," in *Anthropology Today*, A. L. Kroeber, ed. Chicago, Ill.: University of Chicago Press, 1953.

Lewis, O. *Life in a Mexican Village: Tepoztlan Restudied*. Urbana, Ill.: University of Illinois Press, 1963.

McGinn, N. F., E. Harburg, and G. P. Ginsberg. "Responses to Interpersonal Conflict by Middle Class Males in Guadalajara and Michigan," *American Anthropologist* 67:1483–1494 (1965).

Mills, J. E. *Ethno-Sociological Reports of Four Korean Villages.* Seoul: U.S. Operations Mission/Korea, 1960.

Moose, J. R. *Village Life in Korea.* Nashville, Tenn.: Methodist Episcopal Church, 1911.

Murdock, G. P. *Social Structure.* New York: MacMillan Co., 1949.

Nadel, S. F. *The Theory of Social Structure.* London, England: Cohen and West, 1957.

Norbeck, E. "African Rituals of Conflict," *American Anthropologist* 65:1254–79 (1963).

Osgood, C. *The Koreans and Their Culture.* New York: Ronald Press, 1951.

Pak Ki Hyuk and Lee Seung Yun. *Three Clan Villages in Korea.* Seoul: Yonsei University, 1963.

Parsons, K. H. *Issues in Land Tenure Policy for Korea.* Seoul: U.S. Operations Mission/Korea, 1965.

Radcliffe-Brown, A. R. *Structure and Function in Primitive Society.* London, England: Cohen and West, 1959.

Redfield, R. *The Folk Culture of Yucatan.* Chicago, Ill.: University of Chicago Press, 1941.
_____*The Primitive World and Its Transformations.* Ithaca, N.Y.: Cornell University Press, 1953.
_____*Peasant Society and Culture* and *The Little Community.* Chicago, Ill.: University of Chicago Press, 1960.

Rockhill, W. W. "Notes on Some of the Laws, Customs, and Superstitions of Korea," *American Anthropologist* 4:177–187 (1891).

Skinner, G. W. "Marketing and Social Structure in China," *Journal of Asian Studies,* vol. 24, no. 1 (1964).

Turner, V. W. *Schism and Continuity in an African Society.* Manchester, England: Manchester University Press, 1957.
_____*The Ritual Process.* Chicago, Ill.: Aldine, 1969.

van Velsen, J. *The Politics of Kinship.* Manchester, England: Manchester University Press, 1964.

van Velzen, J., H. U. E. Thoden, and W. van Watering. "Residence, Power Groups, and Intra-societal Aggression," *International Archives of Ethnography* 49:169–200 (1960).

Wagner, E. W. "The Literati Purges." Ph.D. thesis, Harvard University, 1959.

Wallace, A. *Culture and Personality*. 2nd ed. New York: Random House, 1970.

Whiting, J. W. M., K. Romney, B. Whiting, E. E. Maccoby, B. Ayres, H. Smith, and E. Lowell. *Field Manual for the Cross-Cultural Study of Child Rearing*. New York: Social Science Research Council, 1953.

Whiting, J. W. M., M. F. Anthonovsky, E. M. Chasdi, and B. C. Ayres. "The Learning of Values," in *Peoples of Rimrock*, vol. 1, E. Vogt and J. M. Roberts, eds. 1961. Final report of the Harvard Values Study, manuscript.

Yang Lien-sheng. "The Concept of *Pao* as a Basis for Social Relations in China," in *Chinese Thought and Institutions*, John Fairbank, ed. Chicago, Ill.: University of Chicago Press, 1957.

# GLOSSARY

ajŏssi 아저씨
ajumŏni 아주머니

ban 반(班)

chagŭn abŏji 작은 아버지
chagŭn chip 작은집
chesa 제사(祭祀)
chiban 집안
ch'in 친(親)
ch'ingu 친구(親舊)
chokpo 족보(族譜)
chong 종(宗)
chongjok 종족(宗族)
ch'osang 초상(初喪)
choŭn kamŭn 좋은 가문(家門)
ch'usŏk 추석 (秋月)

gun 군(郡)
gunch'ŏng 군청(郡廳)

hyŏng 형(兄)
hyŏngnim 형님

ijang 이장(里長)

ilch'e hyŏpcho haji mara 일체 협
　조 하지 마라(一切協助)
insim 인심(人心)

kaoliang (Chinese) 高粱
kisaeng 기생(妓生)
kosa 고사(告祀)
k'ŭn abŏji 큰 아버지
k'ŭn chip 큰집
k'ŭn maŭl 큰 마을
kwahak 과학(科學)
kyŏrŭi hyŏngje 결의형제(結義兄
　弟)

makkŏlli 막걸리
misin 미신(迷信)
mŏn sach'on poda kakkaun iusi
　natta 먼 사촌(四寸)보다 가까
　운 이웃이 낫다
mudang 무당(巫堂)
mun jung 문중(門中)
myŏn 면(面)

oe 외(外)

245

p'a 파(派)
panjang 반장(班長)
pao (Chinese) 報
parŭn haengdong 바른행동 (行動)
ppalgaengi 빨갱이
p'umasi 품앗이
p'umsak 품삯
p'ungsu 풍수(風水)
pyong 평(坪)

sarang pang 사랑방(房)
sije or sisa 시제(時祭) or 시사(時祀)
sijo 시조(始祖)
sillyŏkcha 실력자(實力者)
siyang (alt. suyang) abŏji 시양(수양)아버지
siyang (alt. suyang) ŏmŏni 시양(수양)어머니
sŏllal 설날
sŏri 서리

sŏro towa chunŭn kŏt 서로 도와주는것
sŏsan 서산(瑞山)
sosang 소상(小喪)
ssaum kongjang 싸움공장
sŭpkwan 습관(習慣)

taesang 대상(大喪)
tang 당(堂)
tangnae 당내(堂內)
taptap hada 답답하다
ture 두레

uinammae 의남매(義男妹)
ujŏng 우정(友情)

wŏn 원(円)

yang abŏji 양(養)아버지
yang omŏni 양(養)어머니
yangban 양반(兩班)

# INDEX

Administration: as prestigious function, 179; local, 12–13, 86, 164–165, 170
Adultery, 65, 125, 134, 163
Agnatic relations, 110
Agriculture: as source of income, 101; general description, 49–60; in definition of peasant, 11n; innovation and productivity, 78–79, 81–83, 86–87; practices and skills, 79–81
Aid, from outside village, 87
Ambition, 173n, 178, 179, 191
Ancestor worship, 119–121, 224; and emotional dependence, 138; ritual, 84; welfare of ancestral spirits, 114
Animism, 153, 154, 232
Anthropologist: resident, 163, 168–169; theories of others, 22, 24, 29, 228
Aristocracy, 34, 38, 91, 109, 117. *See also Yangban*
Authority, 27, 94; and kinship ideology, 26, 112, 233; delegation, 105

Behavior: among kin, 136–142; communal, 28, 196, 234–235;

contradictory, 27–28, 196, 234; control of, 86, 94, 239; correct, 17, 28–29; economic, 85; individual, 75, 106; relation to values, 23, 34, 184; with outsiders, 169–171
Birth control, 68–69
Brothers, 139, 187

Capital, 58, 79, 85, 87
Ceremonies, 152–154, 166; cooperation, 154–156; cost, 58, 121; roof raising, 20–21. *See also* Ancestor worship
Change: economic, 83–87, 192; ideological, 22, 191, 192, 237; social, 8, 15–18, 28; structural, 87
Children, 5; ambitions, 99; as source of labor, 68; learning of values, 172–174; punishment, 188
Chinese influence: classics and education, 90, 95; kinship system, 115–117; philosophy, 82; social ethics, 102, 212; traditional administrative practice, 13
Choices, 35, 72, 226
Cities: attitudes towards, 174–

247

175; lure, 223, 237
Clan: definition, 109–110; ideology, 28; solidarity, 141
"Clan" village, 239
Class: consciousness, 92; hereditary divisions, 46, 88–92; status, 18, 238
Cognitive aspects: of class divisions, 189; of cultural code, 24–25, 233; of kinship terminology, 140; of productivity, 78; of relation of village to outside world, 13
Cohesion, 89, 113, 214, 240; clan, 10; of community, 161, 181, 234; of households, 102; territorial, 179; within sub-neighborhoods, 49
Collective institutions: desertion of, 84; norms, 77; responsibility, 86, 166, 181; welfare, 73, 195
Commercial ventures, 77
Commoners, 9, 10, 89, 90, 91, 109
Communists: collaboration with, 149; ideology, 55, 75; occupation of *1950*, 49, 186, 189
Community: as focus of values, 157, 183; development, 10, 11, 192; ethic, 25, 26, 36, 217, 230–233; sanctions, 174; solidarity, 7, 10, 26, 144, 161–163, 235
Concubines, 25, 139, 210–211
Conflict, 158, 184–213; and joint enterprises, 106; domestic, 97, 128–131, 136, 137, 202; institutionalized, 239. *See also* Disputes; Quarrels
Confucianism: classics, 10, 84; ethical tradition, 27, 38, 90, 133, 136, 147, 230, 236, 240; influence on kinship system, 116–117; ritual, 115–121, 234
Consensus, 32, 190, 198, 233; and formal values, 24; process of reaching, 105; village-wide, 164

Contradictions: behavioral, 27–28; personality, 195–196; structural, 189, 191
Cooperation, 10, 21, 28, 76, 86, 89, 91, 145; among kin, 123; among neighbors, 25, 154–161; and values, 137, 174, 175–177, 212; in work, 70, 160, 192–195
Crime and corruption, 42, 163, 200, 210

Debts, 74–75, 141, 208
Dependence, 138, 173, 197
Deviance, 27, 35, 220–221
Disputes, 144, 176, 184, 186, 187, 201–211. *See also* Quarrels
Distribution, of goods, 167–168
Divorce, 125
Drinking, 47, 78, 100, 118, 147–148, 150, 166–167, 206; drunkenness, 57, 65, 145, 163; stratagems, 221; wine shops, 46, 57, 67
Dualism, 29, 30; of Sŏkp'o model, 25, 230, 236

Economics: development of village, 13, 17–18, 83–87, 192–195; relations among kin, 140–151; transactions, 98, 180–181. *See also* Agriculture; Entrepreneurs; Fishing; Wealth
Education, 58, 87; and Confucian ethics, 117; and status, 69, 90, 95–97; cost, 69; lineage support for, 141
Egalitarianism: and status, 216; as political ideology, 18; economic, 53, 233; ethic, 25, 26, 76, 86, 230; outside lineage, 10, 36, 106, 143; pressures, 91
Elders, village, 103
Elections, 42, 164, 194
Emotion: in quarrels, 145, 203; repression, 201; security in family, 138, 202

Entrepreneurs, 78, 159, 181, 223
Equilibrium, among neighborhoods, 165
Ethical systems, 25, 26, 230
Etiquette, 5–6, 91, 94, 126–127, 190
Exchanges: of goods and labor, 168; of oxen, 59
Exogamy, 109, 112, 121; neighborhood, 135; violations, 209

Factionalism, 19–20, 213, 239, 240
Family, as corporate group, 140
Farmers, 22, 84
Filial piety, 97, 114, 116–117, 139, 222, 231
Fish: as food, 65; as gifts, 63; transactions in, 61–63, 169
Fishermen: and community ethic, 232; as farmers, 83; attitudes, 84–85; behavior, 22, 46–47, 105–106; life style and status, 56, 65–66, 98
Fishing, 5, 46–48, 66; boats used, 61, 162; cooperatives, 170; crews and wages, 58, 71, 101; prejudice against, 14, 123, 178; techniques, 43, 48, 57, 60, 61
Food, 49, 51, 65, 78; and hospitality, 150–151, 152, 153; in exchange for labor, 72
Food for Peace Program, 51, 170, 193
Foreigners, in rural Korea, 5–6
Forests, 42, 91
Foster, George, 34, 75–76, 84, 184
Funerals, 120, 155–156

Generosity, 25, 150, 166, 215–216, 222
Geomancy, 84, 179n
Ghosts, malevolent, 120, 155, 200–201
Gossip, 97, 177, 217
Groups: after dark, 148; corporate, 140; informal, 146–

147, 153, 159; loyalties, 213, 235; psychological basis, 192–195; solidarity, 72; work, 70–73

Harmony: domestic, 126, 136; relation to *yangban* lineage, 27; restoration of, 145, 186, 199, 202
Hierarchy: and egalitarianism, 190; and filial piety, 117; kinship structure, 113, 238; organization, 25, 36; relation to leadership, 102–106; rules, 119
Hospitality, 6, 25, 77, 233
Households: collateral, 112; heads, 18, 52–53

Ideology: community, 231–233, 236; lineage, 230–231, 235, 240; of modernization, 18, 22, 28, 237; systems, 25, 28, 36, 76, 234, 239
Incentives, group, 195
Inchŏn, 2
Individuals: ambition, 80, 84, 86; personality, 219; pride, 197; subordination to group, 75, 76, 138
Infant mortality, 115
Informality: of groups, 142, 146–147, 153, 159; of relations, 137
In-laws, 15, 124. *See also* Kinship
Investments, 52, 85, 87, 181
Irrigation, 81

Japanese government: administrative policy, 86, 182; agricultural practices, 7, 79, 81; fishing technology, 60–61, 167; occupation by, 15, 38, 81, 150, 191
Joking, 99, 140, 235

Kim Taik Kyoo, 8
Kinship: affinal relations, 15, 20, 25, 46, 48, 49, 57, 121–

124; behavior, 136–142; collaterals, 139–140; debts, 73; loyalty, 19, 71, 76, 222, 234; organizations, 7, 9, 37, 90, 91, 137, 238–239; property rights, 52–53; rituals, 77, 115–121; values, 16, 26, 108, 142, 217. *See also* Lineage
Korea: cultural homogeneity, 7; government, 14
Kunsan, 2

Labor, division of, 72, 234
Land: as resource, 41–42; distribution, 181–182; ownership, 53; reform law, 38, 55, 56; value, 177
Leach, E. R., 36
Leadership, 102–107, 165, 196–197; and education, 96; arbitrary, 238; conservative, 94n; criteria, 164; lack of strength, 71, 95, 232; of dike project, 194; of kinship organizations, 143; outside village, 86
Lee Hae Young, 11
Lee Man Gap, 9
Leisure: enforced, 47, 65, 67–68, 73; informal groups, 147
Lineage: commoner, 9, 10, 89; composition, 23, 92–93, 94, 103, 109, 111, 114; ethic, 25, 230–231; loyalties, 27, 108, 122, 214–215; mobility, 99–100; rank, 92, 107, 118, 209; *yangban,* 9, 10, 11, 27, 36, 39, 46, 53, 58, 88, 90. *See also* Kinship
Living standards, 57–59, 60, 73, 180–181, 233, 234
Loans, 73. *See also* Debts
Loyalty: lineage, 27, 108, 122, 214–215; regional, 238; village, 177

Malnutrition, 50
Markets, 12, 60, 77, 84, 87
Marriage, 44, 48, 92, 121–124, 130
Migration, village to city, 16, 18,

77, 87, 223–226
Military personnel, 69, 170, 174; GI's, 5, 6
Models: dualistic, 25–29; inadequacy, 235–237; in structural analysis, 24
Money, 165–167, 201, 209
Morale, 71, 178
Murdock, G. P., 109–110

National government, 12–14; economy, 62, 83, 190
Neighborhoods, 45–49, 71, 123, 124, 154, 161, 238
North Korea, 14, 49, 97, 189

Old age, 114, 161
Ostracism, 187, 209
Outside world, relations with, 95, 169–171

Peasants, 11n, 184, 185, 228
Personal relations, 76, 80, 91, 145–150. *See also* Behavior
Police, 171, 181, 199, 204, 210, 224
Population, 43–45, 68, 185
Poverty, 57, 73, 83, 228; exaggeration of, 51; gap between rich and poor, 56
Prestige, 52, 53, 90, 231
Primogeniture, 100
Progress, 79, 80, 85, 192

Quarrels, 47, 65, 145, 157, 198, 221; domestic, 126, 129–131; mediation of, 98. *See also* Disputes

Radios, 16, 58
Reciprocity, 144; among relatives, 141; as internalized value, 168, 175–176; in Confucian tradition, 232n; in rituals, 152; of obligations, 78, 124
Reclamation, of tidal land, 14, 41, 56, 71, 84, 193–195
Redfield, Robert, 11n, 32–34
Regionalism, 7, 239

Residence patterns, 39–40, 45–49, 233
Restraint, 165–166
Rice, 8, 14, 37; land holdings, 53–54; prices, 85, 87; values, 50–52, 80, 82, 91
Roles, of individuals, 214, 234
Rural communities, 8–10, 34

Sailboats, 67
Sanctions, for behavior, 29, 174
Schools, 91, 150. *See also* Education
Self-interest, 35
Sexual customs: contact with opposite sex, 135–136, 208, 209; discrimination against women, 125; jokes, 134; romantic love, 16
Shamanism, 28, 215, 216n, 232
Situational analysis, 34–35
Skills, technical, 2–3, 177
Sociability, 21, 29, 161
Social structure, 93, 229, 237; censure, 29, 77, 174–176, 198, change, 8, 15–18, 28, 239; collectivity, 77, 147; harmony, 7; integration, 214, 217, 218
Socialization, 172
Soil, 41, 42, 79
Solidarity, 32, 182, 190; challenges to, 209; community, 26, 192, 211, 213; lineage, 110, 122, 211
Sons: and fathers, 138–139; eldest, 110, 139, 178, 202, 205–206, 211
Sorcery, 188
Sŏsan, 2
South Ch'ungch'ŏng Province, 2, 4, 37, 38
Status, 77; hereditary, 91; low, 216, 218; of older men, 170; sources, 107
Structural analysis and concepts, 23–24, 30–32, 36, 84, 198
Success, 83, 98, 99, 191
Suicide, 200, 201, 211

Superstition, 121, 179n

T'aean (town), 2
T'aean Peninsula, 1
T'aejong, King, 38, 112
Tenancy, 55, 86
Theft, 188, 199, 209, 216
Tides, 41
Tolerance, 6, 21, 25, 33, 77, 89, 145, 176, 198, 203, 217, 240
Topography, 1–2, 39, 41
Transactions, 83, 98; for fish, 208; speculative, 170; with outsiders, 77–78; within village, 140–141
Transportation, to Sŏkp'o, 2
Turner, Victor, 29–32

Underemployment, 67
Urban society, 33–34, 143

Values, 23–25, 84; attached to land, 81–82; behavior, 106, 137; conflicting, 34, 35, 235; internalization, 137, 143, 175; kinship, 142, 221–222; lineage and community, 157, 236; official, 28, 196; systems, 27, 28, 33
Variation: in basis of groups, 158; in villages, 7–8; neighborhood, 45–49, 142, 147–148
Village head, 13, 103, 161, 163–164
Villages: communalism, 219, 223; contrasts, 7, 22–23; development, 171, 179; endogamy and exogamy, 121–124; meetings, 164; relations with outside world, 12–15, 182
Violence, 203, 204, 211

Wages, 194–195
Warfare, effects, 85
Wealth: amassing, 77; and marriage, 92; distribution, 77, 83, 183; of lineages, 90–91; rice as, 80
Weddings, 153

Widows, 132–133
Wills, 113
Women, 12, 15, 124–133; behavior, 46–48, 134, 203; education, 97; group members,
93, 157–158; status, 109–
110, 232
Work, 48, 72; agricultural, 50,
78; attitudes towards, 65, 68;
collective, 71, 140; efficiency,
68

*Yangban,* 10, 27, 88–91 *passim;*
definition, 11–12; lineage, 20,
46, 53, 230–231, 237–238;
moral superiority, 190; resentment towards, 209; social
control, 197–198. *See also*
Aristocracy
Yellow Sea, 1, 5, 37, 133, 162
Yi dynasty, 37, 38, 61, 91, 182
Yin and yang, 29, 32
Youth, 135–136, 190, 191, 198

# HARVARD
# EAST ASIAN
# SERIES

1. *China's Early Industrialization: Sheng Hsuan-huai (1884–1916) and Mandarin Enterprise.* By Albert Feuerwerker.
2. *Intellectual Trends in the Ch'ing Period.* By Liang Ch'i-ch'ao. Translated by Immanuel C. Y. Hsü.
3. *Reform in Sung China: Wang An-shih (1021–1086) and His New Policies.* By James T. C. Liu.
4. *Studies on the Population of China, 1368–1953.* By Ping-ti Ho.
5. *China's Entrance into the Family of Nations: The Diplomatic Phase, 1858–1880.* By Immanuel C. Y. Hsü.
6. *The May Fourth Movement: Intellectual Revolution in Modern China.* By Chow Tse-tsung.
7. *Ch'ing Administrative Terms: A Translation of the Terminology of the Six Boards with Explanatory Notes.* Translated and edited by E-tu Zen Sun.
8. *Anglo-American Steamship Rivalry in China, 1862–1874.* By Kwang-Ching Liu.
9. *Local Government in China under the Ch'ing.* By T'ung-tsu Ch'ü.
10. *Communist China, 1955–1959: Policy Documents with Analysis.* With a foreword by Robert R. Bowie and John K. Fairbank. (Prepared at Harvard University under the joint auspices of the Center for International Affairs and the East Asian Research Center.)
11. *China and Christianity: The Missionary Movement and the Growth of Chinese Antiforeignism, 1860–1870.* By Paul A. Cohen.
12. *China and the Helping Hand, 1937–1945.* By Arthur N. Young.
13. *Research Guide to the May Fourth Movement: Intellectual Revolution in Modern China, 1915–1924.* By Chow Tse-tsung.
14. *The United States and the Far Eastern Crisis of 1933–1938: From the Manchurian Incident through the Initial Stage of the Undeclared Sino-Japanese War.* By Dorothy Borg.

15. *China and the West, 1858–1861: The Origins of the Tsungli Yamen.* By Masataka Banno.
16. *In Search of Wealth and Power: Yen Fu and the West.* By Benjamin Schwartz.
17. *The Origins of Entrepreneurship in Meiji Japan.* By Johannes Hirschmeier, S.V.D.
18. *Commissioner Lin and the Opium War.* By Hsin-pao Chang.
19. *Money and Monetary Policy in China, 1845–1895.* By Frank H. H. King.
20. *China's Wartime Finance and Inflation, 1937–1945.* By Arthur N. Young.
21. *Foreign Investment and Economic Development in China, 1840–1937.* By Chi-ming Hou.
22. *After Imperialism: The Search for a New Order in the Far East, 1921–1931.* By Akira Iriye.
23. *Foundations of Constitutional Government in Modern Japan, 1868–1900.* By George Akita.
24. *Political Thought in Early Meiji Japan, 1868–1889.* By Joseph Pittau, S.J.
25. *China's Struggle for Naval Development, 1839–1895.* By John L. Rawlinson.
26. *The Practice of Buddhism in China, 1900–1950.* By Holmes Welch.
27. *Li Ta-chao and the Origins of Chinese Marxism.* By Maurice Meisner.
28. *Pa Chin and His Writings: Chinese Youth Between the Two Revolutions.* By Olga Lang.
29. *Literary Dissent in Communist China.* By Merle Goldman.
30. *Politics in the Tokugawa Bakufu, 1600–1843.* By Conrad Totman.
31. *Hara Kei in the Politics of Compromise, 1905–1915.* By Tetsuo Najita.
32. *The Chinese World Order: Traditional China's Foreign Relations.* Edited by John K. Fairbank.
33. *The Buddhist Revival in China.* By Holmes Welch.
34. *Traditional Medicine in Modern China: Science, Nationalism, and the Tensions of Cultural Change.* By Ralph C. Croizier.
35. *Party Rivalry and Political Change in Taishō Japan.* By Peter Duus.
36. *The Rhetoric of Empire: American China Policy, 1895–1901.* By Marilyn B. Young.
37. *Radical Nationalist in Japan: Kita Ikki, 1883–1937.* By George M. Wilson.
38. *While China Faced West: American Reformers in Nationalist China, 1928–1937.* By James C. Thomson, Jr.
39. *The Failure of Freedom: A Portrait of Modern Japanese Intellectuals.* By Tatsuo Arima.
40. *Asian Ideas of East and West: Tagore and His Critics in Japan, China, and India.* By Stephen N. Hay.
41. *Canton under Communism: Programs and Politics in a Provincial Capital, 1949–1968.* By Ezra F. Vogel.
42. *Ting Wen-chiang: Science and China's New Culture.* By Charlotte Furth.
43. *The Manchurian Frontier in Ch'ing History.* By Robert H. G. Lee.
44. *Motoori Norinaga, 1730–1801.* By Shigeru Matsumoto.
45. *The Comprador in Nineteenth Century China: Bridge Between East and West.* By Yen-p'ing Hao.

46. *Hu Shih and the Chinese Renaissance: Liberalism in the Chinese Revolution, 1917–1937.* By Jerome B. Grieder.
47. *The Chinese Peasant Economy: Agricultural Development in Hopei and Shantung, 1890–1949.* By Raymond H. Myers.
48. *Japanese Tradition and Western Law: Emperor, State, and Law in the Thought of Hozumi Yatsuka.* By Richard H. Minear.
49. *Rebellion and Its Enemies in Late Imperial China: Militarization and Social Structure, 1796–1864.* By Philip A. Kuhn.
50. *Early Chinese Revolutionaries: Radical Intellectuals in Shanghai and Chekiang, 1902–1911.* By Mary Backus Rankin.
51. *Communication and Imperial Control in China: Evolution of the Palace Memorial System, 1693–1735.* By Silas H. L. Wu.
52. *Vietnam and the Chinese Model: A Comparative Study of Nguyên and Ch'ing Civil Government in the First Half of the Nineteenth Century.* By Alexander Barton Woodside.
53. *The Modernization of the Chinese Salt Administration, 1900–1920.* By S. A. M. Adshead.
54. *Chang Chih-tung and Educational Reform in China.* By William Ayers.
55. *Kuo Mo-jo: The Early Years.* By David Tod Roy.
56. *Social Reformers in Urban China: The Chinese Y.M.C.A., 1895–1926.* By Shirley S. Garrett.
57. *Biographic Dictionary of Chinese Communism, 1921–1965.* By Donald W. Klein and Anne B. Clark.
58. *Imperialism and Chinese Nationalism: Germany in Shantung.* By John E. Shrecker.
59. *Monarchy in the Emperor's Eyes: Image and Reality in the Ch'ien-lung Reign.* By Harold L. Kahn.
60. *Yamagata Aritomo in the Rise of Modern Japan, 1838–1922.* By Roger F. Hackett.
61. *Russia and China: Their Diplomatic Relations to 1728.* By Mark Mancall.
62. *The Yenan Way in Revolutionary China.* By Mark Selden.
63. *The Mississippi Chinese: Between Black and White.* By James W. Loewen.
64. *Liang Ch'i-ch'ao and Intellectual Transition in China, 1890–1907.* By Hao Chang.
65. *A Korean Village: Between Farm and Sea.* By Vincent S. R. Brandt.